TEXTS

TEXTS: CONTEMPORARY CULTURAL TEXTS AND CRITICAL APPROACHES

Peter Childs

EDINBURGH UNIVERSITY PRESS

84954

© Peter Childs, 2006

Edinburgh University Press Ltd
22 George Square, Edinburgh

Typeset in Sabon and Gill Sans
by Servis Filmsetting Ltd, Manchester, and
printed and bound in Great Britain by
Antony Rowe Ltd, Chippenham, Wilts

A CIP record for this book is
available from the British Library

ISBN-10 0 7486 2043 5 (hardback)
ISBN-13 978 0 7486 2043 2 (hardback)
ISBN-10 0 7486 2044 3 (paperback)
ISBN-13 978 0 7486 2044 9 (paperback)

The right of Peter Childs
to be identified as author of this work
has been asserted in accordance with
the Copyright, Designs and Patents Act 1988.

The Library
University College for the Creative Arts
at Epsom and Farnham

801.
95
CHI

CONTENTS

Introduction: Starting Points   1

1. Film: *The Matrix* and the I-pod   11
   Approach: Cyberphilosophy

2. Building: Shopping in Utopia   21
   Approach: Spatial Criticism

3. Movie Poster: Alien Nature   31
   Approach: Ecocriticism

4. Pop Video: Michael Jackson's 'Thriller' and 'Race'   40
   Approach: 'Race' Studies

5. Celebrity: Diana and Death   49
   Approach: Trauma Theory

6. TV Show: *Big Brother* after the Big Other   60
   Approach: Performativity Theory

7. Newspaper Article: The Gulf War in Real Time and
      Virtual Space   74
   Approach: Hyperreality

8. Photograph(er): Cindy Sherman and the Masquerade   85
   Approach: Feminism

9. Political Speech: Margaret Thatcher's Hymn at the Sermon
      on the Mound   95
   Approach: Historicism

10. Critical Text: Alan Sokal's Sham Transgression   105
    Approach: Reading Postmodernism

11. Popular Novel: The Ethics of Harry Potter   118
    Approach: Ethical Criticism

12. Short Story: Barthelme's Balloon and the Rhizome   128
    Approach: Deleuzian Criticism

13. Lyric: 'Where's my Snare?': Eminem and Sylvia Plath   137
    Approach: Psychoanalytic Criticism

CONTENTS

14. Autobiography: Martin Amis's *Experience*   146
    Approach: Self-Life-Writing

15. Virtual Text: Amazonian Democracy   156
    Approach: Globalization Studies

16. World Media Event: It's About Time: Cultural History at
    the Millennium   164
    Approach: Cultural Studies

    Index   173

[T]hat which limits the *true* is not the *false*, but the *insignificant*. (Paul Virilio)[1]

[1] Virilio, Paul, *Desert Screen: War at the Speed of Light*, trans. Michael Degener, London: Continuum, 2002, p. 17.

INTRODUCTION: STARTING POINTS

In one sense no text is finished, since its potential range is always being extended to every additional reader. (Edward Said)[1]

By 'literature', then, I shall mean the areas of culture which, quite self-consciously, forego agreement on an encompassing critical vocabulary. (Richard Rorty)[2]

Unlike many books in the field, this is not a study of literary texts in cultural contexts but a book about cultural texts of the kind increasingly studied through literary approaches. The chapters analyse a wide range of different texts that are neither poems nor 'literary' novels and offer readings of them in the light of issues that arise in literary studies and elsewhere, from considerations of trauma to questions of time, from ethics to spatial dynamics. A number of pre-selected critical and theoretical perspectives are brought to bear, from ecocriticism to performativity theory to postcolonial studies, but these are used to suggest ways of reading specific texts more than the texts are used to illustrate theories.[3]

Both literary writers and their critics have long taken to the analysis of non-literary texts. Many poets, such as Keats and Yeats, have inscribed the three-dimensional artefact for textual commentary since Sir Thomas Browne provided the metaphor for New Criticism's analysis of the literary work as a 'well-wrought urn'.[4] In David Lodge's novel *Nice Work* (1988), a feminist lecturer offers a semiotic reading of a Silk Cut cigarette-advertising poster that included no words but simply showed a slashed sheet of ruffled purple silk. The poster required the spectator to transform the picture into words in order to understand what it was 'saying', but, like all images, it was susceptible to many readings on several different levels, one of which would place it as an icon of misogyny (in stark contrast to the emasculation suggested by an image of a roll of silk chopped in half which would have served the advertisers just as well). Lodge's book is informed by the 'structuralist' branch of cultural criticism that owed much to the development of linguistics, literary theory and semiotics, employing the work of Louis Althusser, Roland Barthes and Michel Foucault. It is primarily in this context that the contemporary understanding of the 'text' arises in literary and cultural studies.

However, it is also relevant that in Britain writers such as Woolf and Orwell offered readings in the interwar years of postcards and posters that at their time of writing were generally considered to be popular cultural works that lacked the complexity or gravity most contemporary critics considered necessary for serious engagement. Following on from these examples in part, British critics have long since turned to the discussion of culture, most notably in the examples of Raymond Williams's cultural studies work since the 1950s and Richard Hoggart's Centre for Contemporary Cultural Studies established in the 1960s at the University of Birmingham. It is these two strands of cultural criticism, structuralist and Marxist, that have informed the approach to literary studies that understands culture as an assembly of varied and opposed forces coursing through a society at any moment rather than as a value-laden term demarcating the preserve of an elite.

As a series of starting points in a book that proposes to study non-canonical kinds of 'text' from the angles commonly found in literary studies, I want in this Introduction to review some perspectives on texts from literary and cultural criticism. These short sections will amount to a partial genealogy of a number of interventions that put into question three things: the idea that the text is bound; the view that the literary text is substantially different from other texts; the belief that the exclusive object of institutionalised literary study should be the work of literature.

STRUCTURALISM

The distinction between 'work' and 'text' is itself one starting point for considering what critical consensus might now take the latter to be. Prior to the mid-twentieth century most critics would refer to the literary 'work', a product of the author's imagination. Developing on the insights of Saussure, others came to argue that the linguistic codes, rules and structures underlying all language-use were of more significance in the production of meaning than notions of individual creativity. Additionally, this perspective could be applied outside of language to other cultural systems, such that the understanding of a 'text' broadened potentially to include any object of investigation, whether social, spatial, political or historical. Consequently, instead of having a single meaning (and interpretation) as a 'work', the text came to be thought of as involved in a play of dispersed, multiple, variable meanings (and readings) across the full field of other texts, such that it signified intertextually.

The seminal essay in this regard is 'From Work to Text' (1971) by Roland Barthes, whose book *Mythologies* (1957) is perhaps the best-known early example of semiotic discussions of culture, from wrestling and soap powder to motor cars and movie haircuts. In 'From Work to Text', Barthes put forward seven propositions for the delineation of the 'text' in distinction from the traditional literary object, 'the work'.[5] These propositions can be summarised, mainly using Barthes's own words (in translation), as follows:

1. '[T]he work is concrete, occupying a portion of book-space (in a library, for example); the Text, on the other hand, is a methodological field . . . While the work is held in the hand, the Text is held in language' (p. 74). The first is displayed, the second demonstrated. 'A Text can cut across a work, several works (p. 74).'

2. '[T]he Text does not come to a stop with (good) literature; it cannot be apprehended as part of a hierarchy or even a simple division of genres. What constitutes the Text is, on the contrary (or precisely), its subversive force with regard to old classifications' (p. 75). 'If the Text raises problems of classification, that is because it always implies an experience of limits' (p. 75). '[T]he Text is that which goes to the limit of the rules of enunciation (p. 75).'

3. 'Whereas the Text is approached and experienced in relation to the sign, the work closes itself on a signified' (p. 75). '[The Text's] field is that of the signifier' (p. 75): the work is moderately symbolic (the critic is concerned with establishing what a word 'means' in its context), but the Text is radically symbolic (the critic is concerned with exploring what a word can mean in relation to different words and intertexts).

4. 'The Text is plural . . . The Text's plurality does not depend on the ambiguity of its contents, but rather on what could be called the *stereographic plurality* of the signifiers that weave it' (p. 76). The Text is 'completely woven with quotations, references, and echoes' (p. 77).

5. 'The Text . . . is read without the father's [author's] signature' (p. 78). No 'respect' is owed to the Text. The author can only come back to the Text as 'a guest' so to speak. Texts take their place alongside other Texts (intertexts) whereas works simply add to their author's *oeuvre*.

6. The Text 'asks the reader for an active collaboration' (p. 80).[6] The reader should *produce* the Text.

7. 'The Text is linked to enjoyment' (p. 80).

In each of these seven statements Barthes is overturning the 'work' to free the 'Text' and move from a science of interpretation towards the pleasure of reading. The literary work under New Criticism, the dominant approach to literature in the twentieth century up to the 1960s, was a 'verbal icon': a closed structure of meanings which it was the business of the critic to display in all its subtle articulations. Opposing such theories of the autonomous work and the autonomous author, critics since Barthes have more often argued that literary production is not an independent, self-sufficient activity, but a social and an institutional event. Barthes also sees the text as any kind of cultural object that could be decoded or read through its layers of signification. In another key essay 'The Death of the Author' (1968), Barthes asserts that '[T]he text is a tissue of quotations drawn from the innumerable centres of culture.'[7] In such a view, with the text seen as woven from cultural discourse, the author is no longer perceived as creative force but as an adept collator and recycler who is spoken by, rather than speaking, pre-existing linguistic conventions, discourses, signs and codes.

This establishes much of the basis for literary structuralism, which approaches texts as signifying systems within larger cultural structures. From this viewpoint, Jonathan Culler therefore goes on to argue in his *Structuralist Poetics* (1975) that the critic's aim should be to establish not what texts mean but the ways in which readers make texts mean.[8] Culler sees structure lying not simply in texts but in the rules readers with 'literary competence' follow when they study texts.

READER RESPONSE

Building on the structuralist perspective outlined by Culler, another key article in debates over reading the 'text' in literary criticism became the title essay of Stanley Fish's *Is There a Text in This Class?* (1980). A student who asked this question of her new tutor provided Fish's starting point. To her query, the student was given the answer, 'Yes; it's the *Norton Anthology of Literature*'. The student then replied, 'No, no. I mean in this class do we believe in poems and things, or is it just us?' By which, the student was now understood to be voicing her concern over the linguistic turn in literary theory – the tendency of critics like Fish to 'preach the instability of the text and the unavailability of determinate meanings'.[9] In summary of this critical position Fish offers the following assertions: '[N]o text can mean anything in particular' and '[W]e can never just say what anyone means by anything he [or she] writes.'[10]

Fish uses this anecdote to illustrate his belief that what constrains interpretive activities are 'the understood practices and assumptions of the institution and not the rules and fixed meanings of a language system'.[11] How one understands the question 'Is there a text in this class?' is therefore dependent upon what Fish calls an 'interpretive community', which could be otherwise expressed as 'discourse' or 'normalised codes of understandings'. Another term might be institutional, critical or accepted 'context' – the context or set of intertexts that makes the word 'amazon' refer to a river or a parrot, a website or a woman warrior.

In another well-known essay entitled 'How to Recognize a Poem When You See One', also included in *Is There a Text in This Class?*, Fish addresses his title by affirming that a poem is situational. If any list of words is treated as a poem by a group of scholars, then it becomes one – because the interpretive community is approaching the text as a poem.[12] In his example of a classroom experiment, Fish prompts his students to provide a sophisticated reading of a 'religious poem' that is in fact nothing other than a more-or-less arbitrary list of surnames. A literary analysis of the list treats the names as it would a 'poem', and squeezes out an interpretation bristling with religious allusions from the potential of language and the world to interact meaningfully. Fish concludes that words have a significance and an interpretive context before the reader even encounters the text; and so he argues that '[T]he shape of [an analysis] would be constrained not by the names but by the interpretive assumptions that gave them a significance even before they were seen.'[13] Which is to say that the text has a meaning for the reader before it is encountered. The reader's context brings to bear a certain agenda and a set of significances and knowledges that will condition the reading of the text. With regard to the conscious aspects of reading, this may be unrecognised or unacknowledged by the reader, or may be explicitly foregrounded, as I noted by observing that the approaches to be taken to the texts in this book were pre-selected.

DECONSTRUCTION

One of the most famous statements about textuality is Jacques Derrida's assertion that 'Il n'y a pas de hors-text.'[14] Though some critics would wish it to, this does not suggest that there is nothing outside the text but that the text has no outside and there is no experience of the world which is not bound up with textuality and language: the division between text and world becomes untenable because human perception is bounded by sign-systems. Crucially, Derrida implies that meaning is produced (inter)textually and by reference to texts, not to nature or reality.

According to Bernard Harrison, the following might serve as a basic statement of the critical theory of 'deconstruction' associated with Derrida:

1. No text has a determinate meaning
2. A text, though it may refer to other texts, refers to nothing extra-textual
3. Equally legitimate interpretations of a text may be incompatible with one another, or just have nothing in common
4. Since a text gives no access to the conscious states of its author, it gives no access to authorial consciousness *tout court*, and therefore cannot be taken as in any sense a *communication* from author to reader.
5. The job of the critic is not to explain what a text means, but to elaborate it into a new text.[15]

Harrison also concludes that Derrida shows that texts are not bounded by print because human understanding is textual. He goes on to say that those who limit the 'text' to certain objects such as books, branded weak textualists by Richard Rorty, are simply people who cannot bear this much reality:

> [S]uch critics have not grasped that, from a full-fledged pragmatist point of view, there is no interesting difference between tables and texts, between protons and poems. To a pragmatist these are *all* just permanent possibilities for use, and thus for redescription, reinterpretation, manipulation. But the weak textualist thinks . . . that there is a great difference between what scientists do and what critics do . . . The strong textualist simply asks himself the same question about a text which the engineer or physicist asks himself about a puzzling physical object: how shall I describe this in order to get it to do what I want?[16]

A weak textualist position can be illustrated by the stance taken by Richard Freadman and Seumas Miller that 'Literature is a form of communication; as such it involves someone who communicates (the author), someone who is communicated with (the reader), and something that is communicated.' It can immediately be noted that this is at odds with Harrison's succinct notes on deconstruction's view of the text as in no sense a communication between author and reader. Crucially, the weak and strong textualist not only differ in their view of the scope of the term 'text' but also in their understanding of what a text is. So, in line with their emphasis on intention, Freadman and Miller go on to conclude that the text

> is the vehicle by means of which what is to be communicated is in fact communicated. By the text we mean some structured set of speech acts such that each text constitutes a unitary whole and is thereby distinguished from all other texts and from things that are not texts . . . The text may be minimally defined as a series of physical marks which possesses meaning.[17]

Interestingly for the purposes of this book, Freadman and Miller consider another 'act of communication', a conversation, not to be a 'literary text' for these reasons:

> [A] literary text must be conceived as a communicative entity, with the author as communicator and the reader as communicant. However, although the literary text is a structured set of speech acts, it cannot be assimilated to other forms of communicative exchange. There are three reasons for this. First, unlike, for example, a conversation, the text has a definite unity: it has a definite beginning, end and structure. Second, the text transcends the merely pragmatic communicative function of a conversation. Its production involves a concern with aesthetic and other properties. Third, the text is far less context dependent than a conversation. It must have the capacity to communicate across time, to a wider range of readers, and often to persons with very limited knowledge of the author.[18]

The present book would disagree with this position, arguing that: first, a conversation also has a structure and its own form of unity (there are 'rules' of conversation within culture and speakers work within or against these 'rules', even if unconsciously or unknowingly); second, a conversation is also concerned with aesthetic and other properties, though appreciation of conversational strategies, felicities and niceties will vary; and, third, a conversation can be (over)heard or read by people (for example, in published letters) other than the addressee, just as some texts which we know as 'literature' were written not for publication but for private communication.

However, another statement by Freadman and Miller can be given assent, though it might be inflected differently in the present context:

> Most texts have both a literary and a non-literary dimension; and in practice it is very difficult to characterise every given text as either (predominantly) literary or non-literary or to isolate all the literary from the non-literary elements within any individual text.[19]

Consequently, while we have been using the terms 'literary' and 'non-literary' text, this is a conventional, or as Fish would say institutional, distinction that cannot be sustained other than by reference to the history of its usage.

POWER

The perspectives that have been sketched so far are largely both ahistorical and apolitical. A major difficulty with the approach of structuralism has been that it deals with the operational rules of structures that supposedly operate not with specific readers in concrete, material situations but with abstract, ideal readers. Also, analyses drawn from deconstruction seem too often to lock the reader and critic into a textual labyrinth that has little to say about affect and the effects texts have in the world. A last broad point I therefore want to make concerns the relation between the text, the critic and the world. Following the example of Michel Foucault, Edward Said is the literary and cultural theorist who has discussed this most usefully. He argues that 'As Nietzsche had the perspicacity to see, texts are fundamentally facts of power, not of democratic exchange.'[20] Not only is the critic's reading partial and ideological, but the text has no meaning separate from power differentials. No one has access to the text free from the world, nor can it be supposed that the text came into being free from social and political orientation points, however obscure those parameters are, or appear to be, to the twenty-first century reader. In this, Said considers texts to be 'worldly', by which he means they are not self-contained objects but are inevitably and inextricably woven into a broader social and political reality. Said explains, 'Texts have ways of existing, both theoretical and practical, that even in their most rarefied form are always enmeshed in circumstance, time, place, and society – in short, they are in the world, and hence are worldly.'[21] Said's position is that the text is an object whose interpretation has already commenced before it is read because the writer *places* the text in the world. 'Such a text can thereafter be construed as needing at most complementary, as opposed to supplementary, reading.'[22] Said wants to argue that the text always has connection with the world and the text always enacts power differentials – commits discursive violence – while seeming apolitical. Said therefore adds a political gloss to Fish's points above – not least by implicitly revealing Fish's will to power in telling his students that the list of names was a religious poem, thus drawing up the parameters of their response. While Fish sees the meanings of the text as always already pre-prepared by the interpretive community, Said sees the meanings as pre-prepared by the author's circumstances and contexts of writing. Said therefore maintains that critics must scrutinise the will to power inherent in texts. The critic's aim must include paying attention to that which the text has disallowed readers to think or conclude, to reveal the pattern of thought drawn by the text, and to lay bare what has been mapped out in advance.[23]

CONCLUSION: READING

While writing thus involves a will to power, reading a text is not a matter of decoding, but, in Foucault's terminology, of placing a grid over the text to see what effect this recontextualisation has. The grid – theoretical approach, critical focus or descriptive vocabulary – can be of almost any kind and need have nothing to do with the ostensible purposes of the author, even though, as Said says, the critic needs to be alert to the author's deliberate *placing* of the text in the world too. In Harold Bloom's view there are no right readings, only 'strong misreadings'.[24] Another way to look at this is to substitute the idea of interchange for the usual notion of interpretation. Said explains:

> You experience the text making the critic work, and the critic in turn shows the text at work: the product of these interchanges is simply that they have taken place. Critical ingenuity is pretty much confined to transposing the work into an instance of the method.'[25]

Translated into the approach taken by this book, Said's outline of reading by the critic shows it to be a 'production rather than an excavation of meaning':

> [I]t converts what seems to be alien material, or in some cases quixotic and trivial material, into pertinent dimensions of the text . . . The critical method . . . is effective because every aspect of language is significant. And the production of significance is precisely the principal capability of language. What concerns the critic is how language signifies, what it signifies, in what form.[26]

In this book, I consider from the perspectives offered by cultural and literary criticism and theory a sequence of texts that are for the most part not thought of as 'literary', and not always composed solely of words, in order to ask in what ways they 'signify'. The standpoint the book is supporting is one that argues that the skills learned in literature classes can be profitably applied to non-literary objects – if we *treat* them as texts, if we put them in that *situation*. Such an exercise also poses the question of what the point of literary study is; if it is exclusively to learn about the wealth of literature that has been written, then this exercise has no place in a literature classroom. If it is also fundamentally to acquire and hone different practices of reading, then it does have a place, and indeed suggests very well the transferable skills that studying literature cultivates.

The book's purpose is two-fold. On the one hand it seeks to suggest some of the issues involved when a literary critic reads a range of different kinds of text. For example, what are some of the key questions in discussions concerning life-writing? Can one treat an autobiography in the same way as fiction for the purposes of analysis, or are there other issues and factors that could or should be taken into account? On the other hand, *Texts* intends to sketch the perspectives that current theory and criticism can bring to bear on different species of texts, whether it be ethical criticism's reflection on a popular novel or trauma theory's suggestions for a discussion of the death of Diana, Princess of Wales. These sixteen chapters are not meant to be monolithic in their readings of the diverse texts (this would be against the very ideas of the text outlined above), but examples of ways in which a broad spectrum of approaches can be brought to bear on a range of varied *kinds* of text – the sixteen texts and sixteen approaches in the book could be differently aligned with one another, providing 256 permutations or potential different readings. This point is also made by Terry Eagleton in an observation about the specificity of *a* reading in contrast to the plurality of readings: 'We read backwards and forwards simultaneously, predicting and recollecting, perhaps aware of other possible realizations of the text which our reading has negated.'[27] Again, as my opening quotation from Edward Said asserts, texts are never 'finished' because the critical reading of texts is something that never ends, and such a viewpoint applies to the reading of this text, which is meant to engage the reader in a creative dialogue that is most fruitful when alternative readings are suggested.

NOTES

1. Edward Said, 'Roads Taken and Not Taken in Contemporary Criticism', *The World, the Text and the Critic*, London: Vintage, 1991, p. 157.
2. Richard Rorty, 'Nineteenth-Century Idealism and Twentieth-Century Textualism', in *Consequences of Pragmatism*, Brighton, 1982, p. 142.
3. Each text has been picked because it adheres to one of the sixteen different types chosen (which are by no means exhaustive) and might be considered amenable to one of the critical contexts that were also pre-selected. While it is to be hoped that the textual readings are interesting in themselves, the aims of the book are also to illustrate a diversity of critical approaches to what are in general 'non-literary' texts and to raise some of the questions that literary critics keep in mind when examining texts that may or may not be poems or novels or plays.

4. Browne's seventeenth-century analysis of burial urns gave Cleanth Brooks the title of his 1947 book *The Well-Wrought Urn: Studies in the Structure of Poetry*, one of the seminal works of New Criticism.
5. Roland Barthes, 'From Work to Text', in Josue V. Harari (ed.), *Textual Strategies*, Ithaca: Cornell University Press, 1979, pp. 73–81. Page references will be given in the body of the Introduction.
6. This echoes Barthes's notion of the *scriptible* (writerly) text as opposed to the *lisible* (readerly) work.
7. Roland Barthes, 'The Death of the Author', in *Image, Music, Text*, trans. Stephen Heath, New York: Hill and Wang, 1977, p. 146.
8. Jonathan Culler, *Structuralist Poetics*, London: Routledge, 1975.
9. Stanley Fish, 'Is There a Text in This Class?', in *Is There a Text in This Class? The Authority of Interpretive Communities*, Cambridge: Harvard University Press, 1980, p. 305.
10. Fish is quoting M. H. Abrams, 'The Deconstructive Angel', *Critical Inquiry* 3: 3 (Spring) 1977, pp. 431 and 434.
11. Stanley Fish, 'Is There a Text in This Class?' in, *Is There a Text in This Class? The Authority of Interpretive Communities*, Cambridge: Harvard University Press, 1980, p. 306.
12. An unintentional implication of Fish's argument is that literary analysis does not need literature.
13. Fish, *Is There a Text in This Class?*, p. 328.
14. Jacques Derrida, *Of Grammatology*, trans G. C. Spivak, Baltimore: John Hopkins University Press, 1976, p. 163.
15. Bernard Harrison, *Inconvenient Fictions*, New Haven and London: Yale University Press, 1991, p. 123.
16. Ibid., p. 10; on Rorty 'Nineteenth-Century Idealism and Twentieth-Century Textualism' *Consequences of Pragmatism*, Brighton, 1982, p. 153.
17. Richard Freadman and Seumas Miller, *Re-thinking Theory*, Cambridge, Cambridge University Press, 1992, pp. 199–200.
18. Ibid., pp. 210–11.
19. Ibid., p. 201.
20. Edward Said, 'The Text, The World, The Critic', in *Textual Strategies*, ed. Josue V. Harari, Ithaca: Cornell University Press, 1979, p. 178.
21. Ibid., p. 165.
22. Ibid., p. 171.
23. There is also the question of the critic's relation with the text: how does the critic approach the text? (why that text? where to begin?); what are the intentions involved and is the critic wanting to celebrate, explicate, rebuke or enter into dialogue with the text?; what is the critic's sense of their moment and mode of writing, and of their relation to the author(s) of the text and to the readers of both text and criticism?; and what is the critic's sense of changing or seeking to change understandings of the text, (and also of writing another text, making an intertext, or even a parasitic text)?.
24. See *The Anxiety of Influence* (1973) and *A Map of Misreading* (1975).
25. Edward Said, 'Roads Taken and Not Taken in Contemporary Criticism', *The World, the Text and the Critic*, London: Vintage, 1991, p. 145.
26. Ibid., p. 147.
27. Terry Eagleton, *Literary Theory*, Oxford: Blackwell, 1983, p. 77.

FILM: *THE MATRIX* AND THE I-POD

Approach: Cyberphilosophy

Neo: 'I thought it wasn't real.'
Morpheus: 'Your mind makes it real.' (*The Matrix*)

I suffered for a long time, and I suspect many people have, from being told, explicitly or implicitly, that what I 'am' is a copy, an imitation, a derivative example, a shadow of the real. (Judith Butler)[1]

The approaches used by critics to study literary texts, particularly novels, are often equally helpful when considering aspects of film, especially features such as theme, narrative and imagery. There are, of course, significant differences between the two genres: in terms of technology, team production, visual realisation and so forth. A film is the result of multiple efforts from hundreds of individuals, even if they are working towards achieving the vision of one person, a director who may or may not also be the screenwriter.

The film under consideration in this chapter is a key text for a number of reasons. It rivals Stanley Kubrick's *2001: A Space Odyssey* and Ridley Scott's *Blade Runner* in the small canon of Science Fiction films that are extensively discussed in criticism, but, appropriately, it also marks the shift from analogue to digital entertainment by being the film release that more than any other launched the DVD revolution in home technology.[2] *The Matrix* is additionally unusual in being credited to two directors, brothers Larry and Andy Wachowski, and yet this concerted authorship, or auteurship, helps to point up the collaborative nature of film production. While a novel is a kind of technologically 'simple' text whose compositional provenance and physical characteristics are largely taken for granted by literature students, a film is what has been called a 'thick text': one which is technically, creatively and compositionally complex.[3] The technical and design aspects of film production need to be considered carefully in a specialist vocabulary, but the thematic elements of film and its use of plot, narrative and imagery are clearly components that are amenable to literary analysis.

For all its use of cutting-edge techniques such as 'bullet-time', *The Matrix*'s storyline raises questions that have been central to Western philosophy from Plato through Descartes to Baudrillard. The discussion below thus concentrates on the implications of a popular film which students should be able to recognise as exploring philosophical problems and contemporary preoccupations that are also relevant to much literature but especially to twentieth-century fiction and postmodernist criticism.

To begin this discussion, it is pertinent to note that the novelist William Gibson, who wrote a foreword to the filmscript of *The Matrix*, coined the term 'cyberspace' in his novel *Neuromancer* and gave 'the matrix' as its synonym: 'Cyberspace. A consensual hallucination experienced daily by billions of legitimate operators, in every nation.'[4] The premise of the Wachowski brothers' film is thus signalled by its title: that the everyday world with which the audience is familiar exists only in virtual reality (and one reading of the film certainly might focus on the possibility the Internet provides for individuals to 'pass' as other than they physically are)[5]. *The Matrix* is consequently concerned with, among many other things, the synthetic construction of identity and perception, which is placed above an underlying reality to which no one within the matrix has access. The world of the matrix is an artificial one that brings together a programmed computer reality with human mental projections into an immaterial environment. In this it has much in common with cybercriticism and post-humanism, both of which analyse the convergence between the human and the machine, casting doubt on traditional understandings of human identity and reality.[6] As well as questioning humanity's preference for imagined pleasure over real suffering, *The Matrix* exemplifies the postmodernist concern with simulacra, as well as with performed identities, by arguing that human subjectivity exists in role playing and self-delusion.

Alongside essays that compare the Wachowskis's vision to that of idealist philosophers such as Nicolas Malebranche (1638–1715) or George Berkeley (1685–1753), many articles on *The Matrix* discuss whether the film is logically consistent in its presentation of a simulated world, and whether 'existence' can be known to humans as 'real' rather than as part of a computer-generated matrix. Though this latter question perhaps appears in itself somewhat abstruse it is part of the larger question of distinguishing truth from falsity and reality from illusion.[7]

A related issue is the option presented in the film to Cypher between a 'real' world which is unappealing but 'authentic' and a hedonistic world which is simulated: the desert of the real or the comforting illusion of an artificial reality (first explored by Plato in the shadowplay of the Cave in *The Republic*). While Neo's choice between the red and the blue pills is made in pursuit of a 'truth' (the baseline of René Descartes's (1596–1650) *Cogito ergo sum*)[8], despite a complete ignorance of what that truth is, Cypher's choice is radically different. It is made with full knowledge of his options when rejecting the embattled, impoverished real world for the plenitude of simulated cyberspace. Cypher's decision is also different from Neo's in that it comes at the price of deliberately endangering the lives of others and is thus not just an ontological choice but also an ethical one.

In relation to the postmodern condition, however, the categories of the 'real' and the 'simulated' are themselves under scrutiny. Thus, from one perspective *The Matrix* suggests only naturalised artificiality: the illusion of the real in postmodernity. From another perspective the film is far more conservative. It posits not just a hyperreal world, but the desert of the real to which Neo awakes from his lifepod. In other words, *The Matrix* is not concerned with one world but two: the artificiality of the matrix is only possible to identify because of the concrete reality of the machine-dominated world that contains the last 'real' human stonghold, Zion. Such a two-worlds epistemology can be likened to religion's faith on a spiritual plane as well as a material one, to the idealist philosophies of numerous Western and Eastern thinkers, and to the distinction between dreams and reality. The exciting aspect of *The Matrix* is its presentation of the world the audience is familiar with as the insubstantial, delusory world, yet this is precisely the contention of philosophers from Plato to Berkeley.

The Matrix thus becomes fascinating for viewers because, unlike say Buddhism or Lacanian psychoanalysis, it depicts the real world that it claims underlies the illusory or constructed one with which people are familiar. In *The Matrix*, 'the real' is accessible to the filmgoer as viewer even though it is not to the filmgoer as human being. The film's hero, Anderson/Neo, lives in the binaristic Apartment 101, implying that he is already confronting his worst fear, installed in Orwell's room from *1984*. In his first scene, Anderson (meaning 'son of man') takes a minidisc from a hollowed-out copy of a book entitled *Simulacra and Simulations*, one of many indications that the film is indebted to the work of the French postmodernist Jean Baudrillard.

For Baudrillard, the postmodern era is characterised by *the actual* having been replaced by *the virtual* in the constant circulation of signs, or more precisely simulacra: signifiers which do not refer back to original signifieds but only to other signifiers. Baudrillard calls this condition hyperreality and it is most fully expounded in his 1983 book *Simulations*. In this text, Baudrillard argues:

> The very definition of the real becomes: *that of which it is possible to give an equivalent reproduction* . . . At the limit of this process of reproducibility, the real is not only what can be reproduced, *but that which is always already reproduced*. The hyperreal transcends repesentation . . . *It is reality itself today that is hyperrealist* . . . [A]rtifice is at the very heart of reality.[9]

The Matrix also suggests a hyperreal world of simulated images overlaying an inaccessible real world and recycling a long dead culture – in that the simulated world is that of the 1990s but the 'real' world is many decades later.

In hyperreality, simulation takes the place of production: modernity's industrialisation is replaced by postmodernity's imitation of signification. For Baudrillard the traditional distinction between the real and the simulated dissolves, leaving only the circulation of images. Materialism is therefore replaced by idealism in the postmodern world: our conception of reality is based on images, models, idealised versions of life that themselves become the templates or gauges of what is most real. Consequently, everyday life becomes a pale imitation of the artificial: attending the Olympics is a poor substitute for watching it on TV, life is less involving than soap opera, the Grand Canyon is less spectacular than the multimedia experience of its grandeur in an IMAX cinema. In *The Matrix*, a drab ordinary life is portrayed as authentic but only in this respect preferable to the world of the matrix for average Americans. The choice presented to Neo, and later to Cypher, is in a sense between truth and happiness: between unpalatable knowledge about one's own waking reality and a dreamlife where, as Cypher says, 'ignorance is bliss.' The matrix further illustrates Baudrillard's hyperreality because it is a world of simulacra, of signs without referents, which is to say that the late twentieth-century world it imitates has long since passed into history. The matrix reproduces a world that has ceased to be produced; its reality has already disappeared, despite the continued transmission of its own images. In the matrix, because nothing within it is actually happening outside of the minds of its prisoners, the distinctions between politics and entertainment, news and lies, or experience and fantasy, are entirely perceptual. It is a landscape of surfaces in which meaning is meaningless because the matrix refers to nothing in existence other than itself, like the dictionary of an unknown dead language. In line with this, like the matrix's simulation of a dead world, postmodernism for Baudrillard is oriented towards the restoration of the past, trying 'to bring back all past cultures, to bring back everything that one has destroyed'.[10] *The Matrix* similarly reproduces a past that was destroyed – by a war between humans and machines – and the matrix is thus less a reproduction than a simulation.

To simulate, Baudrillard initially says in *Simulacra and Simulations*, is to pretend to have what one has not. He compares pre-postmodern notions of extreme simulation with an essayistic story by Jorge Luis Borges ('Of Exactitude in Science') in which the conceptual (a map) exactly replicates the original (territory). In postmodernity, however, there are simulacra – 'the generation by models of a real without origin or reality: a hyperreal . . . *The desert of the real itself*'.[11] Through this argument, Baudrillard posits the end of metaphysics, of questions of imitation or reduplication of the 'real', and the inauguration of an order of perception that operates by 'substituting signs of the real for the real itself'. Baudrillard makes a comparison here with a religion in which there are only icons or images of a non-existent God. In *The Matrix*,

Thomas Anderson is depicted as having lived in the desert of the real, Borges's 'map' rather than 'territory', until he takes the red pill.

Subsequently, Baudrillard argues that there are four phases of the image: one that reflects a basic reality; one that disguises or perverts a basic reality; one that masks the absence of a basic reality; and one that bears no relation to any reality (and so is its own pure simulacrum). As a development of this, one of Baudrillard's most famous and provocative claims is that 'Illusion is no longer possible.' He gives the example of a bank raid and argues that the apparatus at a Western bank is so geared towards reading the signs of a 'real' bank raid that it would be impossible to simulate one: the established order 'devours' attempts at simulation. This is because simulation is threatening (especially of categories like truth and falsehood, certainty and uncertainty, good and evil): 'Whence the characteristic hysteria of our time: the hysteria of production and reproduction of the real.'[12] In Baudrillard's version of postmodernism, arguments over the authentic or natural cease to have a meaning beyond their operation within a power struggle, as indeed they do in the matrix where there is nothing except simulation. Reality has become its own appearance.

One way to read *The Matrix* is as a playing-out of Baudrillard's theories of postmodernity, in which the artificial has subsumed the real (this develops from Baudrillard's earlier socio-political discussions of 'cyberblitz': 'whereby individuals, objects and society are subjected to the effects of cybernetic codes, models, modulations, and the steering systems of a society which aims at perfecting its instruments of social control')[13]. Of equal interest, however, is the film's presentation of performed identities. When Neo chooses to take the red pill he finds that each person in a pod is jacked into the matrix as if into a role-playing computer game. Human batteries are plugged into the matrix (even those who hack in), where a simulated world is played out using the individual's 'residual self-image', the computerised projection of an electronic and wire-less physical and mental identity.

The idea of performed identities has been explored in the work of the influential philosopher Judith Butler. According to Butler, people do not have fixed identities, and indeed 'identity categories tend to be instruments of regulatory regimes'[14] like the matrix. Which is to say that identity does not precede action, but is constructed through performance within these regulations. It is the repetition of actions or self-presentations that constitutes identity categories, that makes subjects who they are and that creates the signs and effects they believe express them. Thus, for Butler the acts people perform are themselves copies which do not have originals but which have social meanings. Templates of gendered or sexual behaviour mean that the acts subjects perform cause them to understand themselves as 'straight' or 'gay', or 'masculine' or 'feminine' rather than these being character attributes that give rise to their actions (this is further discussed in Chapter 6). These identity effects are themselves always organised in terms of binaries that are socially constructed, reliant upon hierarchical oppositions and promoting a norm and its other. So, even the 'phantasms of "man" and "woman" are theatrically produced effects that posture as grounds, origins, the normative measure of the real'.[15] Similarly, in the matrix the apparently 'real' is no more than the playing out of an original that is absent – individuals are projected or project themselves into a world in which they believe themselves to be living out authentic selves when they are in fact merely imagining their own identities. Thomas Anderson exists only as an imagined life, his identity constructed from a template of behaviour that allows him, in the matrix, to live out and believe in a subjectivity that he does not have except inasmuch as it is performed in his mind. In Butler's theory there is no subject who performs an identity through actions, but a series of actions that construct identity. So, again in *The Matrix*, Thomas Anderson does not exist other than through the actions Neo imagines: he does not exist prior to the matrix and has no identity apart from the matrix. Which is to say that he, Thomas Anderson, does not exist except within a regulated and simulated system of predetermined signs and images. Thomas Anderson is something that Neo does (imagines) rather than is. Identity here is something virtual, as all identity is for Butler. Far from being the cause of his actions in the matrix, Anderson's identity is an imaginary effect of the matrix. It is also important that 'Thomas Anderson' cannot be freely imagined/performed but is imagined/performed within the rules and practices of the matrix.

Here it becomes apparent that the matrix is akin to discourse, which Butler understands in the Foucauldian sense of groups of statements or utterances that govern the way people think about society, history and culture. The matrix is a system of power that conditions what can be said, performed or believed – it is in this sense a discourse in that it exists as a set of rules which the individual is both within and cannot act or speak without (partly because 'matrix' was once a term for the womb, and shares the same latin root as 'mother', in *Gender Trouble* Butler uses the term 'Heterosexual Matrix' to designate the discursive norms within which 'gender' and 'sexuality' are constructed and culturally naturalised).[16]

For Butler in *Gender Trouble*, even the body may not exist prior to discourse and this is also found in *The Matrix* in which Thomas Anderson's body (for example, with hair and without the hose-attachment-holes Neo has in the pod) is imagined according to the norms of the matrix. Thomas Anderson's body is factitious and is manufactured not by the individual but by the matrix, which enables the individual's self-imagination. Also, the matrix writes its system on the pre-imagined body in the sense that it inscribes itself or latches onto the body in the pod, imposing its system and rules upon an individual who firmly believes it has a subjectivity. What Butler says of gender applies more generally to identity: 'Gender is the repeated stylisation of the body, a set of repeated acts within a highly rigid regulatory frame that congeal over time to produce the appearance of substance, of a natural sort of being.'[17]

It is thus only when unplugged from his pod and later replugged into the matrix with different knowledge that Neo can begin to learn the possibility of challenging his identity as constructed by the rules of the matrix. Only then can he subvert the discursive power of the matrix, which then puts him on a par with the agents (sentient programs) like Smith. The term 'agents' is significant because only they have 'agency' within the matrix, everyone else having only the illusion of either free will or subjectivity. Similarly for Butler, human beings have the illusion of agency but are in fact playing out the rules of the heterosexual matrix without realising it.

Thus, from the perspective offered by Baudrillard and Butler *The Matrix* can be a useful illustration of theories of postmodernism or (gender) performativity, both of which rest on the presentation/simulation of a 'real' or an 'identity' which has no original. However, as I mentioned earlier, the film presents two worlds and not one: it posits an artificial world but later introduces a 'real' one with which it is contrasted. This starts to take the film away from analyses indebted to the work of Butler and Baudrillard by introducing more traditional philosophical questions about fantasy, self-delusion and choice.

To explore the questions raised here it is helpful to recall the choices faced by Neo and Cypher that I mentioned earlier. Early on in *The Matrix* Morpheus (the name of the god of sleep and dreams in Greek mythology) asks: 'Have you ever had a dream, Neo, that you were so sure was real? What if you were unable to wake from that dream? How would you know the difference between the dream world and the real world?' This is the point at which Morpheus offers Neo a choice between experiencing 'the truth' and continuing to live (or believing he is living) the simulated life he has known. Neo has to make this choice in ignorance of what 'the truth' is: his decision to choose the unknown over the known is based solely on his desire to discover and live within 'reality'. Later in the film, Cypher takes the opposite decision to Anderson/Neo when faced with the same choice, made under very different conditions. He elects to unlearn 'the truth' in exchange for a privileged, artifical life which he will believe to be real once he is experiencing it. This choice between happy ignorance and 'truth', whatever that truth may be and however it will make the individual feel, is one that has been debated at length by philosophers. An essay that is helpful in this regard is Robert Nozick's 'The Experience Machine' in his book *Anarchy, State and Utopia*. Nozick posits a machine that uses electrodes connected to the central nervous system successfully and unproblematically to provide individuals, suspended in a tank, with the illusion of living any life they choose. Nozick concludes that the individual, unlike Cypher, would not choose to be plugged into this 'experience machine' because humans value authenticity above pleasurable illusion: people wish to live life and not merely believe that they are living it. Which is to say that Nozick believes humans wish to do things, and be a certain way, instead of just feeling it. He argues that people have a deep desire to connect with reality and that they also wish to be certain things – courageous, loyal, loving and so on – which the experience machine deprives them of ever being. For Nozick this decision between authentic living and simulated fantasy is a moral one, just as Cypher's choice is shown in the film to be immoral because he betrays his friends, and Nozick would argue that humans would always be in effect betraying themselves and others by plugging into the experience machine.

Given the perspectives offered by *The Matrix*, there are at least two reasons why Nozick's argument appears less persuasive than it did to most philosophers in 1970. First, Nozick's essay is partly unsatisfying because of the direction in which the experience machine works. The choice is like Cypher's, between a harsh, quotidian reality and an ostensibly superior, near-perfect but artificial life. Neo's choice is more interesting because it is between a known, comfortable but unsatisfying life and an unknown but supposedly truer one. Yet, because the choice is not complicated by knowledge it may be easier. Were Neo to know what awaited him 'down the rabbit-hole' after choosing the red pill, would his decision have been the same? In other words, if an individual were to discover that the life they are now living is merely the effect of having been plugged into Nozick's machine, would they choose to be unplugged and emerge into a world of suffering and pain that was 'real', trading everything they have in this dreamlike existence for an authentic life in agony and penury? Which is to say that Nozick's conclusion, that individuals would not plug into the experience machine, may be right for the wrong reasons, because the decision would not be based on a desire for authenticity but on a preference for an easily tolerable life with which they are already familiar.

Second, from a postmodernist perspective Nozick's conclusion would be considered false because it mistakenly believes that there is an authenticity to which the individual has access, asserting that there is a 'reality' to which the individual wishes to remain true. For Baudrillard by contrast, people are all already in the experience machine where there is a simulated existence but no reality that it is copying. The emphasis on authenticity in Nozick's argument merely betrays a nostalgia for a world in which humans were supposedly able to express their identities in unmediated ways. Again, from Butler's perspective, this belief in an original and true self that is able to exercise free will, presenting its essential being to the world, is a delusion created by the heterosexual matrix (and fostered by *The Matrix*). There is no escape from the experience machine nor are we out of it.

Finally, while it is possible to read the film in myriad terms, such as Buddhist philosophy,[18] postcolonial perspectives (for example, liberation from oppression or slavery), or religious beliefs (for example, Neo is a born-again saviour),[19] it is worth considering *The Matrix* in terms of contemporary politics. On the one hand, if someone were to ask what the matrix represents, a plausible answer would be 'ideology' as defined, for example, by the French Marxist Louis Althusser: 'the Imaginary representation of the subject's relationship to his or her Real conditions of existence'. This is a view proposed by Adam Roberts, who concludes that *The Matrix* is 'one of the most Marxist films ever to come out of Hollywood' because, like capitalist ideology, the matrix operates as a 'fiction obscuring the truth of exploitation' (for another take on this interpretation of *The Matrix* see the discussion of globalisation in Chapter 15).[20] On the other hand, if the film is considered a parable, it might suggest by analogy something more specific about contemporary Western living. In his 2002 book *Welcome to the Desert of the Real*, Slavoj Žižek compares the September 11, 2001 attack on the World Trade Center's Twin Towers to Morpheus's statement to Neo welcoming him to 'the desert of the real', thus suggesting that the terrorist attack in New York was a wake-up call to the West. Euroamerica, this implies, lives in an artificial world protected from the reality of modern post-industrial relations. Through its economic and cultural machinery the West is cocooned from the true state of global affairs, benefiting from inequalities of which it is wilfully ignorant. The conclusion drawn from Žižek's argument would be that the West was so shocked by the attack on the World Trade Center because most people had no idea that groups in the rest of the world might consider them to be as immoral and artificial as the individuals plugged into Nozick's experience machine, ignorant of the global reality that supports consumer capitalism.

REFERENCES AND BIBLIOGRAPHY

Baudrillard, Jean, *Simulations*, New York: Semiotext, 1983.

Bandrillard, Jean, 'Aesthetic Illusion and Virtual Reality', in Julia Thomas (ed.), *Reading Images*, Basingstoke: Palgrave, 2000, pp. 198–206.

Best, Steven and Douglas Kellner, *Postmodern Theory*, London: Macmillan, 1991.

Butler, Judith, *Gender Trouble*, London: Routledge, 1990.

Butler, Judith, 'Imitation and Gender Subordination', in Diana Fuss (ed.), *Inside/Out*, London: Routledge, 1991, pp. 13–31.

Ford, James L., 'Buddhism, Mythology, and *The Matrix*', in Yeffeth (ed.), pp. 150–73.

Haraway, Donna J., *Simians, Cyborgs and Women: The Reinvention of Nature*, London, Routledge, 1991.

Irwin, William (ed.), *'The Matrix' and Philosophy: Welcome to the Desert of the Real*, Chicago: Open Court, 2002.

Kaveney, Roz, *From* Alien *to* The Matrix: *Reading Science Fiction Film*, London: I. B. Tauris, 2005.

Kellner, Douglas, *Jean Baudrillard: From Marxism to Postmodernism and Beyond*, Cambridge: Polity, 1989.

Nozick, Robert, 'The Experience Machine' in *Anarchy, State and Utopia*, New York: Basic Books, 1974, pp. 42–5.

Roberts, Adam, *Fredric Jameson*, London: Routledge, 2000.

Schuchardt, Read Mercer, 'What is the Matrix?', in Yeffeth (ed.), pp. 10–30.

Wachowski, Larry and Andy Wachowski, *The Matrix*, draft film script, 3 June 1997: http://www.scifisctipts.com/scripts/matrix_97_drafttext (accessed 15 Feb. 2006).

Wachowski, Larry and Andy Wachowski, *The Matrix: The Shooting Script*, Foreword, William Gibson, London: Newmarket Press, 2002.

Yeffeth, Glenn (ed.), *Taking the Red Pill: Science, Philosophy and Religion in* The Matrix, Chichester: Summersdale, 2003.

Žižek, Slavoj, *Welcome to the Desert of the Real*, London: Verso, 2002.

Zynda, Lyle, 'Was Cypher Right? Part II: The Nature of Reality and Why it Matters', in Yeffeth (ed.), pp. 43–55.

NOTES

1. Butler, 1991, p. 20.
2. The first film to sell more copies on DVD than VHS, *The Matrix* also remained the highest-selling DVD up to 2003 according to Glenn Yeffeth, p. 289.
3. Kaveney, p. 5.
4. William Gibson, *Neuromancer*, London: Victor Gollancz, 1984, p. 67.
5. For a philosophical discussion of this see Baudrillard in Thomas (ed.).
6. See Haraway.
7. The film can be profitably compared with the comic-strip-derived film *Dark City* (1998, dir. Alex Proyas), in which similar questions of faith, truth and falsity in an artificial world culminate in a maverick hero discovering and overthrowing the powers that are controlling humanity. *Dark City* has numerous plot comparisons with *The Matrix*, including religious overtones of the 'chosen one'.
8. See Zynda.
9. Baudrillard, 1983, pp. 146–7 and p. 151.
10. Quoted in Best and Kellner, p. 127.
11. Baudrillard, 1983, p. 2.
12. Baudrillard, 1983, p. 44.
13. Kellner, p. 77.
14. Butler, 1991, p. 13.
15. Butler, 1991, p. 21.
16. Butler, 1990, p. 151 n. 6.
17. Butler, 1990, p. 33.
18. See Ford.
19. See Schuchardt.
20. Roberts, p. 38.

CHAPTER 2

BUILDING: SHOPPING IN UTOPIA

Approach: Spatial Criticism

[The mall is] the culmination of all the American dreams, both decent and demented; the fulfilment, the model of the postwar paradise. (William Kowinski)[1]

'Can you imagine the guy whose job it is to fight for his right to build a mall on some, like, geological phenomenon.'
'They love their malls here, man.' (Garden State)[2]

Since the late 1980s, cultural geographers have been increasingly reading landscape as text, considering and employing linguistic metaphors, semiotic analyses, and poststructuralist terminology. In particular, the tools of literary analysis and theory have been helpfully employed to consider the built environment. Also, Henri Lefebvre's influential book *The Production of Space* (1974) introduced the idea of 'social space', overturning the traditional understanding of 'space' as an empty area and replacing it with the view that space is always both occupied and meaningful: is always socially, politically and ideologically constructed and interpreted. Rather like the Bakhtinian idea of the chronotope in literature, each society for Lefebvre produces its own forms of space from the Greek world of the *polis* through the city-state of the Renaissance to the present Western urban environment. Because texts inscribe social relations rather than reflecting them it is worthwhile considering the ways in which the mall, the exemplary postmodern space, creates as well as recreates contemporary culture.

The *Encyclopaedia Britannica* defines a shopping mall as a 'collection of independent retail stores, services, and parking areas constructed and maintained by a management firm as a unit' and sees it as a twentieth-century adaptation of the traditional marketplace. Malls arose largely as a response to postwar urban migration to city suburbs alongside widespread car use and the perceived need for shelter from bad weather to attract shoppers. These arcaded smaller versions developed into the colossal regional centres of the late twentieth-century shopping malls but more recent larger examples have attempted to revive the arcade-feel of their forebears by installing atriums or balconies. Malls are noted for internal eclecticism yet they are a feature of the (post)modern city landscape that are themselves differentiated into a number of competing retail models – Meaghan Morris lists 'discount chains, hyper-markets, neo-arcades, ethnic and other "theme" environments, history-zones, speciality malls, multi-use centres and megastructures'.[3]

Malls have many features that can be analysed separately (from their opening hours to their security arrangements), but it is the design of the buildings themselves that attracts most attention, and particularly their spatio-temporal dimensions. Which is to say that the function of shopping mall architecture is usually thought to be to organise consumers' movement through and perception of space in a world that would seek to be free of time. Morris calls the shopping centre:

> a 'place' consecrated to timelessness and stasis (no clocks, perfect weather . . .) yet lived and celebrated, lived and loathed, in intimately historic terms: for some, as ruptural event (catastrophic or Edenic) in the social experience of a community, for others, as the enduring scene (as the cinema once was, and the home still may be) of all the changes fluctuations and repetitions of everyday life.[4]

Consequently, the shopping centre or indoor mall is in fact a multi-purpose space. Its primary function is retail but it also aims to provide amusement and entertainment, takeaways and eat-ins, education and information. It may host fashion shows, cinemas and theatres, libraries and concerts, adult education classes and keep-fit sessions, crèches and funfairs. In a commodified culture, the shopping mall is there to provide everything the consumer needs materially but also spiritually: the marketing of love, fate, happiness, sexual attraction, community and personality all takes place in the mall. According to Jon Pahl, America's 20,000 malls are places to worship a consumer deity: always smelling of fresh-brewed coffee and scented candles, they provide rituals and icons for the capitalist religion.[5]

Though thought of as an exemplary expression of postmodern culture, the mall has its modern predecessors in the outdoor shopping centres that were a notable product of modernity: during the era Le Corbusier (1887–1965) decided the house was a machine for living in, the centre emerged as a machine for shopping in. Its origins lay in buildings such as the Galleria Vittorio Emanuele completed in 1877 in Milan and the first outdoor planned shopping centre in the US which was built in Chicago in 1916. Much later, the first enclosed indoor mall opened in the US in 1956 in Minnesota and the first 'large enclosed shopping centre to be built in the UK' was north-west

London's Brent Cross in 1976. By the end of the twentieth century the number of new malls or indoor shopping centres was in decline but the size was growing: Metrocentre in Gateshead, England described itself in October 2004 as 'Europe's biggest shopping and leisure city' at 1,780,000 sq.ft.[6] This takes the mall to its logical conclusion where it replaces the urban centre and becomes 'a city' in itself, based on shopping but incorporating everything from, in the Metrocentre's case, a transport network to a 'complete leisure experience' dubbed Shoppertainment. For the last twenty-five years, malls have been the most frequented public spaces in the US according to the Bureau of Statistics.

The shopping mall, though its smaller versions have found their way back into the metropolitan heart, developed in opposition to city centre shopping: a suburban rather than urban retail space that would include pedestrianisation, ample free parking, security, climate control, child support and a sense of local community without the inconveniences of cars and congestion, the evils of crime and pollution, or even the vagaries of the weather. As Shields notes, the mall is different from the high street in a number of respects:

> In the high street, there is a much more clearly marked separation between public pavement, where certain types of behaviour and 'crowd' practice are acceptable, and the privately controlled store area where the same behaviour is not. Being in the tightly policed, semiprivate interior of a mall is quite different from being 'on the street'. 'No loitering', as the signs in the mall say. Certain types of comportment are expected. The emotions linked with boisterous behaviour are smothered under a flood of continuous, calming, psychologically tested 'music'.[7]

In distinction from the city centre's availability for public demonstration or organised marches, malls are under constant surveillance and are private buildings to which admittance can be denied. It is nigh impossible, for example, to stage any protest because there is no 'public street' on which to operate. Given the absence of other spaces, it has been argued that this can lead to a lack of rebellion among the young: 'To congregate in such places as the West Edmonton Mall requires that one observe bourgeois norms of social docility and conservatism both in dress and action.'[8] The youth types associated with the mall are thus not rebels but those thought to be either indifferent to or complicit with consumerism: slackers, chavs and mallrats.

Shopping malls, unlike the vast majority of city centres, are purpose-built environments. Often erected on green-field sites, they give few clues to the identity of the locality outside their walls. The mall creates its own sense of space, which it has in common with other malls rather than with its neighbourhood. The mall usually also strives to exist in its own environment without reference to the world outside its doors: clocks are rare and the sky outside is not visible. The primary aim of the centre is to bring the shopper into contact with merchandise as much and as frequently as possible; a secondary aim, to achieve the first, is to keep pedestrians circulating. Free seating is provided for resting and pausing but must not invite the shopper to linger unproductively and so is not too comfortable, private or plentiful. The sense of lanes is created by placing features of different kinds in the centre of main corridors pushing shoppers to left or right, and thus nearer to shopfronts. Corridors themselves are usually straight to allow the shopper a clear line of vision to the department store shopfronts at the end. These are usually openfronted to present no barriers, to detract from the feeling of entering a different space, and to allow the maximum number of entrants. Other retailers have no doors and/or large glass fronts that display the maximum number of goods and seek to attract the department-store bound consumer or the aimless stroller.

From a Foucauldian perspective, the mall is a heterotopia, a placeless place devoted to miniaturising and domesticating diverse other places hygienically and conveniently. Heterotopias have 'the ability to juxtapose in a single real place several emplacements that are incompatible in themselves' and are 'realised utopias': places where the other places of a culture are 'at the same time, represented, contested and reversed, sorts of places that are outside all places'.[9] The overall effect is sometimes seen as pleasantly vertiginous as the shopper loses contact with the preoccupations of the external world and is spatially and temporally disorientated by the movement across levels, passages, galleries and aisles on stairs, elevators, walkways and escalators. The provision of a map enables planning and self-direction but detracts for casual consumers from the feeling of immersion in a leisurely 'shopping experience' that potentially stretches endlessly and enticingly in every direction. However, unlike other maps, these will give almost no sense of distance though mall sizes are dictated by the distance consumers are thought to be willing to walk. Exits, even Fire Exits, are usually poorly marked. Careful control of both the temperature and the lighting, and often also the sound, disable the consumer from sensing any changes outside the mall while, where possible, the mall contrasts itself favourably with the season: cool when it is hot outside, warm when the weather is cold. Some features often also serve as oases in the mall, featuring plants, small trees, fountains and pools or miniature waterfalls. These transport the domestic mundanity of shopping into the illusion of tourism and tropicality, enhanced by the move to natural lighting (to save on the huge costs of electric lighting) and glazed dome or greenhouse effects in later malls, supplemented in some cases by bamboo or palm trees.

A sense of escaping to another place is thus important to the mall, but so is the possibility of feeling oneself lost in another time. The past can be gestured towards by creating the effect of a crystal palace or exhibition centre, or even the themed shopping experience of the souk or village, while nature, especially water and foliage, is incorporated to cultivate the perception that the shopping centre is a more natural environment than the concrete world outside. Mobile 'street' vendors suggest the past of markets and medieval towns.

A further developing feature of malls is apparent in the attempt to make them hygienic, safe, family-friendly and upmarket. All delivery and service areas are kept out of the sight of shoppers. Security is there to keep out not only criminals but also many other distracting non-consumers: the homeless, pamphleteers, charity-workers, unaccompanied children, and so on. Certain retailers are also excluded, such as sellers of alcohol, bookmakers, laundrettes, charity shops, second-hand dealers. As shopping centres have developed, the drive to make them distinctive and cultured has increased. Malls may host even operas or sculpture parks, art centres or museums, and five-star restaurants have appeared in the same mall 'neighbourhood' as food courts.[10]

In his analysis of West Edmonton Mall (WEM), one of the first MegaMalls that combined extensive leisure facilities with retail outlets, Jeffrey Hopkins argues that the Mall owners employ a 'spatial strategy' that seeks to (re)create an environment of 'elsewhere' that amounts to a 'consumer utopia'[11] – hence the quotation with which I began, likening the ideal mall to the American dream. In this spatial strategy, Hopkins stresses 'placial iconization' – a system of resemblance and mimicry that varies from simulation and homage to attempts at direct duplication: ' "Placial icons" attempt to simulate *characteristics* and *uses* of other places; they are "spatial metaphors" of other places in that they act as *substitutes* for the original referent or place.'[12] 'Metonymic icons' by contrast work by associative characteristics that suggest other places and larger settings.

The characteristic tropes of postmodernism, as outlined by Fredric Jameson,[13] are here in play: the stylistic mimicry of pastiche (a nostalgic, largely indiscriminate eclecticism) and the blurring or schizophrenic fragmenting of temporal and spatial boundaries. So, the second part of WEM's three-phase development introduced 'two major placial icons, the skating rink (Ice Palace) and the amusement park (Fantasyland), as well as several other metonymical icons such as the twelve salt-water aquariums, the aviaries and the "Versailles Palace" fountains.'[14] Other signs of elsewhere are an indoor water park, Pebble Beach golf (signifying Miami) and Bourbon Street (signifying New Orleans), Europa Boulevard, a petting zoo, a Middle Eastern bazaar, and a 'deep sea adventure' attraction with submarines and a model of Columbus's Santa Maria.[15] These spectacular zonal evocations of elsewhere are supplemented by smaller synecdochic and metonymic icons: the Crown Jewels, pagodas, rickshaws, Ming vases, safari huts and Dixie Band statues. Promotional material for WEM typically announces that the tourist need not travel to numerous hotspots because they're 'all here at the West Edmonton Mall'.[16] The simple 'mall' has thus developed from a safe, alternative out-of-town shopping environment into a varied and Disnified fantasy experience aimed at maximising the time consumers (a subset of 'people') spend inside the complex through the simulation under one roof of recognisable diverse landscapes and time-periods.

The eclectic consumerism of the shopping mall becomes its chief stylistic characteristic, in which past times and places are available for incorporation as simulacra in the aid of advertising and image-creation.[17] The shopping mall has no ethic, tradition or higher purpose, and aims above all to sell products: WEM accounts for over 1 per cent of all retail sales in Canada. In this pursuit it can appropriate and reify any other available associations, values and emotions from distant places and previous times. As Fredric Jameson argues, this creates a new logic of simulated environments in which time is replaced by space: 'The new spatial logic of the simulacrum can now be expected to have a momentous effect on what used to be historical time. The past is hereby modified: what was once . . . organic genealogy . . . has meanwhile itself become a vast collection of images.'[18] This can be sanitised under the modern preoccupation with 'heritage' but historical accuracy is in no way an aim. The nostalgic use through 'blank quotation' of cultural associations and shorthand styles can be profitable, however, as made plain by restaurants called 'The Taj Mahal' or amusement arcades called 'The Alamo', while the physical, as opposed to nominal, association with romanticised times and places can produce a greater sense of importance in consumers and in their 'experience'.[19]

Duncan and Duncan note that 'One of the most important roles that landscape plays in the social process is ideological, supporting a set of ideas and values, unquestioned assumptions about the way a society *is*, or should be organized.'[20] A shopping mall inevitably implies that shopping is central to society, placing it at the 'centre' of a complex of (simulated) cultural activity whose purpose is to increase consumption, usually of luxury items rather than basics like daily food. Because shopping malls aspire to Utopian consumer spaces they seek both to exclude those without purchasing power and to cosset shoppers in one safe physical place while satisfying their desire for novel and quasi-exotic experiences. The combination of shopping with simulated tourism allows the consumer to experience the pleasures of Miami Beach, Rajasthan or downtown New Orleans without the 'displeasures' of travel and cultural alienation let alone the sensory discomforts (sights, sounds, smells) that might accompany them. For Fredric Jameson, postmodern new space 'involves the suppression of distance . . . and the relentless saturation of any remaining voids and empty places . . . involves our insertion as individual subjects into a multidimensional set of radically discontinuous realities'.[21] The shopping mall works like this because it operates on many levels and in many directions, but there is no logic to its arrangement that is drawn from history or nature. The mall appears to compress as much (leisure) space and (popular) history as possible into one extended building, which like Jameson's reading of the Westin Bonaventure hotel 'aspires to being a total space, a complete world, a kind of miniature city'.[22] Jameson believes this has resulted in a 'postmodern hyperspace' which 'has finally succeeded in transcending the capacities of the individual human body to locate itself, to organise its immediate surroundings perceptually and cognitively to map its position in a mappable external world'.[23] Yet, while this might be disorienting and vertiginous in pejorative ways for the users of a hotel, who are often more purposive than leisure-shoppers, it may be liberating and pleasantly escapist for those in the hypermall.

In terms of a wider culture, malls participate in what has become known as the 'McDonaldization' of society: a flat homogenisation of Western experience:

> [M]alls today have become a kind of community center for both young and old. Many elderly people now use malls as places to both exercise and socialise. Because some parents now take their children to malls to 'play,' malls are providing play rooms, free video games, and free movies. Like many other contributors to the McDonaldization of society, malls strive to engage customers from cradle to grave.[24]

Different theorists conceive of the kind of space found in shopping malls in different ways. Michel Lefebvre has formulated a chronological typology of space, from the 'absolute space' of nature to his concept of the 'abstract space' of capitalism, which is both fragmented and homogeneous at one and the same time, and then the contemporary 'contradictory space' of global capital opposing but often also producing local meaning.[25] Lefebvre's work has been influential on many key theorists of urban space, such as Jameson, Edward Soja and David Harvey, whose shared view of postmodernism rests on:

> a consensus on the importance of the spatial character of a capitalism that increasingly relied on long-distance linkages and attenuated social relations ('distanciation'), bringing places closer together in one sense at the same time as compressing the time allotted for almost every task.[26]

Thus, the shopping centre is a mechanistic space for modernity but under postmodernity it is the appropriate place of spectacle which can use the language of authenticity while solely participating in simulation – to be lost in the shopping mall is to experience it appropriately: to succumb to its all-encompassing multidimensional labyrinths in which there is no need to know where you are because 'everything' is just around one corner or the next, and there is also no need to go 'outside'. The mall's historical and geographical compressions are no longer dizzying for the postmodern flâneur who 'dedicates' time to the mall and finds nothing incongruous in the eclectic assemblage of distant times and places juxtaposed under one roof, with each mock-up claiming to be better than the 'original', thanks to the superior (that is, convenient) environment of the mall. Coherence is supplied by the safety and uniformity of the shopping centre in which every desirable facet of human experience, from Moghul Rajasthan to New Orleans street-prostitution, can be domesticated and sanitised for family consumption. The mall expresses its times, when the West understands the world through tourism, TV and Third World 'trade'. It centres the consumer's world where the consumer shops and plays, overturning ideas of smalltown life or a frontier existence, because the world comes permanently to town in the traditional manner of the circus, travelling merchants or strolling players. This replica experience both demystifies and detracts from the 'originals' it apes, as in hyperreality when mediated experience is the norm and the real most often seems a poor imitation of the simulated. Under postmodernity the grand narratives of the past are no longer subscribed to, and this includes the narratives of history which have fashioned previous beliefs in progress and tradition, cause and effect, frontiers and borders, human alterity and cultural alienation. This applies as much to space as time: '[I]ncremental changes in our basically Cartesian understanding and commonsense conceptions of geographical space as a three-dimensional, seamless, and apparently neutral void have led to a relativised conception of geographical space as a socially constructed convention.'[27]

As Meaghan Morris points out, the shopping centre can be read in other ways than the spatial. Morris's feminist reading also alludes to a psychoanalytic perspective that positions the Imaginary as mirror to the shopping centre spectacle: as 'palaces of dreams, halls of mirrors, galleries of illusion'.[28] However, Morris argues that the shopping centre makes possible that which the separation of spheres (men in public, women in private) in the nineteenth century seemed to make impossible for women in modernity: the female flâneur.[29] But Shields, who has noted that the mall is a 'private-public' space,[30] reads this far less positively:

> [A] shopping centre, such as the Eaton's Centre in Toronto, represents a spatial ensemble that both encourages and requires (for commercial viability) a specific type of 'crowd practice'. The aggregate, wandering consumer crowd of today is complemented by the celebratory and festive galleria-type shopping mall. This type of spatial performance is quite different from the much less commercialised public behaviour of the *boulevardier* or *flâneur* who strolled the nineteenth-century shopping arcades of Paris. This historical model legitimised the new Canadian and American shopping arcades of the 1980s, such as Eaton's, the West Edmonton Mall and Mall of the Americas, even while it was transformed into a new hyper-commercialised model.[31]

Shopping in late capitalism separates consumption from production, and this is increasingly exacerbated by the composite nature of most goods (even foods) and the flows of global capitalist finance. The consumer has little knowledge about where a product was made (it is usually more than one place), who by, or with what, and this in itself has led to counter movements, typified by the contrary pressures for producers to better 'label' foods, in terms of ingredients and miles travelled, and for shoppers to resist designer labels on clothes. Far from being simply a site of leisure activity the mall in the twenty-first century is a site on which wars can be waged: over history, culture and global politics.

REFERENCES AND BIBLIOGRAPHY

De Certeau, Michel, *The Practice of Everday Life*, trans. Steven Randall, Berkeley: University of California Press, 1984.

Duncan, J. and N. Duncan, '(Re)reading the Landscape', *Environment and Planning D: Society and Space*, 6, 1988, pp. 117–26.

Foucault, Michel, 'Questions on Geography', in *Power/Knowledge*, London: Harvester Wheatsheaf, 1980.

Foucault, Michel, 'Different Spaces', in J. B. Faubion (ed.), *Essential Works: Aesthetics*, vol. 2 London: Allen Lane, 1998.

Goss, Jon, 'Modernity and Post-Modernity in the Retail Landscape', *Cultural Geographies: Ways of Seeing the World*, Sydney: Longman Cheshire, 1992, pp. 159–177.

Harvey, David, *The Condition of Postmodernity*, Oxford: Blackwell, 1990.

Hopkins, Jeffrey S. P., 'West Edmonton Mall: Landscapes of Myths and Elsewhereness', *The Canadian Geographer*, 34: 1, 1990, pp. 2–17.

Jameson, Fredric, 'Cognitive Mapping', in Cary Nelson and Lawrence Grossberg (eds), *Marxism and the Interpretation of Culture*, Macmillan: Basingstoke, 1988, pp. 347–57.

Jameson, Fredric, *Postmodernism, or the Cultural Logic of Late Capitalism*, London: Verso, 1991.

Kowinski, William Severini, *The Malling of America*, New York, Morrow, 1985.

Lefebvre, Michel, *The Production of Space*, trans. N. Donaldson-Smith, Oxford: Blackwell, [1974] 1991.

Morris, Meaghan, 'Things to do with Shopping Centres', in Susan Sheridan (ed.), *Grafts: Feminist Cultural Criticism*, London: Verso, 1988, pp. 193–226.

Pahl, Jon, *Shopping Malls and Other Sacred Spaces: Putting God in Place*, Grand Rapids: Brazos, 2003.

Ritzer, George, *The McDonaldization of Society*, revd edn, California: Pine Forge Press, 1996.

Shields, Rob, 'Social Spatialization and the Built Environment: The West Edmonton Mall', *Environment and Planning D: Society and Space*, 7, 1989, pp. 147–64.

Shields, Rob, *Lefebvre, Love and Struggle: Spatial Dialectics*, London: Routledge, 1999.

NOTES

1. Kowinski, p. 25.
2. *Garden State* (2004), written and directed by Zach Braff.
3. Morris, p. 208.
4. Morris, p. 206.
5. See Pahl.
6. http://www.metrocentre-gateshead.co.uk/ (accessed 12 Aug. 2005).
7. Shields, pp. 148–9.
8. Shields, p. 160.
9. Foucault, 1998, p. 181 and p. 178. Conventional examples Foucault gives of heterotopias are fairs, libraries, theatres and museums, but he also cites cemeteries, ships, brothels and colonies.
10. See Goss for an overview of these features.
11. Hopkins, p. 2.
12. Hopkins, p. 4.
13. See Jameson, 1991, Chapter 1.
14. Hopkins, p. 9. Fantasyland is now called Galaxyland.
15. Leisure activity accounts for about 25 per cent of revenue at WEM, nearly all the rest being made from retail.
16. Hopkins, p. 12.

17. Hopkins explains that after home and work/school, the mall is the place where the average Canadian spends most time: Hopkins, p. 7.
18. Jameson, 1991, p. 18.
19. Since at least the 1980s, shopping malls have in part contributed to the widespread acceleration of the heritage industries and in several respects simulate museum culture.
20. Duncan and Duncan, p. 123.
21. Jameson, 1988, p. 351.
22. Jameson, 1991, p. 40.
23. Jameson, 1991, p. 44.
24. Ritzer, p. 29.
25. Lefebvre; see Shields, 1999, pp. 170–85 for discussion.
26. Shields, 1999, p. 143.
27. Shields, 1989, p. 155.
28. Morris, p. 202.
29. Morris, p. 221.
30. Shields, 1989, p. 148.
31. Shields, 1999, p. 163.

MOVIE POSTER: ALIEN NATURE

Approach: Ecocriticism

John Fiske explains that texts are sometimes considered to be used differently in studies of literature and popular culture:

> In popular culture the text is a cultural resource to be plundered or used in ways that are determined by the social interests of the reader/user not by the structure of the text itself, nor by the intentions (however we may discern them) of its author.[1]

This is a relative rather than absolute distinction and one that might be thought to rely too heavily on a certain understanding of literary criticism, but Fiske's distinction between the kinds of texts studied as literature and popular culture is perhaps more helpful. Implicitly, Fiske sees this lying in considerable contemporary social relevance: 'The popularity of a text . . . consists only in its relations with its immediate social and historical conditions: popular texts cannot be transcendent . . . Popular texts, therefore, are evaluated according to their social values, not their universal or aesthetic ones.'[2] While aesthetic considerations play a part in many critics' discussion of literary texts, as many more are interested in literature's social values – conversely, the aesthetic qualities and structural properties of popular texts are certainly amenable to productive analysis. Also, a range of literary critics of different stripes have increasingly analysed poetry, prose and drama as intertexts entwined with social and cultural discourses since the interventions of critical theory in the 1960s. Nonetheless it is helpful to bear in mind the approach that Fiske believes characterises the study of popular culture:

> Analyzing texts that have been made popular involves, then, searching for their contradictions, their rough edges that have not been authorially smoothed out into organic coherence, for these abrasive bits that open a text up to popular uses, and enable it to be seen not as a complete and

unified whole, but as a terrain upon which people can engage in the struggle for meanings. In popular culture the text is not an object of reverence to be understood in all its coherence and completeness, but as a resource to be used. Indeed, the text that is made into popular culture is always incomplete until it is used, it remains at the level of cultural potential until it is selectively taken up and inserted into the social circulation of meanings.[3]

Fiske's division between the reading approaches applied to literary and popular texts seems too rigid and the implication that a text cannot be both popular and literary is open to question. However, Fiske's description could be partly considered an example of Fish's interpretive communities, discussed in the Introduction, because it says how a popular text, however defined, will be read, and also how a canonical or, by implication, 'unpopular' one would be read.

In the reading that follows I will look at a text from popular culture and pay attention to several of the aspects that Fish suggests are the province of literary studies, but I also want to offer a particular angle on its possible signification, suggesting a way of placing it within a wider social circulation of meanings that attends not to its coherence but to its ambiguities. The text is a poster, but the reader may find it helpful to know a little about the film it advertises, Ridley Scott's *Alien* (1979).

> FILM PLOT SYNOPSIS: Halfway home to earth, the mining and refining spaceship *Nostromo* is diverted from its course to investigate an unknown transmission coming from an asteroid. The landing party discovers a crashed spacecraft and a nest of pod-like eggs, one of which dehisces to allow a parasite to shoot out and attach itself to the face of one of the crew, Kane. Later, after Kane has apparently recovered, a baby alien bursts out of his chest and rushes to safety within the bowels of the ship, where it soon grows to full size. The crew are gradually picked off by the alien until there is only one of them remaining, Ripley, played by Sigourney Weaver. During the killing spree, it transpires that the *Nostromo* had been intentionally rerouted by 'the Company' to gather a specimen of the alien life form and return it to earth. The Company is explicit about the fact that the crew's lives are less important than this mission. Finally, escaping the ship in a smaller craft, Ripley blasts the stowaway alien back out into space, but a feeling of menace and threat persists if only because the nest of aliens survives on the asteroid.

In Steven Soderbergh's cerebral 2001 sci-fi film *Solaris*, one character, Gibarian, explains:

> We take off into the cosmos, ready for anything: solitude, hardship, exhaustion, death. We're proud of ourselves, in a way. But when you think about it, our enthusiasm is a sham. We don't want to explore the

cosmos – we want to conquer it, to extend the boundaries of earth to the cosmos, imposing our ideas, our values.

Soderbergh's *Solaris*, in common with Andrei Tarkovsky's earlier 1971 Russian version of Stanislaw Lem's 1961 novel, is concerned with the metaphysical properties of the universe. In this, as suggested by the quotation above, the films share with *Alien* their concern with the human will to power, the desire to control the environment. *Solaris* ultimately postulates a benign universe within which everything is finally forgiven and love exceeds death. However, while the same human urge to explore is present in *Alien*, the universe is also hostile in Ridley Scott's film and the strongest human motive is that of the capitalist pursuit of wealth and weapons, achieved through the further exploitation of mineral resources on other planets.

A film poster is usually designed as part of the post-production process. The major filming has already occurred but aspects such as the score, the credit and title sequences, and the marketing artwork are still to be done. These are all crucial to the atmospherics of the film and will contribute greatly to its image, along with the trailer(s). The poster is to a degree analogous to the book cover: promoting and preceding the film, produced at another time from the body of the text but also bound to it. Film posters are also, of course, aimed at attracting audiences and like book covers vie to entice consumers to part with their money. The poster is thus commercially and creatively linked to the film, but is also an artwork, or text, in its own right. If we consider a film from its poster, particular approaches may be suggested more than others, partly because the poster has many separate meanings from the film, especially for those who have not seen the movie. The poster can also re-accentuate interpretations of the many thousands of single images that comprise the film reels.

The *Alien* poster is pared down: suggestive, allusive, vague but threatening, which is how the barely glimpsed alien is portrayed in the film. The poster uses a combination of elements to achieve its effect: in upper-case, an austere straight-line font for the name of the film; in sentence case, a dissimilar cursive font for the legend 'In space no one can hear you scream'; an ovoid central object that is pitted and spotted; a crack in the object emits both a yellow light and a green gas. What is curious about the poster, however, is that aside from the title it seems to have almost nothing, in terms of story or dialogue, to do with the *Alien* film. For example, nobody in the film says the line 'In space no one can hear you scream', and while a hive or nest of eggs or pods features in the film, the pods are unlike the elliptical object in the poster, which resembles a bird egg in shape, and the poster's object cracks at the bottom rather than unfolding at the top like the pods in the film.[4] Arguably, the poster, though highly suggestive and evocative, has little direct representative meaning with regard to the film except to signal that the narrative is scary and is set in space and is thus a hybrid of the sci-fi and horror genres. The poster fulfils its aim of intriguing and attracting customers, creating a sense of expectation with regard to the film, but signifies differently if not read as either a curtain raiser or a metonym for the film.

Most interestingly, the poster offers an ominous representation of the relationship between nature and science. This is depicted in terms of contrasts, between the egg and the mesh, between the harsh and soft fonts, the dark and the light. Also, though ovoid, the object in space is unlike anything found in nature and is thus 'unnatural' or 'alien'. Absent from the poster are both the humans and the alien creature from the film,[5] though it can be argued that these are signified through the images of the presumably human-made grid at the bottom and the unfamiliar, threatening egg at the centre.[6] In other words, a concept that is suggested by the poster is that of alienation – isolation and an estrangement from what should be familiar.

Taking such a reading back to the film, *Alien* from this perspective seems not just to portray isolation in space but to posit the failed attempt of humanity (or rather, transglobal corporatism), to exploit with impunity the mineral resources of the universe, to contain nature, which reasserts itself as radically unknowable, all-powerful, and fundamentally inimical to human domestication. The film thus seems a futuristic take on the continuing 'alienation' of an exploitative humanity from nature whose origins are generally ascribed to the eighteenth-century 'enlightenment' period that saw the advancement of technology and the market economy in a spirit of 'objective-scientific' exploration.

Marx writes at some length on the subject in the *Economic-Philosophical Manuscripts* (1844),[7] and critics of the film have read its narration and characterisation in terms of Marxist alienation but have primarily focused on that of the workers from their work, not that of the humans from nature – seen as the planets mined for resources but also the creature they attempt to domesticate for scientific analysis. Marx writes, for example, of the product manufactured under industrialisation as an 'alien being, as a power independent of the producer . . . the worker is related to the product of his labour as to an alien object'.[8] The alien creature thus can be considered as a manifestation of the alienated labour of the Company's disaffected mining workers on the *Nostromo*: '[T]he product of labour is alien to me and confronts me as an alien power.'[9] To Marx, this alien power is capitalism, private property and those who benefit from the labour of the worker. 'The greed, militarism, and amorality of the Company that owns the *Nostromo* is the main basis for the anti-capitalist readings.'[10] For some critics, 'the Alien is the double, we might say the *biological analogue*, of the Company.'[11] They are both amoral, ruthless, exploitative, parasitic, self-replicating and mortally competitive. Both have reached out into space in an attempt to control, conquer and colonise it.

Given its class and gender representations, the film, coming at the end of the 1970s, can be read in the light of the feminist and environmentalist agenda of that decade, which considered neither science nor capitalism to be liberating, with the self-interested domination of nature appearing as the scientific drive of patriarchy, such that the exploitative mining in *Alien* can stand for the masculinist penetration of women and the Earth.[12] This is mimicked in the 'rape' of John Hurt's character, Kane, in the film – and Kane's subsequent 'birth' of the alien (just as the ship's computer is called 'Mother' – a technological parent as opposed to a natural one, 'mother Earth'). On the poster, the egg is birth and death; representing the womb in its association with hatching but also intimating a threat. Beneath the egg is stretched out the cage or wire of containment, suggesting the patriarchal domestication of the environment and yet unrelated to any image that appears in the movie.

Science Fiction is from one point of view about technology, but this is arguably a male reading – that of technology-driven films such as *2001* which place exploration and weaponry to the fore.[13] In contrast, Elizabeth Fisher in *Man's Creation* explains that 'the first cultural device was probably a recipient . . . Many theorisers feel that the earliest cultural inventions must have been a container to hold gathered products and some kind of sling or net-carrier.'[14] Like so many travel narratives, whether set on earth, sea or in space, *Alien* indeed draws on the archetype of travellers carried through peril in a womb-like container or ship of some kind (containers feature throughout the film but the alien moves through receptacles from pod to human via the protective shell of the facehugger). Agreeing with Fisher, Ursula Le Guin argues that it should be possible to:

> redefine technology and science as primarily cultural carrier bag rather than weapon of domination . . . Science Fiction is a way of describing what is in fact going on . . . how people relate to everything else in this vast sack, this belly of the universe, this womb of things to be and tomb of things that were, this unending story. In it, as in all fiction, there is room enough to keep even Man where he belongs, in his place in the scheme of things.[15]

This alternative perspective provides one way of reading the *Alien* poster. The sphere cracking open is an egg, a carrier bag, a womb, or simply the Earth breaking apart (the 'fragile earth' campaigns often depicted the planet as an egg in danger of cracking). From this viewpoint it becomes apparent that the only menacing aspect of the poster is in fact the strapline because the object cracking open is in itself mysterious rather than necessarily aggressive. Laurence Coupe writes that:

> [Green studies in invoking nature] challenges the logic of industrialism, which assumes that nothing matters beyond technological progress. Thus, it offers a radical alternative to both 'right' and 'left' political positions, both of which assume that the means of production must always be developed, no matter what the cost. Second, in insisting that the non-human world matters, it challenges the complacent culturalism which renders other species, as well as flora and fauna, subordinate to the human capacity for signification. Thus, it queries the validity of treating nature as

something which is 'produced' by language . . . Thus the appeal to ecology is ultimately a matter of ethics. As Aldo Leopold long ago reminded us: 'All ethics so far evolved rest upon a single premise: that the land is a member of a community of interdependent parts . . .'. The land ethic simply enlarges the boundaries of the community to include soils, waters, plants, and animals, or collectively: the land . . . A thing is right when it tends to preserve the integrity, stability and beauty of the biotic community. It is wrong when it tends to do otherwise.[16]

There are thus possible thematic connections between poster and film even though in *Alien* only the graphic design of the title sequence, by the same artists in this case, Stephen Frankfurt and Richard Greenberg, complements the poster. Another part of the post-production process, the film's titles form a link between the poster and the main narrative because the design echoes the poster while the slow development of the word 'Alien' on the dark screen mimics the growth and evolution of the creature itself in the film, as the camera pans across deep space to arrive at the *Nostromo* spacecraft. Thus the artwork forms a segue into the film through the title sequence, which also creates a bridge from the iconography and trademarked typeface of the poster to the somewhat different design features and imagery of the movie. The *Alien* poster, arguably like all film posters, book covers and similar cultural texts, is in some ways most interesting because of its tangential relationship to a 'host' text.

The final image and design of the poster was arrived at only after rejecting many others. These range from a simple space shot with only a blurry planet-shaped central object and the threat 'Prepare Yourself. ALIEN, Arriving May 23, 1979' through to those that use the image of Kane's chest-explosion or Ripley about to scream.[17] Taglines vary from 'No one should be allowed to even imagine that thing which is now headed our way' through 'Please listen Mankind, you have so little time' to 'Once again something has come from space and this time it's not a friend.'[18] All of these lines seem to draw on the established tropes of sci-fi horror to present a clearer threat than the eeriness conveyed by the final poster.

The information left on screen at the end of the title sequence boldly states several facts as prologue: the '*Nostromo*', which can be dimly seen in the background, is a mining company's commercial towing vehicle returning to Earth with a crew of seven. It is an 'aircraft carrier/refinery' and its cargo comprises 20 million tons of refined material ore.

The name of the vehicle refers to Joseph Conrad's 1904 novel *Nostromo* which offers a critique of a colonial silver mining company in South America. In Conrad's novel the silver brings only death to those who possess it, and this is clearly a parallel with the creature discovered by the mining crew in *Alien*.[19] As has been noted, the theme of mining, with its rapacious and penetrative associations, is itself embedded in the film in many different ways. A whimsical example is the hugely anachronistic nose-diving plastic toy birds – cranes perhaps – who continuously nod up and down, as though in imitation of mining cranes, on the dining table of the crew's common room. Though this is minor detail, these artificial birds can lead the viewer into the bird and egg imagery of the film which, while suggesting no resemblances to the poster object, is present elsewhere. For example, there are mechanical birds on springs suspended from the ceiling in one room and the egg/pod symbolism encompasses the human sleep chambers, from the ones out of which the crew emerge at the start to the one in which Ripley lies down at the end, in the escape shuttle.[20]

This element of the film can be placed in terms of many different readings: a pro-feminist one with Ripley as hero, a phallocentric one that contrasts the ova imagery with that of rape/penises, and a masculinist critique which concentrates on how men are shown to usurp the reproductive process. It is an element that can also be linked to the poster and an ecocritical reading.

While Fiske says that popular texts are evaluated according to their social values, not their universal or aesthetic ones, this is a matter of the reading and not the text. Arguably, *Alien* has become a canonical text that Fiske would think has transcended its historical moment, yet it remains an extremely popular one. The film undoubtedly repays detailed social, cultural, aesthetic and formal readings, as critics have found. It is multi-layered in terms of imagery and amenable to a range of approaches, making it far more of a *scriptible* than a *lisible* text, in Barthes's terms (discussed in the Introduction). The film's poster is more ephemeral but nonetheless intriguing, seen as a peritext to the film,[21] and/or as a signifying intertext itself.[22] While the reading offered here seeks to place the poster – and by implication the film – in an ecocritical frame of reference, the poster's separate appeal from the movie lies in its aesthetic construction but also its ambiguous symbolism, as the images that feature in the design are allusive with regard to the film but elusive with regard to their desired or possible meanings.

REFERENCES AND BIBLIOGRAPHY

Coupe, Laurence, *The Green Studies Reader*, London: Routledge, 2000.

Fiske, John, 'Popular Culture', in Frank Lentricchia and Thomas McLaughlin (eds), *Critical Terms for Literary Study*, 2nd edn, Chicago: University of Chicago Press, 1995.

Garrard, Greg, *Ecocriticism*, London: Routledge, 2004.

Kaveney, Roz, *From* Alien *to* The Matrix: *Reading Science Fiction Film*, London: I. B. Tauris, 2005.

Le Guin, Ursula, 'The Carrier Bag Theory of Fiction' [1986], in Cheryll Glotfelty and Harold Fromm (eds), *The Ecocriticism Reader*, Athens: University of Georgia Press, 1996, pp. 149–54.

O'Bannon, Dan, *Alien: Illustrated Screenplay*, Orion: London, 2001.

Scanlon, Paul and Michael Gross, *The Book of Alien*, London: Titan, 1993.

Schwartz, Richard A., *The Films of Ridley Scott*, Westport: Greenwood Press, 2001.

NOTES

1. Fiske, p. 331.
2. Fiske, p. 334.
3. Fiske, p. 332.
4. Following director Ridley Scott, Roz Kaveney uses the term 'egg' to describe what I am calling a pod (H. R. Giger, the designer, used the term 'organic footballs' to describe the spore pods but his initial design was for an 'egg chamber'), underlining the difficulty with naming in *Alien*. The object splits like a pod, but contains a creature, known as a face-hugger. This face-hugger, which springs from the pod, is however not a fully gestated creature but a parasite that itself lays an egg of some kind in the host. Kaveney refers to the face-hugger after it detaches from the host as a 'husk' (p. 139), suggesting the external green or membranous covering of certain fruits and seeds rather than the corpse of a creature from an egg. The biotechnical alien is also indeterminate in terms of usual divisions of animal, vegetable and mineral, placed somewhere between the humans in the film and the 'synthetic' crewmember Kane.
5. This is not the case with many of the earlier versions of the poster, which featured a range of different images and taglines, many of which are clearly referential or announce the arrival of the film in terms of the alien's imminent arrival to terrorise humans/filmgoers.
6. The film is open to feminist readings and the contrast between 'manmade' grid and female egg in the poster is similarly amenable to a gender analysis.
7. Karl Marx, 'Alienated Labour' in Alasdair Clayre (ed.), *Nature and Industrialization*, Oxford: Oxford University Press, 1977, pp. 245–50; excerpted from *Economic-Philosophical Manuscripts*.
8. Ibid., p. 246.
9. Ibid., p. 249.
10. Schwartz, p. 23.
11. Schwartz, p. 25.
12. The equation between women and nature is, of course, one that is culturally established as a stereotype (as in mother nature) and one that is open to feminist critique.
13. Ursula Le Guin explains:

> Where is that wonderful, big, long, hard thing, a bone, I believe, that the Ape Man first bashed somebody with in the movie and then, grunting with ecstasy at having achieved the first proper murder, flung up into the sky and whirling there it became a space ship thrusting its way into the cosmos to fertilise it and produce at the end of the movie a lovely fetus, a boy of course, drifting around the milky way without (oddly) any womb, any matrix at all? . . . we've all heard all about all the sticks and spears and swords, the things to bash and poke and hit with, the long, hard things, but we have not heard about the thing to put things in, the container for the thing contained. (Le Guin, Athens: p. 153)

14. Elizabeth Fisher in *Man's Creation*, McGraw-Hill, 1975, p. 56.
15. Le Guin, pp. 153–4.
16. Coupe, p. 4, quoting Aldo Leopold, *A Sand Country Almanac*, Oxford: Oxford University Press, 1949, pp. 204, 224–5.
17. This last uses the strapline 'In space no one can hear you scream' – but with the image of Ripley rather than an image of the threat itself. The poster image suggests Fay Wray about to scream at King Kong, or countless other screen heroines in promotional stills.
18. 'Once again something has come from space and this time it's not a friend' may be an allusion to Stanley Kubrick's *2001*, a major influence on Scott when he was making *Alien*, but from a contemporary perspective it could more likely be a reference to *Close Encounters of the Third Kind*, released in 1977.
19. To call the spaceship after a Conrad novel was Scott's decision. In the first outline

treatment by Dan O'Bannon, it was to be called the *Snark* after Lewis Carroll's poem 'The Hunting of the Snark'. Scott had just finished his first feature film, *The Duellists*, an adaptation of a Conrad short story and his original strapline for *Alien* was 'We live as we dream – alone', a quotation from Conrad's *Heart of Darkness*. The final strapline 'In space no one can hear you scream' is a variant on the sentiment of Conrad's line concerning human isolation, and *Heart of Darkness* remains a clear influence on *Alien*.

20. Kaveney considers the computer room to be 'another egg or womb' (p. 134). The main computer itself is called 'Mother', emphasising both reproduction and the film's conflation of the natural and the artificial.

21. Nearly all books have what are called 'peritexts' – headings, subtitles, prefaces, dedications, forewords, and so on – which are arguably part of 'the text' and sometimes just as arguably not a part of it.

22. Cf. in the Introduction, the semiotic reading of a Silk Cut advertising poster from David Lodge's novel *Nice Work* (1988).

POP VIDEO: MICHAEL JACKSON'S 'THRILLER' AND 'RACE'

Approach: 'Race' Studies

'Mama, see the Negro! I'm frightened!' (Frantz Fanon)[1]

'All black people in the United States, irrespective of their class status or politics, live with the possibility that they will be terrorized by whiteness.' (bell hooks)[2]

Video synopsis: One evening, Michael and his girlfriend Ola are driving along a dirt road in the woods when the car stops and Michael says they are out of gas. After they leave the car and start walking under the full moon, Michael presents Ola with an engagement ring before claiming that he's different from other people. All of a sudden, Michael falls to his knees and then looks up with solid yellow eyes, causing Ola to run. Michael transforms into a werewolf and then chases after her. Following a cut to a movie theatre, it transpires that the 'real' Michael and Ola are watching themselves in a film at the cinema. The movie is *Thriller*, starring Vincent Price. Michael is greedily enjoying the film, but Ola insists they leave. The song starts on the soundtrack as they walk the streets, with Michael apparently singing to Ola about *Thriller*. From the cemeteries they walk past, zombies rise from graves and begin to close in on the couple. Michael now transforms into a zombie and suddenly starts to dance and sing with the others. Ola is chased into an old house and is close to being attacked when she awakens from what has evidently been a dream. Michael is with her and offers to take her home. They go to leave but the shot freezes as Michael turns back to face the camera with unhuman glowing yellow eyes.

One of Michael Jackson's hit singles has the consistent line in its chorus, 'It Don't Matter If You're Black Or White': the statement of an ideal rather than a social fact.[3] In Western society, white has been generally portrayed as a norm against which blackness is positioned as aberrant – threatening and perhaps even monstrous. As well as telling a mini-story familiar from teen horror, Michael Jackson's music video for his song 'Thriller' invokes a number of discourses about 'race' and race relations in the US. Riffing on 1950s horror movies, it divides small-town America between respectable cinemagoers, fascinated and appalled by celluloid monsters, and unseen street zombies who recolonise the night. By drawing on the xenophobia of Cold War America and its continuing segregationist racial policies, 'Thriller', like many 1950s sci-fi movies, preaches both a fear and acceptance of 'the Other' outside and within society. Jackson's own troubled relationship with chromatism forms a further context for readings of the video, as does his position in both black and white popular music. It is in this light that this chapter will look at 'Thriller'.

Ed Guerrero notes that after the Blaxploitation movies of the period 1969–74 (sixty or so vehicles for narratives of the black ghetto), Hollywood studios moved towards 'crossover' films. These were stories that would appeal to white as well as black audiences, would rely on one or two big-name black stars (like Sydney Poitier) and accommodate white sensibilities and values. The effect was to incorporate the margin into the mainstream and so neutralise the commercial and ideological threat of the 'black' movie. Guerrero concludes that 'by 1978 the only major production with any kind of black focus was the musical *The Wiz*.'[4] In this film (dir. Sidney Lumet, 1978) an urban African American version of *The Wizard of Oz*, just four years before 'Thriller', Michael Jackson played the part of the scarecrow to Diana Ross's Dorothy. The film's transformations of identity and location can be seen as a precursor to 'Thriller' but so can the attempt to engage with political issues concerning the black American community. Its writing credited to Jackson and John Landis, the 'Thriller' video was directed by Landis who had previously directed the film *An American Werewolf in London* (1981). Having seen the film, Jackson wanted Landis to shoot his music video, starring Jackson and Ola Ray, for the song, written by Rod Temperton (from the British mixed-race disco group Heatwave).

The *Thriller* (1982) album is associated with record-breaking because it became the biggest selling LP in pop's history. The fourteen-minute video accompanying the single 'Thriller' was released as part of a videocassette, 'The Making of Michael Jackson's *Thriller*' (1983), which in turn became the largest-selling home video at the time, according to the *Guinness Book of Records*. An unprecedented seven top-ten singles were released from the album. Also, music videos from the album were the first by a black artist to be shown on MTV, which had hitherto been a *segregationist* white-only rock music channel – consequently, Kobena Mercer argues that the designs used by Jackson in his music videos are important 'because they breached the boundaries of race on which the music industry have been based'.[5] Music videos after 'Thriller' increasingly used a story-telling mode, now common, that was previously rare in the promotion of pop music.

The 'Thriller' video has been read by Kobena Mercer in terms of sexuality. I will summarise aspects of Mercer's reading and then outline an alternative way of considering 'Thriller' as a text as much concerned with 'race' as 'sex'. Mercer argues that the interpellative second-person address of the lyric is explained in the third verse only when it becomes clear that this 'you', or another 'you', is the 'Girl' watching a horror movie with the singer. Mercer believes that the 'thriller' element is split into a second meaning of 'thrill', largely sexual, which is conveyed by the passion of Jackson's voice and the erotics of dancing, rather than the lyric, which is somewhat coyer, simply suggesting that being frightened is a good 'time for you and I to cuddle close together'.[6] In this reading, 'Thriller' concerns the predatory seduction of Ola by Michael. The frightening aspect to it is the group pressure on Ola to submit to Michael's sexual advances, which are presented as aggressive while the body is more generally presented in terms of disgust and decay.

These are elements of a reading applicable to many, if not most horror films, from 1960s Hammer horror to the present. What is more interesting to me about 'Thriller' is its use of racial signifiers and imagery. It is also productive to consider the film's interaction with the lyrics that provide most of its dialogue and commentary.

Though the film shows a young man and woman at the cinema, the song lyric refers to a couple at home watching a horror film on TV. The implication of the lyric is of a threat that will find you out in your living room rather than the bedroom setting of the video's end. The story narrative of the music video has three parts on different narrative levels: in the first, 1950s-styled scene, college student 'Michael' is transformed into a werewolf when he is out in the woods with his girlfriend after their car has run out of gas. The 1950s setting alludes to the sci-fi horror films of the Cold War period but also inevitably brings to mind the history of the civil rights movement, which in modern times swung into full force from 1954, when the US Supreme Court declared school segregation unconstitutional, to 1962 when President Kennedy had to send federal troops to quell riots so that James Meredith, the school's first black student, could attend the University of Mississippi.

This first sequence then turns out to be a film within the video as the narrative cuts to part two, which takes place in the present of 1983, the year the civil rights movement was officially recognised by the establishing of a federal holiday to honour the birthday of Martin Luther King Jr. This second, main section is initially set in a cinema where the first part has become a horror film watched by a couple in contemporary 1980s dress (who are in fact the same couple as in the film). It is in this part that the music begins as Jackson teases his girlfriend for being frightened by the werewolf-movie but then transforms into a zombie, along with others who have surrounded the couple. The closing third part reveals all that has gone before to be a dream but then the final flash of Jackson's eyes implies otherwise.

While Kobena Mercer appropriately reads the first part of the video in terms of sexuality – the male (were)wolf in the forest is a traditional fairy tale symbol of masculine rapacity – the second part, when the music begins, shifts from the isolated boy–girl story of sexual menace to a night-time urban scene of a neighbourhood terrorised by zombies. This draws on alternative narrative traditions and films, such as George Romero's *Night of the Living Dead* (1968), which signify differently from the werewolf movie – Mercer sees the zombie simply as an asexual image[7] – and concern the overthrow of society by 'aliens'. *Night of the Living Dead*, in which people hiding in a house are terrorised by zombies, is also notable for casting a black hero,[8] still rare in 1968, and is surrounded by racial tensions: it concludes with the hero, played by Duane Jones, being shot by the white authorities for no apparent reason, when they arrive outside the house. The implication is that Jones, the black man, is a threat akin to the zombie – despite having been the hero who has saved the other (white) survivors. 'Thriller' in part plays with whites' perceptions of blacks in the way that Jackson is repeatedly shown not to be what he seems – at the start he is dressed as a regular 1950s college student but is in fact a werewolf; in the main part of the film he is a boyfriend who turns out to be a zombie; and at the end he appears, like Jones in *Night of the Living Dead*, to be the small-town hero of the piece – but then is revealed to be monstrous in the closing shot. In each of these story segments – film, dream and 'reality' – the black man is a monster pretending not to be.[9]

While Jackson's earlier transformation into a werewolf reminds the viewer of Landis's work on *An American Werewolf in London*, his second transformation into a zombie recalls 1940s and 1950s horror movies, such as *I Walked With a Zombie* (1943), which play on white fears of 'black magic'. The origins of the word 'zombie' lie in the African religion of voodoo, where the zombie represents a threatening in-between life: a re-animated dead body that inspires dread among the living. Romero introduced the idea that zombies eat the living and thus created a terrorising aspect to what might previously have been seen as mere revenants under the control of a magician, witch-doctor or other person with supernatural power.

The lyrics to 'Thriller' juxtapose the voyeuristic thrill of watching a film with sexual thrills: 'I can thrill you more than any ghost would dare to try.' The song works by using puns and juxtapositions to the extent that its title is a self-conscious catachresis because the genre with which it deals is horror and not thriller movies. Also, in the lyric, the threat that creatures will 'terrorise y'awl's neighbourhood' plays on the etymological connection between terror and terrorising, between the supernatural threat of the monstrous undead and the everyday threat to neighbourhoods of urban gangs attacking or mugging citizens. The ones at danger are those 'Without the soul for getting down', punning once more on soul as metaphysical concept and black music form. Danger comes from 'the funk of forty thousand years', suggesting black music seeking vengeance through the zombie rite that is the central set-piece of the film. The ritualistic dance routine in the streets draws on the racial battle between the rival gangs of Jets and Sharks in Leonard Bernstein's *West Side Story*, which was the direct inspiration for Jackson's previous video, 'Beat It'. There are many reasons, then, why the zombie might appear as a racialised image in the film – as the threatening other of mainstream white society – implying a 'sleeper' in the midst of small-town America that will arise at night to stage a riot or revolution. In line with this reading, bell hooks notes that, for reasons of safety, blacks growing up as servants in white households in the southern US 'learned to appear before whites as though they were zombies' in order to seem subservient and invisible.[10] This is an act that in the light of modern versions of the zombie suggests a threat that masquerades under what Homi Bhabha calls a 'sly civility' which challenges authority by its exaggerated formality.

The director of 'Thriller', John Landis, is best known for *An American Werewolf in London*, but his main film of 1983, the year of the 'Thriller' video, was *Trading Places*, a role-reversal comedy about a homeless black man swapping places with a white stockbroker. This modern urban reworking of the basic formula of a 'white' classic (cf. *The Wiz*), Mark Twain's *The Prince and the Pauper*, is given a further twist by its racial casting, which can be read in terms of a white fear of black appropriation and usurpation. This transformation can be related in two ways to the video for 'Thriller', aside from the implicit threat of a black presence, signalled by the zombies, that might exchange places with the affluent white majority. On the one hand, there is Michael Jackson's lightening skin colour. According to Richard Dyer: 'Few things have delighted the white press as much as the disfigurement of Michael Jackson's face through what have been supposed to be his attempts to become white.'[11] If 'Thriller' can be considered to play out a racial narrative then Jackson's own transformations in the film from homely fratboy to monster suggest the conflict in identity played out in his relations with cosmetic surgery, which he denies, and racial politics.[12] Jackson says he has a condition, vitiligo, a fairly common non-contagious skin condition affecting pigmentation, which began to whiten his skin around the time he made the album *Thriller*. On the other hand, there is Frantz Fanon's psychoanalytic analyses of the problems facing black men and women in a white world in *Black Skin, White Masks*. Building on W. E. B. DuBois's theory of African American 'double consciousness', Fanon sees a 'self-division', or fundamental self-alienation in black people as a result of subjugation, which can lead to both resistance and the desire for acceptance and assimilation into white culture.

Both of these aspects to self-division can be seen in Jackson's videos. For example, the next time that Jackson and Landis worked together was in the early 1990s on the video for Jackson's song 'Black Or White', which I mentioned at the start of this chapter. The song was taken to be a plea for racial tolerance and understanding but the subsequent accompanying video, released two days before the LA riots, had to have its finale cut on release. This was because it ends with Jackson smashing all the windows of a car with a crowbar and then slinking into the night as he transforms into a black panther, the symbolism of which is certainly provocative and again contains a clear sexual referent but also a racial-political one.[13]

The racial aspect to 'Thriller', and other videos by mainstream black artists like Jackson, is brought to the fore only by considering history and discourse outside the film and by linking the 'monstrous' within the film with white demonisation of blacks in US society. As E. Ann Kaplan notes of white responses to blacks, derived from the discourse of colonialism: '[W]hites split off the inner hatred and violent part of themselves – negation turned inward – and project it onto blacks.'[14] Which is to say that:

> when black people are visualised, it is most frequently in terms of what Edward Said calls 'Orientalism,' a stereotypical and hierarchical construction of Africans and Asians culture as savage, mysterious and exotic that serves to define white EuroAmerica as rational and superior. One might consider the representation of blacks in advertising today, of the way that . . . black men are defined in terms of an uncontrollable and threatening sexuality.[15]

Jackson's video for 'Thriller' is a prime example of this, in that it simultaneously portrays Jackson as nice all-American boy, three times, only to unmask him repeatedly as both sexually predatory and threateningly monstrous.

To conclude, this reading of the video is not about intention (a method of meaning-making associated with the 'work'), but signification (associated with the 'text' and intertextuality): reading the text in the light of selected overlapping discourses and texts. Also, sex and 'race' are not separate discourses but imbricated ones, in which black, particularly male, sexuality is perceived as a constant threat to white society.[16] The reasons for viewing the video in terms of 'race' are to do with the civil rights movement from the 1950s to the 1980s and the exclusion of black artists from MTV, plus the racial message of the 1950s' B Movies that the 'Thriller' video draws on, combined with the history of representations of the zombie.

Finally, Paul Gilroy upbraids readings of music videos such as Mercer's for forsaking 'discussion of music and its attendant dramaturgy, performance, ritual, and gesture in favour of an obsessive fascination with the bodies of the performers themselves'.[17] According to Gilroy, Mercer 'steadily reduces Michael Jackson's voice first to his body, then to his hair, and eventually to his emphatically disembodied image'.[18] All readings are reductive, but a way of avoiding this is to read the text in terms of intertexts, theory or history. For example, in her introduction to *Reading Images*, Julia Thomas explains how 'bell hooks has drawn on Foucault's ideas that vision is complicit with power and discipline to argue that the subordination of blacks has been achieved by refusing them the right to look and by constructing whiteness as the ideal.'[19] The 'Thriller' video works against this by celebrating the monstrous, by making the black characters in the video both actors and viewers, and by staging the final 'monstrous' shot of the movie as a threatening stare back at the audience of the film by Jackson.

APPENDIX

'Thriller', written and composed by Rod Temperton

Verse 1
It's close to midnight and something evil's lurking in the dark
Under the moonlight you see a sight that almost stops your heart
You try to scream but terror takes the sound before you make it
You start to freeze as horror looks you right between the eyes,
You're paralysed.

Chorus
'cause this is thriller, thriller night
And no one's gonna save you from the beast about to strike
You know it's thriller, thriller night
You're fighting for your life inside a killer, thriller tonight.

Verse 2
You hear the door slam and realise there's nowhere left to run
You feel the cold hand and wonder if you'll ever see the sun
You close your eyes and hope that this is just imagination
But all the while you hear the creature creepin' up behind
You're out of time.

Chorus
'cause this is thriller, thriller night
There ain't no second chance against the thing with forty eyes
You know it's thriller, thriller night
You're fighting for your life inside of killer, thriller tonight.

Bridge
Night creatures call
And the dead start to walk in their masquerade
There's no escapin' the jaws of the alien this time
(they're open wide)
This is the end of your life.

Verse 3
They're out to get you, there's demons closing in on every side
They will possess you unless you change the number on your dial
Now is the time for you and I to cuddle close together
All thru the night I'll save you from the terror on the screen
I'll make you see.

Chorus
That this is thriller, thriller night
'cause I can thrill you more than any ghost would dare to try
Girl, this is thriller, thriller night
So let me hold you tight and share a killer, diller, chiller
Thriller here tonight.

Rap performed by Vincent Price
Darkness falls across the land
The midnight hour is close at hand
Creatures crawl in search of blood
To terrorise y'awl's neighbourhood
And whosoever shall be found
Without the soul for getting down
Must stand and face the hounds of hell
And rot inside a corpse's shell
The foulest stench is in the air
The funk of forty thousand years
And grizzly ghouls from every tomb
Are closing in to seal your doom
And though you fight to stay alive
Your body starts to shiver
For no mere mortal can resist
The evil of the thriller.

REFERENCES AND BIBLIOGRAPHY

Aschroft, Bill, *The Post-Colonial Studies Reader*, London: Routledge, 1995.
Bhabha, Homi, 'Sly Civility', in *The Location of Culture*, London: Routledge, 1993, pp. 93–101.
Dyer, Richard, *Whiteness*, London: Routledge, 1997.
Gilroy, Paul, *The Black Atlantic*, London: Verso, 1993.
Guerrero, Ed, 'The Rise and Fall of Blaxploitation', in Steven J. Rose (ed.), *Movies and American Society*, Oxford: Blackwell, 2002, pp. 250–73.
hooks, bell, *Black Looks: Race and Representation*, Boston: South End Press, 1992.
Kaplan, E. Ann, *Looking for the Other: Feminism, Film and the Imperial Gaze*, London: Routledge, 1997.
Mercer, Kobena, 'Monster Metaphors – Notes on Michael Jackson's *Thriller*', in Christine Gledhill (ed.), *Stardom: Industry of Desire*, London: Routledge, 1991, pp. 300–16. Also reprinted in Thomas (ed.), pp. 17–32.
Thomas, Julia (ed.), *Reading Images*, Basingstoke: Palgrave, 2000.

NOTES

1. Frantz Fanon, *Black Skin, White Masks*, quotation cited from excerpt in Ashcroft et al., 1995, p. 324.
2. bell hooks, p. 175.
3. Michael Jackson, 'Black or White', from the 1991 *Dangerous* album.

4. Guerrero, p. 272.
5. Mercer, p. 303.
6. 'Thriller' was written and composed by Rod Temperton from the British band Heatwave.
7. Mercer, p. 311
8. This was the first time an African American actor had played the lead in a horror film.
9. That a white horror-film actor, Vincent Price, intones the rap that closes the song, again sets up a binary between a white audience and the black zombies on screen they are in danger from.
10. hooks, p. 168.
11. Dyer, p. 50.
12. In 1996, Jackson starred in the short film 'Ghosts' (dir. Stan Winston) where he again plays many 'made-up' characters (maestro, mayor, ghoul mayor, superghoul, skeleton).
13. The Black Panther Group was an African American revolutionary party founded in the US in the mid-1960s to protect blacks from acts of police brutality. Eventually the Panthers developed into a Marxist revolutionary group that called for compensation to African Americans for centuries of white exploitation.
14. Kaplan, p. 295.
15. Thomas, p. 7.
16. See hooks, pp. 87–114.
17. Gilroy, p. 101.
18. Ibid.
19. Julia Thomas, p. 7.

CHAPTER 5

CELEBRITY: DIANA AND DEATH

Approach: Trauma Theory

There was no end to grief. It is worth recalling some details. William Hague wanted Heathrow to be renamed Diana Airport, Gordon Brown was said to be seriously considering the idea that August Bank Holiday be renamed Diana Day. Three foreign tourists were sentenced to jail for taking a few old teddy bears from the tribute heap. Newspapers instructed the Queen and her family to grieve, and to be seen grieving. Many people were recorded saying that they grieved more for Diana than for their dead mothers and husbands. Not to grieve was to be odd, cynical, wicked. (Ian Jack)[1]

Trauma is neutralised as product, something you can buy (Elton John saccharine, albums of sentiment), or somewhere you can boast of visiting. (Iain Sinclair)[2]

In this chapter, I want to consider a public event involving a celebrity in order to discuss the ways in which famous people take on a significant role in the emotional life of others. In particular I want to look at how Diana's death was received in Britain in terms of a pervasive sense of trauma. Which is to say I want to explore why polls 'even a year after her death, showed that many still believed themselves and their country to have been significantly changed by the Diana phenomenon'.[3]

The public grief that followed in the wake of Princess Diana's death on 31 August 1997 can be understood in terms of various perspectives on grief and trauma. For example, it gave rise to Bernie Taupin and Elton John's refashioning of their tribute to Marilyn Monroe (who also died aged 36 in much-debated circumstances) 'Candle in the Wind' as 'England's Rose', which became the biggest selling single to date and which, according to William Watkin, placed

Diana's death 'directly within the context of ritual mourning of the dead celebrity who died too soon because of the demands society placed upon them'.[4] Diana's position as, in Tony Blair's phrase, the 'people's princess', also made the reception of her death seem in some ways akin to that of John F. Kennedy's, the 'people's president', and resulted in documented life crises for many people who received the news of her death as a personal tragedy. Some critics argue that the mourning for Diana, though intense, passed quickly, but there is evidence to suggest that she long remained as much a celebrity in death as she was in life: she appeared in the top ten of the BBC's 'Greatest Britons' poll in 2002 and a huge commemorative fountain/moat unveiled by the Queen in London's Hyde Park in 2004 immediately became one of the nation's top attractions, attracting 5,000 people an hour.[5]

Diana died along with Dodi Al-Fayed, her lover with whom she had been dining at the Paris Ritz Hotel in the Place Vendome, and their driver Henri Paul (a security guard from the Mohammed Al-Fayed-owned hotel), from injuries suffered in a car accident in the Alma road tunnel beside the Seine. The only survivor, Dodi Al-Fayed's body guard Trevor Rees-Jones, says he recalls nothing of the accident. Various 'factual' details have been put forward as the cause of the accident, but all have also been refuted: the car was travelling at more than twice the speed limit, it was being hotly pursued by reporters, and its driver was extremely drunk. Henri Paul lost control of the Mercedes and it struck one of the pillar supports within the tunnel. Accounts of the crash and of Diana's death a few hours later dominated news reports around the world. The accident immediately became part of what Gilles Deleuze has called 'world memory', a term 'intended to echo the globalizing tendency of media reports echoing from the cultural and economic centres'.[6] According to some rumours, Diana was pregnant, and conspiracy theorists have claimed that the 'accident' was in fact a murder arranged by MI6 and the CIA (Diana's butler, Paul Burrell, claimed in October 2003 to have a letter in which Diana predicted her death). Almost no detail about the incident is universally agreed upon. Photographers who arrived on the scene shortly after the accident took photographs of Diana, but these were refused by all newspapers around the world and have never been printed.[7] An inquest into the death was opened by the Queen's coroner, Michael Burgess, in January 2004.

The week between the accident and the funeral was marked for many people by the Royal Family's silence while members of the public brought their tributes to Kensington Palace and other sites. On 4 September the *Daily Express* ran the front-page headline 'Show Us You Care' alongside a picture of the Queen, while the *Sun*'s front page asked 'Where is Our Queen? Where is Her Flag?' On the day of the funeral service on 6 September, Diana's coffin was drawn on a gun carriage from Kensington Palace to Westminster Abbey, where her brother Charles, Earl Spencer, criticised in his eulogy both the media's pursuit of Diana and the Royal Family's muted mourning for a woman they had undervalued (his speech was roundly applauded by the crowds outside to whom it was broadcast live). London's streets were packed with millions of mourners, who watched largely in silence as the cortege proceeded, though many tossed flowers into the road and others wept.[8] Nearly fifty members of the Royal Family stood together outside Buckingham Palace as the cortege passed and the Union Flag at the Palace hung at halfmast for the first time. Over the last mile, Earl Spencer, Prince Charles, Princes William and Harry, and the Queen's husband Prince Philip, walked behind the coffin, joined by representatives from charities patronised by Diana. Crowds in Regent's Park and Hyde Park watched the TV broadcast of the funeral on huge screens and listened to hymns, readings and prayers. Supermarkets and museums were closed, and many sporting events were cancelled.

Diana's funeral was watched on TV by an estimated one in three of the world's population,[9] and thirty countries issued Diana commemorative stamps within a month of her death.[10] The perceived importance of her death was evident in films across the world made in the following years, such as the French *Amélie* (dir: Jean-Pierre Jeunet, 1999), where news of Diana's death is a life-changing event, and the Australian *Diana and Me* (dir: David Parker, 1997), which begins and ends with floral tributes to Diana outside of Kensington Palace.[11] In its most extreme form, this hagiography resulted in Jeremy Paxman declaring the response to Diana's funeral as a sign that the English were acquiring a new sense of self:[12] one in which restraint and the traditional stiff upper-lip were replaced by open displays of public grief. This was also an occasion on which collective displays of emotion, produced by perceived pain and loss rather than ostensible strength and authority, resulted in small but perceptible changes at the highest social level of British society. For Small and Hockey, Diana's death created an 'affective enclave' or 'community of pain and healing' empowered by collective grief at the margins of the social structure (mourning was supposedly most common among women, gays and ethnic minorities and was also largely confined to social groups C1, C2 and D):[13]

> One of the most dramatic examples of the formation of alternative social structures occurred immediately after the death of Diana, Princess of Wales, in 1997 when the monarch and members of her household yielded to public pressure to change the arrangements for Diana's funeral and to express their grief publicly. The funeral itself was appropriated by Diana's brother, Earl Spencer, as an occasion to question if not attack the Royal Family and the resounding applause of members of the public not only augmented the force of his words but also represented an entirely innovative mourning practice.[14]

Small and Hockey identify here the perceived link between grief and truth: someone in pain is accorded a privileged right to speak out and to be respected as speaking from a position of veracity based on the force of feeling. It is also important here to consider the way in which a death can lead on to a political struggle over the meaning of a life: Spencer evidently felt he had a right to allude to disagreements between the Royal Family and his sister in what was both a public broadcast and a private ceremony attended by Diana's sons. This could be construed as an exploitation of her death, and her inability to represent herself, or as speaking out truthfully from a position of strength conferred on him by the special right to testify accorded to the bereaved. It was certainly unusual at a funeral to mount a none-too-veiled attack on some of the mourners present, but the force of public feeling as represented by the media was behind Spencer's words, and some of the grief over Diana's death seemed to be based on an insistence that the monarchy not return to the standoffishness and insularity to which Diana was thought to have been a threat and of which a victim.

It has been observed that the collective response to Diana's death in some ways amounted to the behaviour associated with community disasters: visits to special places and the laying of flowers and mementoes (not necessarily at the scene of the disaster – after Diana's death flowers were left at Kensington Palace but also at town halls, supermarkets and war memorials), a memorial service, pilgrimage to an unmarked grave, the lighting of candles, the establishment of permanent memorials (at Althorp and then at the Diana memorial fountain in London), anniversary events and a widespread view that the disaster had some significance. It is also arguable that the significance of the grief experienced at the death of Diana can be explained in different terms for men and women. Sarah Coleman considers this in terms of men's inability to see the death as important, or at best to see it as sad that a woman they found attractive had died.[15] This is in contrast to women's mourning for numerous reasons: the death of a fairytale princess, of a single mother, of someone who brought food related illnesses to media attention, and of someone who worked for charitable causes while standing up to the monarchy. As a woman in her mid-thirties who had well-publicised problems with relationships, weight issues, career opportunities, in-laws and media perceptions, she could represent something of women's struggle against patriarchal social structures, especially as in her final years she seemed to be living a socially productive and personally satisfying independent life. Irrespective of the inevitable conspiracy stories that have surrounded the circumstances of the car crash in which she died, her death suggested that the forces she had been fighting against had in some sense succeeded in silencing her, and in doing so had made Diana into a martyr – or even a saint: '[T]he astonishing public reaction to her death indicated that some kind of apotheosis had taken place.'[16] Here, the story runs that Diana's death allowed people to mourn for greater and often abstract things that they felt were missing from their own lives: community, generosity, empathy, love, emotion and compassion. Perhaps most paradoxically a princess seemed to have embodied a general anti-materialist, anti-hierarchical spiritual and moral feeling – as well as being a gay icon, a sex symbol, and in some quarters a feminist heroine. Her charitable works for children, the sick, AIDS patients, and most famously land-mine victims were thought to stretch beyond a national context, making this most privileged of women a campaigner for some of the most disenfranchised sections of global society.

Alternatively, for Ian Jack the demonstrative response to Diana's death was 'recreational grieving',[17] in which the death of one of the most famous people on the planet was an opportunity to observe and also participate in a spectacle, to feel important by associating oneself physically and emotionally with a media event of enormous proportions (at its most frivolous, attending the funeral could be seen as an opportunity to be on TV). Death always has a fascination – as is evident from the reactions of passing motorists to highway accidents – and the death of someone so famous can exert a powerful attraction as well as prompt an unprecedented degree of reflection on one's own mortality – particularly given the confusion over who was to be held (most) responsible for Diana's death. Another powerful factor may have been guilt as the pursuit of Diana by paparazzi eager to feed the public's hunger for news of her was contributory to her death. Calls for tightened privacy laws after Diana's death and attacks on journalists and photographers at her funeral seemed to contrast with the consumer support for press intrusion prior to it.

In some ways similarly to Ian Jack, Alvin Cohan argues that 'what Diana's death may have involved was mourning without grief, largely public display with little private feeling.'[18] Cohan's own private experience, away from the scenes of public mourning, was of London going about its business untouched by the 'tragedy' and of little evidence in people's outward behaviour of any internal sense of loss. This he contrasts with surveys after Kennedy's assassination, which recorded respondents expressing an almost total preoccupation with the death, and nine out of ten Americans reporting an experience of physical symptoms such as headaches, tiredness, loss of appetite or dizziness, likening their experience of the assassination of Kennedy to personal grief over a private bereavement.[19] Cohan believes that mourning over Diana's death was largely confined to particular public spaces (particularly Buckingham, Kensington and St James's Palaces), and the media's announcement of a general state of mourning was unfounded in the sense that it was spatially localised even if widely felt, which is to say that those who were particularly moved by her death made a journey or pilgrimage to identified places rather than mourning in their own environments. This may say something about what Diana represented (she was not a head of state or representative of a country) or about the time at which her death occurred in the late 1990s, when part of the world's population felt that a display of feeling was more important than private grief.

It is also out-of-step with Jeremy Paxman's view that grief at the funeral seemed to be more aimed at invoking demonstrations of emotion in others than at self-exhibition. While there were few expressive displays there were many calls for the Royal Family to show its own grief. Crowds were mainly characterised by respectful silence and expressions of feeling were mostly made through tokens: flowers, toys and written messages. Perhaps, rather than overturning traditional ways of displaying grief in England, this was the most well-attended example of public but undemonstrative mourning. The signs of mourning were not breakdowns, wailing and crises but more muted evidence in the West of an affluent late-twentieth-century consumer culture in which people's lives are dominated by the media: '31.5 million viewers of Diana's funeral in Britain and an estimated 1 billion world-wide, the carpet of flowers, the sale of 40 million copies of "Good-bye England's Rose", over £100 million donated to Diana's memorial fund'.[20]

For Therese Davis in 2004, the grief over Diana's death has to be put in the context of media representation and fading memory:

> The deep sense of shock experienced by millions of people around the world upon hearing about the death of Diana has long since dissipated. The intensity of the mass outpouring of grief that followed this news is utterly expended. But, looking back, those few days in September 1997 when it seemed that the entire whole world mourned the death of Diana are, surely, more than cause for embarrassment. Rather than reduce this global cultural phenomenon to 'mass hysteria' we might instead reflect on the way in which the media event of Diana's death reveals the way in which modern image hunger conceals death.[21]

Davis is here partly alluding to the fact that no pictures of Diana after the crash were published in the press. The images printed and broadcast of her remained those of an unassuming, healthy young woman, adding to the sense of shock and disorientation over her death, and fuelling a climate of mass bereavement for a life inexplicably cut short. The collective mourning for Diana was as much a subject for debate in the media at the time as Diana or the death itself. To some, this mourning, in terms of an event and in terms of the emotions ascribed to it, was itself fostered by the media.[22] The first anniversary was marked by letters and articles querying or denying the universality of grief, suggesting that the supposed mourning was instead a diversity of responses homogenised by the media into one emotion. While some individuals were deeply moved, others were simply caught up in the spectacle: witnesses, onlookers and tourists rather than mourners.[23] This can be understood in different ways: these individuals may have felt unable to speak out at the time because they thought they would have been vilified for displaying an insensitivity out of step with the majority, or they may have been inclined a year later to reject their own feelings of September 1997, speaking out less against the press than against their own complicity with it through an excessive grief for a famous stranger who had provoked an emotional response out of proportion to her significance. Yet, Diana was only a 'stranger' in the sense that most people who mourned her death had never met her – they had however, via the media, borne witness to her life, at least since her marriage to Prince Charles, and quite probably felt more strongly about her than about many of their acquaintances. Consequently, Jeanne Katz believes that 'members of the public made their need for visible emotional expression paramount'[24] and for Simon Critchley, 'what is at issue here is the question of feeling, emotion or affect and the seemingly overwhelming requirement on the part of countless millions of people, to find a *meaning* for this affect.'[25]

This perceived force of feeling in 1997 can be illustrated by Critchley's own response soon after the funeral: 'There is much to say about Diana's death, which is possibly the biggest single *event* in world history, if we define an event as something contemporary which living human beings share, whether immediately or through the various media.'[26] This seems hyperbole but not if one thinks of an event in media terms rather than, for example, political significance. Which is to say that the death of one of the most famous people on the planet, in a car crash that would have become the top news story in almost every country in the world, becomes an emotional occasion partly because of the sheer number of people exposed to an event that was universally portrayed as tragic.

This is one way in which to consider the accident's emotional aftermath: 'Isn't the trauma and drama of Diana's death the *risk of the potential meaninglessness of pain*?'[27] By this Critchley means that it was Diana's own sense of pain and lack of self-worth that caused people to identify with and love her: a symbol of their own agony and of its meaning:

> Her death, then, is the trauma of the disappearance of this symbol, of this means of identification, where meaning collapses, and the subject is left with the *noesis* [the process of meaning] of substantive affect without the *noema* [that which is meant] of an intentional object.[28]

Grief here, then, is a signifier without a signified, but what Critchley sees in the expression of grief is a demand – a demand for the world, life and death to *mean* something. People outside of the media had little to say – because death is the negation of expression – but had a powerful desire for something appropriate and important to be said or done. Diana's funeral was thus like almost any other funeral but on a larger scale, involving the public display of emotional pain, in an effort towards amelioration through sharing. But Critchley thinks there was also here a demand for (political) justice of some kind, which he thinks can only be rationalised as a demand for the primacy of compassion; though it may also be seen as the irrational demand for vengeance from mourners who wished to direct at someone their sense of anger at the brute natural fact of mortality, here compounded by the unnatural fact of an untimely death. The proliferation of conspiracy theories around deaths such as Diana's is arguably a response to this – a way to make the seemingly inexplicable meaningful by ascribing a hidden cause to it.

Trauma or traumatic stress is the name given to people's reactions to disturbing or overwhelming events, such as a road accident, rape, assault or the death of a relative. Critchley is one of the critics who uses the word 'trauma' to describe a collective response to Diana's death, and, according to one psychotherapist, Dennis Neill, certain:

> events can leave people feeling unsafe and less secure than they were and fearful about life in general. The terrorist attack on the twin towers in New York and the following psychological effects on entire communities,

is a good example of a community wide traumatic stress reaction. So was the death of Princess Diana.[29]

For Kirby Farrell, Diana's death, like that of Prince Albert for the Victorian age, focused dominant themes of the 1990s in a modern 'fairy-tale' that resonates in popular culture from 'Beauty and the Beast' to *Pretty Woman*:

> a feminist story about a shy nursery school teacher who married a prince, suffered betrayal, eating disorders, and divorce, but then became a respected mother and moral leader . . . In Diana's story the trope of trauma supported fantasies that one good woman could heal an injured world.[30]

It is to the ways in which Diana's death could be considered psychologically traumatic for groups as well as individuals that I now want to turn.

Traditionally understood, trauma (from the Greek word for 'wound') centres on an injury or disturbance and arises from some kind of blow to the body, but more often nowadays to the mind. For Freud in 'Beyond the Pleasure Principle', mental trauma or 'traumatic neurosis' is a response to some stimulation of anxiety experienced too suddenly and unexpectedly to be assimilated and so is not available to consciousness until it is remembered and acted out mentally or physically in ritualistic repetition. It possesses the individual and threatens to drain or empty them, resulting in feelings that oscillate between restlessness and numbness, in which 'memory repeats to us what we haven't yet come to terms with'.[31] For the traumatised individual, chronology is disturbed in the sense that a past event repeatedly slips into the mental present. From a social perspective, trauma can both damage and forge a community, the latter being a response to the former, and trauma's effect of isolation, a personal sense of grief, gives rise to a desire to come together with others who feel similarly marked because perhaps only they can recognise and sympathise with one's own pain. Trauma, according to Erikson, therefore has a centripetal and a centrifugal force, drawing the individual apart from one group, those who do not share or understand, and towards another, those who do: '[O]therwise unconnected persons who share a traumatic experience seek one another out and develop a form of fellowship on the strength of that common tie . . . a gathering of the wounded.'[32]

Now, Diana's death seemed to cut across existing communities and relationships, separating those who felt affected from those who didn't: those who felt grief, for whatever reasons, arguably experienced a strong drive to join together with others who were also mourning, the vast majority of whom they had never met, but who were linked by the media's power to communicate to them individually across the globe. The calls for the monarchy to display strong emotion can be read as a call to strengthen the national bonds of fellowship that some people thought were harmed by the death of a 'people's princess' or by 'England's Rose'. This provides a therapeutic environment for those affected by the death but also highlights the divide between those in the community affected (the mourners) and those not (many members of the Royal Family and others): 'The fault lines usually open to divide the people affected by the event from the people spared . . . Those not touched try to distance themselves from those touched, almost as if they are escaping something spoiled.'[33] Those who went about their daily lives after the news of Diana's death can thus be understood not just to be emotionally unaffected but, at least in some cases, to be distinguishing themselves from those who were affected, and who congregated in specific places to share their grief. For many, their sense of disorientation may of course have had little to do with Diana but were none the less genuine. The effect of a widely publicised, unnatural and unforeseen death can bring sharply to mind the risks that surround people but which the conduct of daily life requires individuals to put at the back of their minds. To be reminded of the hazards and contingencies of existence can in itself be traumatising, and if even a highly privileged and famous person is vulnerable to the vicissitudes of life then others may well suddenly feel significantly less safe. Calls to the Royal Family to speak out can thus be understood as a desire to see them break their traditional reserve but also as a request, because trauma is characterised by a loss of confidence and faith, for them to reassure people about the state and security of the country they symbolised. As Cathy Caruth explains, there is in trauma an 'oscillation between a *crisis of death* and the correlative *crisis of life*'.[34]

Finally, there is also here the smack of superstition. In contemporary culture, where the media compete for viewers, angles and exclusives, there is an inevitable shift towards exaggerated meaning-making. A big news story cannot be allowed to rest simply as the communication of a fact such as the death of Diana, but must be made portentous: to some degree symbolic and meaningful. Which is to say that the media that many held responsible for Diana's death[35] were also responsible for the frenzied signs of mourning that circulated in the weeks after her death, in an effort to feed their own (and the public's) desire for spectacle. Yet, that is not to suggest that the mourning was insincere or fabricated, but that it might have been displaced. As Richard Johnson says, Diana, known as 'the most photographed woman in the world', was available through her excessive media exposure for so many feelings to be projected onto her life, making her the object of 'feelings that had little to do with her own life and death, and everything to do with the lives of members of her public'.[36] For many critics, the cultural function of celebrity is to provide opportunities and outlets for personal displays of emotion and mass ritualistic behaviour, such as public mourning, of a kind that are restricted in secular societies.[37]

REFERENCES AND BIBLIOGRAPHY

Bennett, Jill and Rosanne Kennedy (eds), *World Memory: Personal Trajectories in Global Time*, London: Palgrave, 2003.

Caruth, Cathy, *Unclaimed Experience: Trauma, Narrative and History*, Baltimore: Johns Hopkins University Press, 1996.

Caruth, Cathy, (ed.), *Trauma: Explorations in Memory*, Baltimore: Johns Hopkins University Press, 1995.

Clayton, Tim and Phil Craig, *Diana: Story of a Princess*, London: Hodder and Stoughton, 2001.

Cohan, Alvin, 'The Spatial Diana', in Richards et al., pp. 163–76.

Coleman, Sarah, 'Princess Diana's Death: A Feminist Response', http://www.feminista.com/archives/v1n6/coleman.html (accessed 23 September 2005).

Critchley, Simon, 'Di and Dodi die', in Richards et al., pp. 154–62.

Davis, Therese, *The Face on the Screen: Death, Recognition and Spectatorship*, Bristol: Intellect, 2004.

Erikson, Kai, 'Notes on Trauma and Community', in Caruth (ed.), pp. 183–99.

Farrell, Kirby, *Post-Traumatic Culture*, Baltimore: Johns Hopkins University Press, 1998.

Freud, Sigmund, 'Beyond the Pleasure Principle', in *The Essentials of Psychoanalysis*, trans. James Strachey, Harmondsworth: Pelican, 1986, pp. 218–68.

Gilbert, J, D. Glover, C. Kaplan, J. Bourne Taylor and W. Wheeler, *Diana and Democracy*, special edition of *New Formations* 36, 1999.

Hallam, Elizabeth and Jenny Hockey, *Death, Memory and Material Culture*, Oxford: Berg, 2001.

Hockey, Jenny, Jeanne Katz and Neil Small (eds), *Grief, Mourning and Death Ritual*, Buckingham: Open University, 2001.

Johnson, Richard, 'Exemplary Differences: Mourning (and not Mourning) a Princess', in Kear and Steinberg, pp. 15–39.

Katz, Jeanne, 'Conclusion', in Hockey et al., 2001, pp. 267–73.

Kear, A. and D. L. Steinberg, *Mourning Diana: Nation, Culture and the Performance of Grief*, London: Routledge, 1999.

Merrin, W., 'Crash, Bang, Wallop! What a Picture! The Death of Diana and the Media', *Mortality*, 4: 1, 1999, pp. 41–62.

Neill, Dennis, 'Traumatic Stress and Post-Traumatic Stress Disorder', http://www.medicdirect.co.uk/clinics/default.ihtml?step=4&pid=1792 (accessed 23 September 2005).

Richards, Jeffrey, Scott Wilson and Linda Woodhead (eds), *Diana: The Making of a Media Saint*, London: I. B. Tauris, 1999.

Rushdie, Salman, 'Crash', in *Step Across this Line*, London: Vintage, 2002, pp. 118–21.

Small, David and Jenny Hockey, 'Discouse into Practice: The Production of Bereavement Care', in Hockey et al., 2001, pp. 97–124.

Turner, Graeme, *Understanding Celebrity*, London: Sage, 2004.

NOTES

1. Ian Jack, 'A Sentimental Education', *The Guardian*, Review Section, 16 April 2005, p. 7.
2. Iain Sinclair, *Sorry Meniscus*, London: Profile, 1999, pp. 43–4.
3. Richards et al., p. 10.
4. William Watkin, *On Mourning: Theories of Loss in Modern Literature*, Edinburgh: Edinburgh University Press, 2004, p. 47.
5. For the 'Greatest Britons' poll see the BBC News Website, http://news.bbc.co.uk/1/hi/entertainment/tv_and_radio/2341661.stm (accessed 30 Sept. 2005).
6. Bennett and Kennedy, p. 5.
7. Clayton and Craig, pp. 343–56.
8. Ibid., pp. 357–74.
9. Davis, p. 75.

10. Richards et al., p. 1.
11. The government estimated that the floral tributes would reach one million at Kensington Palace by the time of the funeral. In France, the response to Diana's death was considered to have an intensity unequalled since the death of de Gaulle thirty years earlier (Andrew Pierce, 'As the Nation Mourned', *The Times*, 16 March, 2005, p. 3).
12. Jeremy Paxman, *The English: A Portrait of a People*, London: Penguin, 1999, pp. 240–3.
13. Richards et al., p. 8.
14. Small and Hockey, pp. 119–20.
15. See Coleman.
16. Richards et al., p. 1.
17. Richards et al., p. 7.
18. Cohan, p. 164.
19. Cohan, p. 171.
20. Richards et al, p. 10.
21. Davis, p. 81.
22. Merrin, 1999.
23. Hallam and Hockey, p. 6.
24. Katz, p. 271.
25. Critchley, p. 155.
26. Ibid., p. 155.
27. Ibid., p. 155.
28. Ibid., p. 156.
29. See Neill.
30. Farrell, p. 276.
31. Erikson, pp. 183–4.
32. Ibid., pp. 186–7.
33. Ibid., p. 189.
34. Caruth, p. 7.
35. For example, see Rushdie.
36. Johnson, p. 33.
37. For an extended discussion of this see Turner, Chapter 5.

CHAPTER 6

TV SHOW: *BIG BROTHER* AFTER THE BIG OTHER

Approach: Performativity Theory

In everyday reality, life may be dreadful and dull, but all is well as long as this remains hidden from the gaze of 'the big Other'. (Slavoj Žižek)[1]

'It's amazing to think the whole nation is watching *us*.' (*Big Brother* contestant, 2002)[2]

In this chapter I will consider the TV programme *Big Brother* in the context of performative gendered identity. This will involve a consideration of the mediation of gender and sexuality in terms of normativity and transgression, and the complex negotiation of identity between the personal, conceived in terms of intimacy and privacy, and the public, conceived in terms of gossip and surveillance.

Big Brother was the first of the high-profile 'Reality Television' shows. Pioneered in Holland, it was imported to Britain by the production company Endemol.[3] From the first, the programme was presented as a sociological experiment, in the vein of Stanley Milgram's socio-psychological 1960s research to measure the willingness of participants to obey instructions conflicting with personal conscience if directed by an authority figure.[4] However, as the show's popularity increased, the pretext of studying how people behave and interact in a house under 'laboratory conditions' diminished while criticisms of the programme's repetitiveness encouraged changes in the show that raised its level of artificiality. Like the televised input of experimental psychologists such as Oxford University's Dr Peter Collett, interest in people's social psychology had all but disappeared after a couple of series and been entirely replaced by a fascination with game-show elements allied to the promise of sex and conflict. *Big Brother* has thus been considered part of a growing phenomenon known as the 'television of cruelty', with some contestants diagnosed as suffering from post traumatic stress disorder after appearing.[5]

With a programme such as *Big Brother* there is a complex question to be addressed in terms of textuality:

> What and where exactly . . . was 'the text' of *Big Brother*? First, rather than being confined to a single TV show, the programme itself offered multiple sites for the production of meaning. Second, it was taken up by other media outside the control of the TV producers, including independent websites and tabloid newspapers, which became the source for the development of different meanings about the programme. Third, participants who had been voted out of the house – and later those who stayed longest – began to offer their own versions of the story in various memoirs, interviews, and exposés. All of these different texts contributed to the wider text that was *Big Brother* while helping to develop different and sometimes contesting meanings about it.[6]

After its first incarnation in the Netherlands a year earlier, *Big Brother* was initially screened in Britain on Channel 4 in summer 2000. Ten contestants shared a security-fenced house next to the River Lea in East London, where they were allowed no contact without the outside world. As the householders were voted out one by one, those remaining had a greater chance of winning £70,000 in prize money. Presented as a combination of reality soap-opera, game show and chat/confession talk show, the programme assembled contestants in a specially constructed house where cameras had been installed to record their every move round the clock. While the show is now successfully made in over seventy countries from Venezuela to Thailand, in the UK the programme has run each year in the summer since 2000 on Channel 4, attracting millions of viewers to a minority station with a public service broadcasting remit.

The makers of the original Dutch show, Endemol, call *Big Brother* a 'real life soap', and they emphasise that 'Every week there are tasks to perform which test [the contestants] community spirit and team-work.' They describe the format as centred on:

> 4 elements: 1) The environment in which the contestants live – it's stripped-back to basics; 2) The knock-out system by which the contestants are voted out of the house by the audience at home; 3) The tasks, set by the editorial team, which the contestants must complete on a weekly basis; 4) The diary room, in which the contestants are required to record their feelings, frustrations, thoughts and their nominations. '*Big Brother*' is a format with a wide range of applications including Internet exploitation and programme spin-offs.[7]

In part imitating the experience of those people who become housemates through advertisements, *Big Brother* intentionally creates a closed community of strangers, almost invariably young adults (the first UK show included people aged between 20 and 40), that reflects the wider social experience of house sharing. However, where a similarly groundbreaking *fictional* drama such as

This Life (1996) played out its mixed-house relationships in the context of home and work, *Big Brother* uses 'real people', or amateur performers, in living arrangements that remove not only work but news, family and distractions such as music systems, recreating and distorting a model most familiar in the UK from squats, communal student households, institutions from borstals to boarding schools, and comedy shows such as *The Young Ones* (1982–4). The *Big Brother* programme also operates in two modes. One broadcasts around-the-clock coverage in which the principal mediation by the production company involves selecting which camera shots can be viewed. The other is a mainstream evening programme, watched by far greater numbers: a short digest of the day's events with a voiceover to present and narrativise the selected 'highlights', usually focused on emotional but especially sexual or confrontational interaction. The audience is drawn into the performance not just through viewing, but voting, attending in the adjacent evictees' studio or outside the house, and offering themselves as potential contestants.

In *Big Brother*, appearing on TV is the participants' one reason for being together and so it is unsurprising therefore that the model for the format is largely TV itself (game show, soap or talk show), rather than any of the templates used in previous documentary (until *Big Brother*, reality TV usually filmed an event, such as a talent show, or individuals in their normal daily lives – docusoap – instead of placing *contestants* in a TV studio-cum-laboratory environment). Echoing Lacan's point about the never-ending promise of the striptease,[8] the psychiatrist Raj Persaud argues that the popularity of what he calls voyeur TV 'reveals how conscious we have become of the artifice behind the media. Ironically, TV is constantly attempting to reseduce us by offering to strip away the next layer of artifice and show us the reality beneath.'[9] The sociological premise of the programme is thus that it depicts 'ordinary' people behaving ordinarily, and so holds a mirror up to both the audience and their everyday experience. Yet this is in a specially constructed house, whose design serves the purposes of a place of habitation but is equally a TV studio (hence not only the cameras but non-domestic features of the house such as the diary/interview room).

Sexuality has been a key ingredient of *Big Brother* from its inception.[10] Publicity and reporting of the first series, in which men and women slept in separate rooms, focused on a series of heterosexual romances within the house. According to Jane Arthurs, *Big Brother* is one of a number of programmes that are central to contemporary 'lifestyle' programming and 'simultaneously offer "fun" entertainment while educating the audience in the appropriate "performance" of the sexualised self'.[11] To illustrate how this operates, Arthurs quotes Mark Jankovitch's observation of how this 'liberated sexuality' is 'only ever achieved through education, discipline and intense self-surveillance. The "liberation" of the body from its "repression" is therefore experienced simultaneously as the rediscovery of a natural self and as the enactment of a carefully controlled performance.'[12]

By the fifth series, the producers had removed one of the beds from the single-room sleeping quarters in order to provoke greater intimacy and ensured that the mix of sexual orientation among contestants was much richer. So, while the first series was won by Craig, a heterosexual Liverpudlian, the fifth series was won by Nadia, a Portuguese transsexual.[13] According to Tincknell and Raghuram, the contestants 'were often available to be sexualised' and 'produced themselves in largely sexualised terms'.[14] Tincknell and Raghuram suggest that this was a key part of how members of the *Big Brother* house were perceived and judged: 'Women who were produced (or produced themselves) as working class, "stroppy", sexually undesirable, or as heterosexually desiring in unconventional ways (such as Caroline and Nichola in the first UK series) were voted out of the house as the weeks went by.'[15]

The sense of performance, or self-production, on *Big Brother* is heightened by several factors: interaction and intimacy with strangers; the element of competition for both popularity and money; the presence of cameras; the hermetically sealed social environment; the lack of feedback and interaction with friends, family or others. There is also the effect on individuals of being institutionalised. The situation is not directly comparable with, but has some similarities to that of not only a holiday-camp or retreat, but also a prison or other enclosed, surveilled and disciplined environment. Additionally, it is a principle of anthropological investigation that the observer not only interprets and filters what is observed from a particular angle but affects it through the act of observation. As will be discussed in Chapter 8, individuals under observation – anyone who is being looked at – structures their behaviour towards the eye and the opinion of the observer. To a degree, this delineates the difference between private and public, between what is legitimately or consciously open to public view and what is not. *Big Brother*, in effect, purports to show the minutiae of a private situation – every moment of the behaviour of a group of people in their temporary 'home' – but necessarily operates by making it a public one. Thus, by observation, it undermines and arguably even negates its own premise, altering the 'normal' behaviour it aims to show. The only way to minimise this effect would be to conceal from the contestants the fact that they were being filmed, which is the premise in Peter Weir's 1998 movie *The Truman Show*.

Noel Coward famously quipped that 'Television is for appearing on – not for looking at.' His remark identifies the traditional difference between the view of the performer and the non-performer. However, reality television blurs this distinction by complicating the signs of difference as the 'ordinary person' is transformed into a 'celebrity' on and by the screen. This move into celebrity status is occasioned not just by appearing on television, but by media interest, especially in the tabloids and 'celebrity magazines' like *OK!* and *heat*, and also by the C4 and E4 channels that broadcast the show. These work in the opposite direction, offering to reveal the 'real', as opposed to 'ordinary', person behind the celebrity, reinforcing common-sense notions of 'individualism' and 'authenticity' as well as drawing on traditional discourses surrounding (Hollywood) 'stars'.

Where reality TV differs from cinema, however, is that the individuals on screen are presented by the programme-makers as 'themselves' to begin with – this is one of the bases on which the show is marketed – and not as acting or playing someone other than 'themselves' (discussion of whether an actor or mole has been planted among the contestants constantly attaches to *Big Brother*). While part of the aura surrounding actors (or pop stars) is predicated upon a distinction between their self-presentation on stage or screen, where they are 'performing', and their 'authentic' selves in 'real life', where they are 'not performing', this division is not supposed to apply to individuals who are deemed not to be 'performing' on screen. However, similar kinds of interest in the show are generated when it is proposed that *Big Brother* contestants are not behaving as they have outside the house, because they are shy, guarded, nervous, in unfamiliar surroundings, disingenuous or 'performing' for the other contestants and/or the cameras. An aura of mystery or intrigue may then attach to the contestant who is open to rereading by the TV audience looking for signs of authenticity or dissemblance; but there is also a media-split created between the on-screen 'inauthentic performance' and the 'real person', who is usually purported to be *exclusively* revealed in the competing story of their 'true' identity (presented in terms of background or personality or past behaviour), most often reported in a different medium – print rather than broadcast.

Competing versions of authenticity and identity such as these necessarily become a primary discussion point and engender the assertion of integrity on the part of some participants. These contestants, who commonly see themselves as transparently authentic rather than as having *presented* themselves authentically, may or may not identify with the screen images of themselves they see after leaving the house, depending on whether they feel the programme *represented* them authentically. Su Holmes observes how one contestant referred to the screen images he saw of himself after release from the house as 'just me': 'Spencer draws here on his status as simply an "ordinary" person in an extraordinary situation to authenticate what is now effectively his celebrity persona.'[16] As Holmes observes, such claims and counter-claims are rooted in a view of the self's continuity and essential characteristics while downplaying or emphasising the effects of celebrity.

Such debates serve as prelude to wider discussion of the mediated and performative aspects to identity per se. In her book *Gender Trouble*, discussed briefly in Chapter 1, Judith Butler asks: '[W]hat grounds the presumption that identities are self-identical, persisting through time as the same, unified and internally coherent?'[17] A further question, which points towards a possible answer, is: 'To what extent do *regulatory practices* of gender formation and division constitute identity, the internal coherence of the subject, indeed, the self-identical status of the person?'[18] Butler argues that identity is assured by the three 'stabilizing concepts' of gender, sex and sexuality, such that the prevailing understanding of identity itself is put into question by those individuals who do not conform to the expected continuity between the three, which normalises heterosexual desire and assumes gender follows from sex within a binary system of male or female, feminine or masculine. Such naturalised continuity enables the unity of identity to be asserted in terms of polar differences that are kept in place by heteronormativity, such that the mutually exclusive and oppositional positioning of male and female, feminine and masculine, is reinforced by the hegemony of heterosexual desire.

Most importantly, Butler goes on to argue that, compelled by these regulatory practices, 'gender is performatively produced . . . constituting the identity it is purported to be.'[19] Butler believes that 'gender' is not something that underlies gender expressions. Which is to say that there is no behaviour that is an expression of gender identity but instead 'gender' identity is performatively constituted by behaviour – identity is a signifying practice.

In considering this theoretical position, we need to stress that performativity, 'that aspect of discourse that has the capacity to produce what it names' through physical and verbal repetition,[20] is different from performance. Performativity is 'something everyone does in order to inhabit a gendered identity, without which one can't be a meaningful subject'.[21] The term 'performative' comes from the writings of J. L. Austin, a British philosopher. Austin's work on speech-act theory distinguished between constative and performative statements. The former are those that describe the world, and so might be considered passive, in the sense that they depict rather than intervene in events: examples would be 'The door is open' or 'You are early'. By contrast, the latter, performative statements, are those that *do* something in the world and so might be considered active because they have an effect, as in 'I declare this building open', 'I pronounce you husband and wife', or 'I hereby sentence you to life in prison'.[22] Austin's theory develops into one in which this seeming binary division between categories is revised into an acknowledgement that all utterances are performative because they selectively construct the world and (seek to) affect it.

In Butler's view, it is similarly true that gender-identity is always performative: gender is an act (of speech) that brings into being the identity it purports to describe. As Sara Salih puts it, Butler denies that gender precedes action 'by claiming that gender acts are not performed by the subject, but they performatively constitute a subject that is the effect of discourse rather than the cause of it'.[23] Also, for Butler, if gender 'is a fantasy instituted and inscribed on the surface of bodies, then it seems that genders can be neither true nor false, but are only produced as the truth effects of a discourse of primary and stable identity'.[24] Gender identity for Butler is located in and not behind practices of signification, and is therefore 'an "act," as it were, that is open to splittings, self-parody, self-criticism, and those hyperbolic exhibitions of "the natural" that, in their very exaggeration, reveal its fundamentally phantasmatic status'.[25] Thus, for example, exaggerated displays of 'masculinity' through vehement assertions of heterosexuality or aversions to homosexuality not only suggest an insecurity over sexuality but also reveal the fantasy of authentic gender-identity.

That gender is a construction is in itself not a surprising assertion, given that gender is usually considered to be the qualities ascribed to men and women by culture. A person's sex, by contrast, is usually understood as a biological given. For Butler, however, it is the interpellation of the child as female or male that categorises and conditions its sex. The theory of interpellation in use here is that developed by the French theorist Louis Althusser, who argued that subjectivity was created through being interpellated, or hailed, by others. In other words, we come to subjectivity through the different ways we are called into language (that is, we do not have an identity prior to the identifications made by others). Much of this interpellation will explicitly, and arguably all of it will implicitly, address the individual in terms of their sex. Which is to say that not only gender, but also sex is ideological, and the fetishised reiterations of (the supreme importance of) sexual difference create the girl/boy they purport to name. This is not to deny bodily differences but to observe that 'sex' is a discursive construction, like judgemental divisions between people on the basis of skin colour, or any other physical feature – which is always for political rather than 'natural' reasons.

Christopher Pullen argues that TV, and particularly reality TV, has increasingly taken the sexual 'outsider identity' out of the basement or the closet 'and *seemingly* welcomed it into the space of the living room [my emphasis]'.[26] He gives the example of Brian Dowling, an openly gay householder who won *Big Brother 2* in 2001. For John McGrath, there is a connection to be made here, in that Dowling's sexual self-presentation showed him to be well-equipped for the programme's intense surveillance: 'As a gay man he seemed already to understand and to have practised how to engage socially in the post-private world. He seemed to be teaching everyone how they could survive and prosper in surveillance space.'[27] However, while McGrath thinks that Dowling's 'exhibitionism and humorous self-engagement' made him engaging to the audience, Pullen argues that through a 'portfolio of theatrical antics, pantomime cross-dressing and child-like behaviour, Brian presents himself as a comic, if somewhat absurd, entertaining character for the audience's consumption'.[28] For Pullen, this showed Dowling to be both 'failing' to challenge identity structures and also fully aware of the performative nature of the programme by imitating the behaviour of camp gay performers familiar to TV audiences. When another gay man, Josh Rafter, was voted into the house, his performance of sexual identity was very different: intensely sexual, highly fashion conscious. Where Dowling is domesticated and child-like, Rafter is threatening and sexualised. Dowling, the ultimate winner, presents the acceptable, entertaining image of gay identity, as in numerous Hollywood films where comparisons can be made with traditional, unthreatening representations of African-American identity. Chinn observes that:

> [T]here are times when incoherent gender performativity can expose the constructedness of gender and (hetero)sexuality. Butler lands on drag as a possible place this can happen. Drag is a self-conscious, larger-than-life realisation of heterosexual normativity. By performing gender in

a hyperbolic, stylized way, drag queens don't simply imitate femininity, they reveal how women imitate femininity as well, and what hard work it is. Through parody, drag can expose the seeming naturalness of gender itself; it doesn't imitate an original, but reveals that there is no original, only layers of performance.[29]

Thus, Dowling's camp entertainment was well-received by a TV audience who recognised and felt comfortable with a stereotype, while Rafter's less obvious but more threatening sexuality was soon rejected by viewers. The programme in this way does not reflect a wider social view but constructs it.

The different receptions of Dowling and Rafter, which McGrath summarises as Rafter 'being punished by everyone for the sexual confusion he caused',[30] can be usefully considered in terms of queer theory which *queries* all dominant schemes of sexual and gender normativity and breaks the link between gay sexuality and 'queer' or deviant sexuality.[31] Queer sexuality recognises the polymorphous sexual impulses and desires that go against the push to regulate, control and organise. It sees the binary division of heterosexual/gay sexuality (which enables the latter to be chastised as transgressive) as reductive of actual sexual fantasies and practices. The site of intervention here is that of 'identity' which is seen not as foundational, but as imitative, contingent and unstable.

For example, Butler sees lesbianism as a postmodern pastiche of heterosexuality: not straight sexuality's other but its parody. She also adopts Joan Riviere's idea of a feminine masquerade that either subverts or reinforces norms of masculinity, and applies it to lesbianism, arguing that repetition with a difference – parody – can reveal the fictions of normativity or can bolster its foundations.[32] A similar argument can be applied to the effects of Dowling and Rafter on *Big Brother 2*. Because male homosexual identity is expected to reinforce norms of masculinity by offering a caricature of feminine identity (the performance given by Dowling), Rafter's performance of an intensely masculine and heterosexually attractive yet gay identity met with audience disapproval.

Eve Kosofsky Sedgwick says that one of the things 'queer' refers to is 'the open mesh of possibilities, gaps, overlaps, dissonances and resonances, lapses and excesses of meaning when the constituent elements of anyone's gender, of anyone's sexuality aren't made (or *can't be* made) to signify monolithically'.[33] This applies to the term 'queer' itself, which does not denote or connote so much as open up, deviate and *query* what Alan Sinfield, taking a term from the novelist Nicholson Baker, calls the 'straightgeist'.[34] Also, when writing about heterosexuality, queer analyses specifically work, as Sedgwick puts it, not at 'reconfirming the self-evidence and "naturalness" of heterosexual identity and desire, but rather at rendering those culturally central, apparently monolithic constructions newly accessible to analysis and interrogation'.[35] However, with regard to *Big Brother* and other cult TV programmes, critics note how 'queer' loses its radical political force when it is so visible and permissible that it is domesticated within ' heterosexual camp'. When co-opted by postmodern visual culture, 'queer' simply becomes the latest novelty of a commercial culture.

Big Brother, of course, takes its name from the surveillance system in George Orwell's novel *1984*. Here, the purpose of constant observation is not just to check that citizens are behaving according to the prevailing orthodoxy, but also to ensure that they internalise its values. Complementary to Althusser's theory of interpellation,[36] and like Foucault's comments on such devices as the panopticon in *Discipline and Punish*,[37] the purpose of constant observation in the *Big Brother* house is not to allow the audience to view people behaving as they do in their lives outside the house, but simultaneously to produce and witness certain kinds of behaviour through surveillance. This is a technological avatar of the reminder given to parishioners of God's constant observation, which itself is framed as a threat that regulates behaviour. Any observing presence also has a regulatory purpose for surveillance.

Moving from metaphysical to secular observation, in school or prison for example, belief in the possibility of observation is an end in itself because it encourages the observed to think about the demands of the observer – to self-regulate in the knowledge that someone who wishes to observe certain behaviour may be watching. From a psychoanalytic viewpoint this can also be considered in terms of the development of the superego through the internalisation of parental or social injunctions in the form of a regulating force on the ego counterbalancing the selfish demands of the id. Thus the question arises of what the role of surveillance is for the observers of *Big Brother*. Tony Myers sketches one response to this articulated by Slavoj Žižek:

> Constantly bombarded with images of, and invitations to indulge in, sexual enjoyment, it can no longer be claimed that sexual pleasure is in any way prohibited. On the contrary, for Slavoj Žižek, sensual gratification has been elevated to the status of an official ideology. We are compelled to enjoy sex. The compunction – the injunction 'Enjoy!' – marks the return of the superego.[38]

However, for Žižek the superego is not an internalised mechanism of prohibition but an invocation to act which is opposed to the repressive invocations of social rules. For the postmodern subject, enjoyment becomes compulsory, and it is the superego that sustains this imperative. Enjoyment is no longer 'normal' or spontaneous but a social injunction. For Žižek this is the consequence of the passing of what he calls 'the big Other', his name for the social network of laws, conventions and customs.[39] Just as a post-Christian society no longer believes in the law of God, a postmodern society no longer believes in the grand narratives that previously conditioned community living. The big Other of social authority, which never was materially embodied but existed as an accepted symbolic order, operated as a fiction of authorisation that gave access to what Foucault would call 'being in the true' – the consensual hegemony over meaning that validated, among other things, identity. Only this official and authorised recognition confers 'reality' because the big Other is that which has the power to make those performative speech acts that will be socially recognised, authorising the subject's status, which is to say 'identity', as a criminal, an adult, a lawyer, a poet, or as mad, beautiful, unemployed and so on. Identity is thus not a matter of a real self underneath a fantasy or mask. Instead:

> [W]e are dealing with a symbolic fiction, but a fiction which, for contingent reasons that have nothing to do with its inherent structure, possesses performative power – is socially operative, structures the socio-symbolic reality in which I participate. The status of the same person, inclusive of his/her very 'real' features, can appear in an entirely different light the moment the modality of his/her relationship to the big Other changes.[40]

With the decline in power of this overarching authority, the postmodern subject is left with vertiginous choice, with the necessity constantly to make decisions without efficacious injunctions of the big Other directing and legitimating the parameters of conduct. For Žižek, this dizzying freedom has led to, among other things, a desire for authority and subjection in private lives, the most obvious of which is the higher profile, if not necessarily incidence, of BDSM (Bondage Discipline Submission/Sadism Masochism), but another is arguably the desire to be observed, surveilled or televised (often with the argument that, as with the comforting authority of the big Other, it feels safer). As with BDSM, in *Big Brother* contestants freely agree to be constrained and regulated in return for the pleasure they will gain from the audience and media attention the show guarantees (the cash prize is no longer a necessary incentive, if ever it was).

While incredulity towards ideological subservience to the big Other occasions postmodern freedom, Žižek argues that this is replaced by the stipulation to enjoy. At the heart of the obligations placed on the willing *Big Brother* contestants by their surveillance is thus the obligation to (be seen to) enjoy sex – and of course one of the meanings of the verb 'to enjoy' is 'to have sexual intercourse with'. The media scrutiny of the show is centred on this injunction, which Žižek sees as the superego imperative. The contestants are often selected and promoted in the light of their willingness to bring sex into the show, which, seemingly paradoxically, has been largely absent from the programmes, leading to increased pressure to perform (more) sexually as each series passes. For Žižek, this is the conclusion of making enjoyment compulsory. As for wider Western society, for the *Big Brother* contestants, despite the rhetoric that surrounds the show and their participation in it, 'the injunction of the superego to "Enjoy!" is stultifying in its effect, leaving the addressees of the injunction either indifferent or unable to enjoy what they are told to enjoy'.[41] The liberal stipulation to enjoy undermines its own injunction as previously transgressive acts become obligatory – 'the *obligation* to enjoy . . . is the most effective way to block access to enjoyment.'[42]

Finally, an alternative view would be that the programme is driven by judgemental attitudes of scrutiny and shame in the 'television of cruelty' I mentioned at the start. According to a *Guardian* newspaper column in 2004:

> Nowhere is the cruelty of today's shows more apparent than in their treatment of female contestants: a selection of ever-more lads'-mag-friendly 'babes' are popping up in *Big Brother* and *I'm A Celebrity*, only to be branded as sluts in tabloid gossip columns and on-line chat rooms. In the pantomime world of reality TV, the days of affable cheats such as Nasty Nick [who had to leave the *Big Brother* programme in shame for 'cheating' in the first series] are gone. The new villains are female: *Pop Idol's* Michelle McManus (too fat), *Hell's Kitchen's* Edwina Currie (too old) and *Big Brother's* Kitten (too gay, too loud).[43]

If programmes like *Big Brother* illustrate in detail how everyone is opened up to judgement in a culture of surveillance that in fact stretches far beyond TV studios, then the relationship between gender and performativity in the construction of identity will be increasingly significant. In *Big Brother*, participants are contestants who are voted in or out of the house by millions of viewers on the basis of their gendered performance. The much-vaunted upside to media exposure is the possibility of a career as a 'celebrity', but the downside includes cruelty and humiliation. Making the most private aspects of people's lives public means exposing their sense of identity to judgement, ridicule and possible shame, which several theorists of performativity also see as a focal point for understanding how gender works:

> Eve Kosofsky Sedgwick has speculated that experiencing shame has a foundational role in subject formation. In her essay 'Queer Performativity' (1993) she argues that 'shame is a bad feeling attached to what one is: one therefore is *something*, in experiencing shame. The place of identity, the structure "identity" . . . may be established and naturalized in the first instance *through shame*'[44] For Sedgwick, then, shame is a constitutive element of all the things that make up identity, most centrally gender and sexuality; it is woven into the parts of ourselves that feel the most personal and the most important.[45]

REFERENCES AND BIBLIOGRAPHY

Allen, Robert C. and Annette Hill, *The Television Studies Reader*, London: Routledge, 2004.

Arthurs, Jane, *Television and Sexuality: Regulation and the Politics of Taste*, Berkshire: Open University Press, 2004.

Butler, Judith, *Gender Trouble*, London: Routledge, 1990.

Chinn, Sarah E. 'Gender Performativity', in Andy Medhurst and Sally R. Munt (eds), *Lesbian and Gay Studies: A Critical Introduction*, London: Cassell, 1997, pp. 294–308.

Holmes, Su, ' "All you've got to worry about is the task, having a cup of tea, and doing a bit of sunbathing": Approaching Celebrity in *Big Brother*', in Holmes and Jermyn (eds), pp. 111–35.

Holmes, Su and Deborah Jermyn (eds), *Understanding Reality Television*, London: Routledge, 2004.

McGrath, John E., *Loving Big Brother: Performance, Privacy and Surveillance Space*, London: Routledge, 2004.

Myers, Tony, *Slavoj Žižek*, London: Routledge, 2003.

Persaud, Raj, 'Car-Crash Television', *The Guardian*, Media section, 17 July 2000, pp. 6–7

Pullen, Christopher, 'The Household, the Basement and *The Real World*', in Holmes and Jermyn (eds), pp. 211–32.

Ritchie, Jean, *Big Brother: The Official Unseen Story*, London: Macmillan Channel 4 Books, 2000.

Roscoe, Jane, '*Big Brother* Australia: Performing the "real" Twenty-Four-Seven', in Allen and Hill (eds), pp. 311–21.

Salih, Sara, *Judith Butler*, London: Routledge, 2002.

Sedgwick, Eve Kosofsky, *Tendencies*, Durham: Duke University Press, 1993.

Sinfield, Alan, *Gay and After: Gender, Culture and Consumption*, London: Serpents Tail, 1998.

Tincknell, Estella and Parvati Raghuram, '*Big Brother*: Reconfiguring the Active Audience of Cultural Studies', in Holmes and Jermyn (eds), pp. 252–69.

Žižek, Slavoj, *For They Know Not What They Do: Enjoyment as a Political Factor*, London: Verso, 1991.

Žižek, Slavoj, *The Ticklish Subject: The Absent Centre of Political Ontology*, London: Verso, 1999.

Žižek, Slavoj, *Enjoy Your Symptom!: Jacques Lacan in Hollywood and Out*, revd edn, London: Routledge, 2001.

NOTES

1. Žižek, 2001, p. 40.
2. Quoted in Holmes, p. 118.
3. See Endemol television, http://www.endemol.com/current_tv_hits.xml (accessed 10 Aug. 2005).
4. A good place to start examining Milgram's experiment is Wikipedia's entry: http://en.wikipedia.org/wiki/Milgram_experiment (accessed 5 Oct. 2005).
5. One of the programme's consultant editors, David Wilson, a former prison governor and Professor of Criminology at the University of Central England in Birmingham, resigned from the programme after recognising that the producers wished to provoke rather than reduce conflict of a psychologically damaging nature. Wilson called for all such programmes to have an Ethics Committee. See Wilson's article 'Big Brother Damages Our Health' at http://www.guardian.co.uk/pda/story/0,8884,1548422-Comment,00.html (accessed 12 Oct. 2005).
6. Tincknell and Raghuram, p. 261.
7. http://www.gamesindustry.biz/press_release.php?aid=4673 (accessed 10 Aug. 2005).
8. See Chapter 13.
9. Persaud, p. 7.
10. It has also been an important part of voting trends. An advertisement in *Gay Times* 'urged readers to vote for the lesbian contestant, Anna, wholly on the grounds of

her sexuality' (Tincknell and Raghuram, p. 262). Again, differences are apparent between the first and fifth series in that Anna a shy ex-nun, was replaced by the fifth series with 'Kitten' an outspoken lesbian political activist.

11. Arthurs, p. 45.
12. Ibid.
13. In the fifth series security guards were required to enter the house after a fight broke out between contestants. This had been highly probable when two evicted participants were reintroduced after watching, for several days, some of the remaining house members criticise them heavily from an annexe to the main house. The producers of the show had promised excitement in the fifth series after the previous year's series had been criticised as dull. The 2004 series was thus noted in the press for violence and sex, both of which had been largely absent in previous years. After the fight, psychotherapists and psychologists counselled the contestants. The fifth series was notable for the choice of individuals with extreme views during the selection process.
14. Tincknell and Raghuram, p. 266.
15. Ibid. In terms of a reading of resistance, Tincknell and Raghuram point out Anna's comparative success in the first series, noting however that she finished second to a heterosexual male, and Brian's winning of the second series. But, '[A] closer reading of Brian's persona suggests that only a performative, camp version of homosexuality sufficiently unthreatening to contemporary heteronormative sexual discourse could be endorsed'(Tincknell and Raghuram, p. 266).
16. Holmes, p. 131.
17. Butler, p. 16.
18. Ibid.
19. Ibid., pp. 24–5.
20. Judith Butler, 'Gender as Performance: An Interview with Judith Butler', *Radical Philosophy* 67, 1994, pp. 32–9; p. 33.
21. Chinn, p. 294.
22. Of course it is significant that the performative statements I mention, such as 'I hereby sentence you to life in prison', only achieve the effect we expect if they are performed in the right context. They have to be official – to be recognised as uttered by an authorised person at a legitimised place at a correct time.
23. Salih, p. 65.
24. Butler, p. 136.
25. Ibid., p. 147.
26. Pullen, p. 211.
27. McGrath, p. 74.
28. Pullen, p. 222.
29. Chinn, p. 301. This is not to say that drag is inherently subversive – as Butler notes, it can also reinforce norms.
30. McGrath, p. 75.
31. Indebted to Michel Foucault's *History of Sexuality* (1976–86), queer theory arose in the 1990s, particularly out of the work of Judith Butler (e.g. *Gender Trouble*) and Eve Kosofsky Sedgwick (e.g. *Epistemology of the Closet*).
32. Butler was greatly influenced by Joan Riviere's paper 'Womanliness as Masquerade' in the *International Journal of Psycho-analysis* in 1929 (see Chapter 8).
33. Sedgwick, p. 8.
34. See Alan Sinfield, *Gay and After: Gender, Culture and Consumption*, London: Serpent's Tail, 1998.
35. Ibid., p. 9.
36. Althusser's theory of interpellation says that 'individuals are persuaded that that which is presented to them actually represesents their own identity or self.' Interpellation happens when a statement of some kind, verbal or in a political manifesto, an advert, or a literary text, places the listener/viewer/reader in a subject

position with which they identify. Like the words on the Lord Kitchener First World War poster that proclaimed 'Your country needs YOU', all language addresses individuals and asks them to see themselves in a certain role: patriot, activist, consumer or whatever. See Louis Althusser's essay 'Ideology and Ideological State Apparatuses' in *Lenin and Philosophy and Other Essays* (1970).The essay is available on-line at http://www.marx2mao.com/Other/LPOE70ii.html#s5 (accessed 12 Aug. 2005).

37. Juliet Mitchell in her ground-breaking *Psychoanalysis and Feminism* (1974) outlines how Freudian analysis shows that gender roles are a consequence of power relations. However, Foucault argues that a dominated group is complicit in its domination because it participates in the status quo. It also exercises its own power where it can – power is not a top-down hierarchy but a diffuse, ever-present series of micro-actions. On *Big Brother* everyone is being watched by the audience, but they are also always watching each other and themselves, aware of being watched they check themselves in mirrors, but have also internalised self-observation.

38. Myers, p. 53.

39. As a concept the big Other is most easily aligned with the symbolic order in Lacanian psychoanalysis.

40. Žižek, 1999, p. 330.

41. Myers, p. 54.

42. Žižek, 1991, p. 237.

43. *The Guardian*, Education Section, 22 June 2004, p. 12.

44. Eve Kosofsky Sedgwick, 'Queer Performativity: Henry James's *The Art of the Novel*' *GLQ: A Journal of Lesbian and Gay Studies* 1: 1, 1993, pp. 1–16; p. 12.

45. Chinn, p. 302.

NEWSPAPER ARTICLE: THE GULF WAR IN REAL TIME AND VIRTUAL SPACE

Approach: Hyperreality

'The war, therefore, if we judge it by the standards of previous wars, is merely an imposture.'
'[N]o Inner Party member wavers for an instant in his mystical belief that the war *is* real.' (George Orwell)[1]

The literary, however identified, may be said to include many examples of non-fiction, including works of journalism. Given the reporter's quasi-objective relationship to history, the journalistic article was in some ways seen as a model for much literature in the 1930s, with a writer such as George Orwell specialising equally in fiction, essay-writing and reportage, and a novelist such as Christopher Isherwood fashioning himself in fiction as a news camera 'recording, not thinking'.[2] Newspaper articles are, in fact, defined by their place of publication rather than their content, but there are certain likely formal characteristics or principles of journalistic writing to do with information-content, length, veracity, verisimilitude, argument, and so forth, though these are also highly variable and differ from feature writing to editorial and so on. The article that will be looked at in this chapter is the first in a series of three pieces written by Jean Baudrillard in 1991 about the war in the Gulf, or rather the lack of it. The articles are unusual inasmuch as they are a rare example of what might be called postmodernist journalism, in which journalism's relation to reality is not the issue, as it would have been earlier in the twentieth century, but the entire modern Western world's relationship to 'reality' is called into question, and considered in terms of the hyperreality discussed in Chapter 1 with regard to *The Matrix*.

Baudrillard's articles appeared in a national newspaper, and thus were published to a large and general audience. The articles implicitly contest the very reporting that appeared elsewhere in the newspaper and attempt to convince a country's population that the 'reality' they take for granted is not as it appears. Above all, the articles seek to persuade the reader to think otherwise, to see that a vast media machinery, like the Ministry of Truth in *1984*, is creating rather than reporting the news.

After a costly war with Iran between 1980 and 1988, fought in the name of collective Arab interests opposing Islamic fundamentalism, Iraq sought to rebuild its economy. Iraq had been supported politically and militarily (with equipment not soldiers) by the US during the war with Iran:

> The state Department talked of the importance of the US relationship with Iraq and US senators visited Iraq for Saddam Hussein's birthday in 1990, advising him that his image problem was merely a product of the Western media that could be corrected with a better public-relations (PR) policy.[3]

Oil was central to rebuilding the Iraqi economy, such that, when Kuwait reduced the price of its oil below that agreed by OPEC, after having both upheld Iraq's war debts and declined to negotiate the long-running border dispute between the countries, Iraq began to amass troops and weaponry along the Kuwaiti frontier. When the move led to no censure or threat from the US, Iraq invaded in early August 1990. Within six months, the world response to this invasion, in the context of the oil reserves at risk, the stability of the Middle East, and the potential further military threats to US allies, particularly Saudi Arabia, culminated in military action: the Gulf War.

When, in January 1991, Jean Baudrillard published an article entitled 'The Gulf War Will Not Take Place' in the French newspaper *Libération*, most readers would have imagined him to be claiming that diplomatic or other political interventions would cause the US and its allies not to attack Iraq. Most probably, Iraq would begin to remove its troops from Kuwait before the UN Security Council's deadline of 15 January. When the attacks began to be reported in the media, however, Baudrillard, far from admitting he was wrong, published a further article asking: 'The Gulf War: Is It Really Taking Place?' In March, when hostilities were over, Baudrillard produced a third article asserting 'The Gulf War Did Not Take Place.' As a triptych of journalism, Baudrillard's articles draw attention to the media's role in creating the public's version of 'war' and 'reality' while adding to its sense of incredulity, in some ways anticipating the scepticism over war journalism and political rhetoric in the second Gulf War. The principal objection to the arguments of Baudrillard is that they leave no room for truth or reality, perceiving everything in terms of simulation. Thus, Christopher Norris summarises Baudrillard's view of the Gulf War as:

> In short, the whole campaign is a media benefit, an extension of video war games technology by alternative means, a 'hyperreal' scenario (Baudrillard's phrase) where truth is defined solely in performative or

rhetorical terms, i.e. as what presently counts as such according to the latest feedback consensus. Nor can we complain, in the time-honoured fashion, that 'truth is always the first "casualty of war"' . . . Anyone who continues to invoke such standards is plainly in the grip of a nostalgic desire for some ultimate truth-telling discourse.[4]

Bearing Norris's comment in mind, I would think that the first word to pick up on from the second of Baudrillard's titles is 'really'. This is not a synonym for 'actually' but an antonym to 'virtually'. Baudrillard might therefore be considered to be arguing that there neither would be nor was a real war. This is not the same as saying, for example, that the 'Falklands War' was not a war because 'war' was never declared, but that the 'Gulf War' was neither like a hot war, such as the Second World War, nor like the Cold War. So, we need to ask what was different? To begin with, there was the media saturation of 'live' events. The conflict was inseparable in the West from its coverage to the extent that the 'war' could be considered to have happened on TV, in real time, with round-the-clock coverage. There is a parallel to be made here with 'reality television', whose advent in the late 1990s signalled the commercial simulation of real life in the name of sociological experiment. A reverse logic occurs here as, for example, the *Big Brother* cameras are not installed to record the activities of the housemates but the housemates are installed in the house so that they can be filmed (see Chapter 6). A similar argument would claim that reporters and cameras were not simply sent to cover a war that had started in the Gulf but that the war was waged while it was also staged for the cameras. But Baudrillard is also concerned with the absence of the signs of war as usually understood. The screening of the Gulf War was choreographed like a Hollywood movie, containing few images of human suffering but many of weapons, destroyed buildings and military targets. Viewers' TV screens were filled by pictures of other screens as the war was planned, monitored, reviewed and explained with computer technology. For many of the military personnel involved in this process there could be no difference between this 'war' and the simulations of their training programmes. For the viewer, despite the 24/7 coverage, the comparatively few images of casualties also minimised perceptions that a 'war' was taking place.[5] For Baudrillard this is a necessary consequence of the West's rhetoric, which has replaced war with 'deterrence', defining its own military action in terms of the liberation of both Kuwait and the people of Iraq, just as in the second Gulf War 'Weapons of Mass Destruction' were something the West's enemies owned in contrast to its own 'defence systems'.

A 'real' war differs from a 'virtual' war in that the former relies on direct physical engagement while the latter uses technology to simulate, and thus prevent, 'war' by interposing hardware and software between the combatants. In Orson Welles's film *Citizen Kane* (1941) a correspondent is told to boost sales by reporting a South American war. When the correspondent replies that there is no war he is told to make one. The 'war reporter' is not asked to make one up but to make one appear: to simulate one. While simulation may some-times seem to be little more than an imitation of life, like a computer game that has little impact on the 'real' world, this is of course far from the case. The virtual is not a parallel world but an interlocking one which can have devas-tating consequences and effects. In war, this has historically been associated with 'propaganda', an increasingly dominant feature of the twentieth century which has spawned 'misinformation', 'fabrication' and 'spin'. Paul Patton writes: 'The images of war nonetheless have real effects and become enmeshed in the ensuing material and social reality. In this sense, Baudrillard argues, we live in a hyperreality which results from a fusion of the virtual and the real into a third order of reality.'[6] It is in this order of reality that the Gulf War was waged, in the transmission and manipulation of information and images where the virtual circulates more quickly and more widely than the real. Most import-antly for Baudrillard, the virtual is substituted for the real as the authoritative version of events (whereas for other critics information is a weapon in war)[7]. The authority of the real is strategically invoked to claim moral superiority or factual truth but for the viewer the real is always mediated, always represented, always virtual. In an information age, events are interpretive means to political ends, and when even the combatants are reliant on CNN for news of the war, direct or indirect control of the media is essential to a successful campaign.[8]

It is also worth thinking about what remains of a war in its aftermath. There are the physical and political effects and the memories, but for most people the conflict persists as a series of textual reports, an archive that replaces the events it documents. In terms of the Gulf War, this is what Baudrillard argues also hap-pened at the time, and his more important points are about the mediation of the war rather than its existence. This is only partly to argue, with Noam Chomsky and others, that the Gulf War did not take place because it was a totally unequal and predictable one-sided but not open-armed conflict (to call it a 'war' means that it is not (called) a suppression, a religious crusade, or a capitalist assertion of oil rights, just as the 'Indian Mutiny' of 1857 is not the same as the 'First Indian War of Independence'). For Baudrillard it was also a simulation: clean, virtual, and computerised.

I want to turn now to a discussion of one of the articles in detail, or rather of its translation into English. For the purposes of the analysis I will treat the translation as the 'original' document while here acknowledging that it is itself a simulacrum – a representation – of something that will remain absent.

Baudrillard's first article is the shortest of the three. It is allusive and ellip-tical, trades in shorthand expressions and blunt assertions, and relies on metaphor and wordplay. It is also rhetorical. The opening statement claims that 'we' knew the Gulf War would 'never happen'. The rest of the article retains this first person plural, thus making the reader complicit with its argument, and its use of the word 'never' is crucial: Baudrillard is not saying just that it won't happen but that it can't happen. The rest of the first paragraph explains this stance by claiming the principal effect of war for war itself: war is now *dead*.

This has arisen after the hot war – that which complies with the dictionary definitions of open armed conflict – and the Cold War of the superpowers' standoff in which espionage, nuclear proliferation and imperial expansion substituted for direct engagement between enemies. A crucial context for Baudrillard's argument, therefore, is the fall of the Berlin Wall and the Soviet Union's capitulation to democracy. While Francis Fukuyama considers this the end of history, Baudrillard sees it as the termination of war as such: 'There will be no other.'[9]

The transition from 'hot' to 'cold' war was from the violence of conflict to the deterrence of proliferation. One way to read this is indeed in the context of nuclear weaponry. Both the US and the USSR had sufficient weaponry to annihilate each other. War remained a possibility but would have taken place in the context of mutually assured destruction. War was thus replaced with economic and military might: the winner being the one with the greater amount of reserves and resources, wealth and weaponry, intelligence and technology, on show. This was 'reciprocal deterrence' (p. 23) in which too much was at stake for the cold war to escalate into armed conflict. For Baudrillard, though the Cold War has ended, deterrence has remained. The apex of deterrence was the Soviet Bloc's self-dissolution: an extreme form of deterrence in which the USSR disabled itself from waging war. Its aftermath is Western self-deterrence: 'paralysed by its own strength and incapable of assuming it in the form of relations of force' (p. 24).

Baudrillard then claims that this is why the Gulf War will not take place: because the West will not use its 'strength' to wage war against Iraq. Neither its nuclear weapons nor its military personnel will be sent to war, for political and pragmatic reasons: the Cold War period has made the use of either unacceptable but the development of technology has also made the use of them unnecessary. Baudrillard then substitutes for the 'Gulf War' the terms 'non-event' and 'non-war', and he likens the period of waiting for the attacks on Iraq to 'the highly toxic period which affects a rotting corpse and which can cause nausea and powerless stupor' because we do not know how to deal with the death of war (p. 24). He speaks of a 'uniform shameless indifference', which is not to war but to its absence.

His delineation of non-war is its substitution of 'blackmail', 'hostage manipulation and negotiation' for armed conflict. These are the tactics and actions of not war but the deterrence of war. Hostages are not combatants in war but human bargaining chips in its avoidance: 'the protagoniser of non-war' (p. 24). In non-war the hostage replaces the warrior as the means of influence. However, the hostage is used to prevent war and so is the antithesis of the warrior: the warrior cannot wage war until the position of the hostage is bargained over, decided upon and/or resolved, and so the hostage is a deterrent to war.

In this non-war, Baudrillard positions 'us' as information hostages. This is because the media audience is similarly deployed to how hostages are, as central protagonisers of the non-war: 'phantom actors' on the stage of war where war is not waged. In Baudrillard's scenario, the hyperreal war turns citizens into non-combatants who occupy 'the powerless stage of war' because the non-war is fought in terms of information, manipulation and negotiation. In contrast to war, the non-war is won by the side that can win over the non-combatants: those who do not want 'war' and have to be persuaded that war has been deterred. In the non-war or weak-war information hostages are strategically fought over for their exchange value and are market commodities to be 'traded' while the reasons for or against war are heatedly debated in the media.

In Orwell's *1984*, war is waged constantly.[10] The citizens of Oceania are information-manipulated to believe in war against a changing opponent who is deployed as an enemy to justify war, or in Baudrillard's terms non-war, as required by the state. As with the 'war on terror' that has been created after the September 11 attacks on the New York World Trade Center in 2001, both the question of who the war is against and the fact that it can never be won, are irrelevant to the usefulness of public opinion, whose force can justify arms production and fuel governmental power. For Baudrillard as for Orwell, to control the media is to control the minds of the populace and so to gain a mandate for action.[11]

Baudrillard introduces a historical class-dimension into his analysis by likening the trade in (information) hostages to previous markets in slaves and workers. Saddam Hussein is positioned by Baudrillard as a trader in this hostage market: the accomplice in the West's 'staging' of war, where the bombardment of cities is substituted with the daily bombardment of screen images, replacing the 'stage of war' with a 'grotesque vaudeville' (p. 25). The hard terrorism of bombings is replaced by the soft terrorism of media bombardment, in which war is diverted into non-war and the struggle over images, representations and discourse, in which the chief weapons are blackmail and negotiation.[12] The 'nobility' of war fades into the 'vulgarity' of non-war: '[R]eligious challenge has become fake holy war, the sacrificial hostage a commercial hostage, the violent refusal of the West a nationalistic scam and war an impossible comedy' (p. 25)

To gloss further his term 'non-war', Baudrillard explains again that 'We are in neither a logic of war nor a logic of peace but in a logic of deterrence' (p. 26). What Baudrillard seems to mean by this is that the object of the conflict is not peace or the conquering of another country, but the disciplining of its regime. The logic of war would necessitate action but the logic of deterrence seeks only 'the right to war under the green light of the UN and with an abundance of precautions and concessions' (p. 26). In the non-war staged as spectacle, in which mediation precedes rather than follows conflict, Baudrillard sees all the mechanisms of warfare working towards simulation rather than action. Armies and bombs are not meant to wage war but deter it, just as technology has been developed to simulate and distance war, and the media stages more than reports the war. War does not happen (the real) so much as circulate in an economy of information and representation (the hyperreal). In this, Baudrillard sees the virtual (non-war) deterring the real (war):

> The most widespread belief is in a logical progression from virtual to actual, according to which no available weapon will not one day be used and such a concentration of force cannot but lead to conflict. However, this is an Aristotelian logic which is no longer our own. Our virtuality has definitively overtaken the actual and we must be content with this extreme virtuality which, unlike the Aristotelian, deters any passage to action. We are no longer in a logic of the passage from virtual to actual but in a hyper-realist logic of the deterrence of the real by the virtual. (p. 27)

Hostages, from the Old French word *hoste* meaning guest, become a symbol of this logic as they make manifest the 'degradation of real hostility (war) into virtual hospitality (Saddam Hussein's "guests")' (p. 27). Hostages are not prisoners or combatants of war, or guests (peace), but people used for their exchange-value: which is to say, they are substitutes for combat, deployed in an attempt to achieve what in a 'real' war would be accomplished by force. Thus, alongside the myriad technological changes that replace the real with the virtual, hostages are part of a 'war' fought outside of war, 'in vitro' (a biological process made to occur outside the body in an artificial environment).

Baudrillard ends by saying that his essay is a 'stupid gamble' to take when the Gulf War looks about to start. This can remind the reader that Baudrillard is in part arguing that he thinks conflict will not happen, but will continue to be deterred. But this is not all of the argument by any means. His main point concerns the changes in warfare brought about by postmodernity: changes in technology, in media communications and in global relations. He claims that war as previously understood can no longer happen.

In the second essay in his trilogy, Baudrillard says: 'We have still not left the virtual war, in other words a sophisticated although often laughable build-up against the backdrop of a global indeterminacy of will to make war' (p. 30). Thus, having lost the 'gamble', Baudrillard is nonetheless interested in trying to force the reader to consider the Gulf War in the light of its mediation, largely because there is no other way for 'us' to access it. This echoes Douglas Kellner's book *The Persian Gulf TV War*, in which he says: '[W]ith the whole world watching and following the events of the day, TV directly constituted the viewers' conceptions of the war . . . the Gulf War was primarily a media propaganda war.'[13] Kellner also thinks the Gulf War represented a change in war itself, as the US video accounts presented by Norman Schwarzkopf sought to demonstrate that bombs only ever struck their (military) targets and led to no collateral damage: 'This was intended to change the public perception of war itself, that the new technowar was clean, precise, and surgical, that the very nature of war had changed.'[14] The oxymoronic expression that encapsulates this is 'clean war', which distinguishes itself from 'dirty war' (a covert offensive conducted by secret police and militia against individuals suspected of insurgency), but also implies that it leaves no marks, stains or blood.

The arguments of Kellner and Baudrillard are not just about mediation – they concern the particular kinds of media newsreporting that dominate Western TV. A comparison can be made with Chris Morris's British TV programmes *The Day Today* and *Brass Eye* which satirise the media's sensationalising and self-important reporting: the substitution of statistics and graphs for factual information; the avoidance of upsetting images of intense or large-scale human suffering alongside the sentimental treatment of minor stories; the manipulation of language to create partisan feeling; the euphemisms for killing, bombing and other military actions; the attempt to portray an invasion as a moral crusade of liberation; and the near complete absence of dissenting voices.

The extremity of Baudrillard's argument has had at least two consequences. On the one hand, it has brought considerable comment and notoriety. On the other, it has obscured important points because critics have focused on the seeming absurdity of the essays, encapsulated in their titles.[15] Another critic who perhaps more helpfully brings out several similar points to Baudrillard is Paul Virilio, who also asks, for example, 'How can we fail to recognize, after a month of standoff, that the true *intervention force* in the Gulf is TV?'[16] However, Virilio disagrees with Baudrillard's basic contention that the war did not take place and sees instead an example of modern warfare which has moved into space. Virilio also perceives changes in modern warfare that redefine what war is. He says, for example, of the war in Kosovo: 'It was a war that took place almost entirely in the air. There were hardly any Allied armed personnel on the ground. There was, for example, no real state of siege and practically no blockade.'[17] Virilio makes a similar point in his expanded comments on the Gulf War's relation to space:

> The Gulf War was a world war in miniature. Let me explain. The monitoring of the globe by American satellites was required to win a local war. Therefore we can say that this was a fractal war: at once local and global. With the new technologies and with the new logistics of perception, the battlefield was also developing the field of perception. The Gulf War, for example, was a local war in comparison with the Second World War, with regard to its battlefield. But it was a worldwide war on the temporal level of representation, on the level of media, thanks to the satellite acquisition of targets, thanks to the tele-command of the war. I am thinking of Patriot anti-missiles which were commanded from the Pentagon and from a satellite positioned high above the Gulf countries. On the one side, it was a local war, of little interest, without many deaths, without many consequences. But, by contrast, on the other side, it was a unique field of perception. For the first time, as opposed to the Vietnam War, it was a war rendered live, worldwide – with, of course, the special effects, all the

information processing organized by the Pentagon and the censorship by the major states. In fact, it is a war that took place in the artifice of TV, much more than in the reality of the field of battle, in the sense that real time prevailed over real space.[18]

Virilio sees a development from previous types of warfare inasmuch as the wars in Kosovo and the Gulf took place not just before the ears (like the Second World War) or the eyes of the world (as with the Vietnam War) but in ways that involved the audience: '[I]t is now a matter of *tele-action*, where the opposing parties are engaged in an *absolute interactive situation*, before the eyes of all, thanks to the broadcast transmissions of TV networks, CNN among others.'[19] For Virilio, modern warfare thus marks a substitution in which technology replaces human reality. In this, deterrence has also changed, from nuclear deterrence to deterrence associated with what Virilio calls 'the information bomb', which is no longer a local phenomenon but a global, virtual one allowed by the reach of communication technologies: ' "Cyberwar" has nothing to do with the destruction brought about by bombs and grenades and so on. It is specifically linked to the information systems of life itself.'[20]

Virilio here returns the argument to the significant political dimension of Baudrillard's position, which can be read as a provocative response to the intense media coverage of the war. The saturation coverage is so insistent and self-important in its creation of a technological reality that to claim it is indistinguishable from an artificial or virtual reality masking the absence of a war beneath is to testify to the power of its illusory quality. The audience is bombarded with information to convince it that this is an important news media event rather than that there is a war going on.

Finally, for a critic who was discussed in the last chapter, Slavoj Žižek, the Gulf War was symptomatic of a pervasive and antiseptic Western political correctness in which everything is 'lite'. Just as contemporary culture delivers coffee without caffeine, beer without alcohol, cakes without sugar, the war was initially conceived as 'a decaffeinated conflict – a war without victims, at least on our side'.[21] Which is presumably to say, with Baudrillard, that it was not conceived as a war at all.

REFERENCES AND BIBLIOGRAPHY

Amis, Martin, *Einstein's Monsters*, Harmondsworth: Penguin, 1988.

Baudrillard, Jean, 'The Gulf War Will Not Take Place', in *The Gulf War Did Not Take Place*, pp. 23–8 (first publ. in *Libération*, 4 Jan. 1991).

Baudrillard, Jean, 'The Gulf War: Is It Really Taking Place', in *The Gulf War Did Not Take Place*, pp. 29–59 (first publ. in *Libération*, 6 Feb. 1991).

Baudrillard, Jean, 'The Gulf War Did Not Take Place', in *The Gulf War Did Not Take Place*, pp. 61–87 (first publ. in *Libération*, 29 Mar. 1991).

Baudrillard, Jean, *The Gulf War Did Not Take Place*, Bloomington: Indiana University Press, 1995.

Centre for Economic and Social Rights (CESR), *The Human Costs of War in Iraq*, Cambridge: CESR, 2003.

Fukuyama, Francis, *The End of History and the Last Man*, London: Hamish Hamilton, 1992.

Kellner, Douglas, *The Persian Gulf TV War*, Boulder: Westview Press, 1992.

Norris, Christopher, *Uncritical Theory: Postmodernism, Intellectuals and the Gulf War*, London: Lawrence and Wishart, 1992.

Patton, Paul, 'Introduction', in *The Gulf War Did Not Take Place*, Bloomington: Indiana University Press, 1995, pp. 1–21.

Virilio, Paul, *Desert Screen: War at the Speed of Light*, trans. Michael Degener, London: Continuum, 2002.

Virilio, Paul, 'Ctheory Interview with Paul Virilio: The Kosovo War Took Place In Orbital Space', Paul Virilio in conversation with John Armitage, trans. Patrice Riemens, published 18 October 2000, http://www.ctheory.net/text_file.asp?pick=132 (accessed 12 Aug. 2005).

Virilio, Paul, 'Future War: A Discussion with Paul Virilio', Dialogues: An Interview with James der Derian, http://www.watsoninstitute.org/infopeace/vy2k/futurewar.cfm (accessed 12 Aug. 2005).

Virilio, Paul and Sylvère Lotringer, *Pure War*, trans. Mark Polizzotti and Brian O'Keefe, revd edn, New York: Semiotext(e), 1997.

NOTES

1. George Orwell, *1984*, London: Folio, 2001, pp. 207 and p. 200.
2. Christopher Isherwood, *Goodbye to Berlin* (1939), London: Minerva, 1989, p. 3.
3. Kellner, p. 12.
4. Norris, p. 13.
5. Other things can contribute to this perception, especially with regard to the different experiences of the two sides (one entirely military, the other in many ways largely civilian). On the one hand, for example, the majority of British casualties in the second Gulf War were caused not by enemy fire but by friendly fire, poor training and faulty equipment. On the other hand, taking his data from the report by the 'Centre for Economic and Social Rights' on *The Human Costs of War in Iraq*, Ben Wisner concludes:

   > During the 1991 war, the US destroyed electricity supplies, shutting off power to hospitals, water treatment facilities, etc., with the excuse of destroying Iraq's 'command and control' ability. This began a series of disastrous events that undermined public health. Transportation networks were also targeted, so that distribution of food and other essential items to Iraq's primarily urban civilian pop ulation was disrupted. Because humanitarian organizations could not cope with the large number of civilians whose lives were put in danger by this wholesale destruction of lifeline infrastructure, there were 47,000 avoidable child deaths within 8 months of the 1991 war.' (Wisner, Ben, 'Notes on the Ideas of "Clean War" and "Collateral Damage"', 17 March 2003, http://online.northumbria.ac.uk/geography_research/radix/resources/there-is-no-clean-war-iraq2003.doc(accessed 12 Aug. 2005)).

6. Patton, p. 11.
7. Virilio and Lotringer, p. 183.
8. The second Gulf War accentuated this viewpoint when the highly controversial information (known colloquially as the 'dodgy dossier') supplied to the British government established the pretext for war. Subsequently, the Hutton Inquiry into the reporting of the Blair government's use of the information led to the resignation of the BBC Director General Greg Dyke and the BBC Chairman Gavyn

Davies (after parts of Andrew Gilligan's BBC reports of claims Downing Street 'sexed up' a dossier on Iraq's illegal weapons were branded 'unfounded' by Lord Hutton's report). See http://www.the-hutton-inquiry.org.uk/

9. Baudrillard, 1995, p. 23. Further page references will be given in the text. See Chapter 16 for further comment on Fukuyama.

10. War is continuously being fought between the three global hyperstates in *1984*, with two allied powers always fighting against a third.

11. It is later explained in Orwell's novel that the war can never be won by any of the three superpowers, and that its function is to maintain the status quo through destruction and hatred.

12. It is important that the war has been discussed, dissected and deterred before any conflict has been initiated.

13. Kellner, p. 6.

14. Kellner, p. 159.

15. Christopher Norris has dubbed Baudrillard's arguments 'nonsense' (see Norris, pp. 15–16).

16. Virilio, 2002, p. 20.

17. Virilio, http://www.ctheory.net/text_file.asp?pick=132

18. Virilio, http://www.watsoninstitute.org/infopeace/vy2k/futurewar.cfm

19. Virilio, 2002, p. 22.

20. Virilio, http://www.ctheory.net/text_file.asp?pick=132

21. James Harkin with Slavoj Žižek, 'Saturday Interview: Joker Apart', *The Guardian*, Main Section, 8 October 2005, p. 27.

CHAPTER

8

PHOTOGRAPH(ER): CINDY SHERMAN AND THE MASQUERADE

Approach: Feminism

Fig. 8.1: **Cindy Sherman**, Untitled Film Still #10, 1978. Courtesy of the Artist and Metro Pictures Gallery.

In Sherman's pictures, the way the woman is *affected* by something makes her like an *effect*, her face stamped by events. (Judith Williamson)[1]

[T]he masquerade . . . is what women do . . . in order to participate in man's desire, but at the cost of giving up theirs. (Luce Irigaray)[2]

Actively reading or analysing images is an uncommon experience even though – or perhaps because – in a visual culture everyone sees thousands of them every-day. Pictures, with or without words, are presented in newspapers, in advertis-ing, on TV and elsewhere, yet when discussing images we have to turn exclusively to words. It is in language that social meaning-making occurs and appraising images is a function of language. However, every seeing child encounters images before learning language and the subject has a complex relationship with the visual field that needs exploring before we consider the meaning of particular images.

The French psychoanalyst Jacques Lacan maintains that it is in relation to the surrounding world that selfhood arises.[3] This relationship is first perceived by the child when it sees its reflection and is able to delineate in this image a self with which it identifies: an act of recognition which is also a misrecognition (the child is not its image).[4] Thus, before entering the world of language, where it will be socialised,[5] the child enters the world of images where its sense of identity is first established by its reflection.

Through this 'mirror-stage', the self both sees and objectifies itself in the act of seeing, and is thus inserted into a specular order that precedes it. The infant, though lacking co-ordination or the ability to stand, sees itself in its reflection as autonomous, whole and distinct from everything else. It is thus simultaneously subject and object, seeing and seen: located in a visual system. The subject is thus situated in a world of images, where the eye is the organ of sight for the subject but the look or gaze ('le regard') is the condition of looking: is the eye of the other objectifying and constituting the I of the subject. Crucially, therefore, Lacan discriminates between the eye's act of seeing and the effect of the 'gaze' or look, which is *subjectivity*. This is to say that, rather as language is a pre-existing system into which any individual becomes located (as an 'I'), the subject is first the effect of sight (an 'eye' and an object of the gaze). Photography can suggest this inasmuch as the photograph precedes the audience's act of viewing it: the photograph is an object made to be seen, and this grammatical construction can illustrate the passive rather than active relation that the seeing subject has towards the image.

However, just as language is naturalised in society as a medium for self-expression, the act of seeing is naturalised to the extent that viewers rarely think of the condition of seeing (what Lacan calls 'the inside-out structure of the gaze'). Unless we are already inclined, for whatever reason, to consider the dynamics of vision, it is only when confronted with a person or an image that in some way calls attention to the act of seeing that we become self-conscious about our own place within the specular realm and about what we are doing, or participating in, when we look. This is most acute when we unexpectedly discover someone watching us looking, but can occur when we see an image of an eye, catch our reflection, or look at a picture that involves either an internal recognition of vision (one person viewing another, for example) or an external recognition (such as a portrait that stares out at the spectator).

Yet, as Ros Coward remarks with regard to gender, visual relations are also power relations: 'In this society, looking has become a crucial aspect of sexual relations, not because of any natural impulse, but because it is one of the ways in which domination and subordination are expressed.'[6] Coward argues that for men, the visual consumption of women's images allows a feeling of secure sexual control through the distance of voyeuristic pleasure. For women, by contrast, the relation with these, often idealised, images is:

> a relation of narcissistic damage . . . an ambivalence between fascination and damage in looking at themselves and images of other women . . . Where women's behaviour was previously controlled directly by state, family or church, control of women is now also effected through the scrutiny of women by visual ideals.[7]

Thus, the practice of looking at women has been naturalised in society as much as heterosexuality, making a power relation appear to be simply a norm, which is reinforced by common-sense arguments that assert a universal aesthetic difference between the sexes.

Cindy Sherman, a postwar American artist, uses multiple images of herself to explore the ways in which women are represented in popular culture, especially film.[8] The individual portrayed in the photographs, Sherman herself, multiplies into dozens of widely differing identities, defined by the masks and roles women are assigned in society. Born in New York in 1954, Sherman studied photography at the University of Buffalo.[9] Initially inspired by stereotypical representations of women in 1950s films, she masqueraded as iconic female characters drawn from the movies, and took photographs of herself in poses that evoked such roles.

Sherman began her photographic career at college in 1975 with the series Untitled A–E, in which she used makeup and hats to adopt different roles from 'the clown' to 'the little girl'. Her works have usually been without titles as she prefers viewers of the photographs to construct their own titles and narratives for the images. In 1977, Sherman began her best-known series, 'Untitled Film Stills', which includes the one shown above (Fig. 8.1): 'Untitled Film Still #10' (sixty-nine in total). In these photographs, which mimic authentic film stills, she takes on the role of women from B movies and film noir. Her touchstones are the images of the media, particularly TV (including reruns of black and white films), and she seems most interested to explore the ways in which women are portrayed in forms that have wide popular appeal and mass distribution.[10]

Many early viewers thought these photographs were stills from real films, initially unaware that the person in each shot was the same woman, let alone the photographer herself. As Laura Mulvey explains, '[T]he viewer of Sherman's *Film Stills* . . . looks, recognises a style, doubts, does a double take, then recognises that the style is a citation, and meanings shift and change their reference like shifting perceptions of perspective from an optical illusion.'[11] Sherman's attitude to these stills was that they depicted the ambivalence towards female sexuality current in media and film representations alongside the popular discourse of passive female sexuality. In this, she identified a contradiction between the images of film noir and the dominant view of female innocence, implying a split-identity in which women were both predatory and innocent.

The 'Untitled Film Stills' feature women in poses that suggest the narratives of unmade films they might accompany. The construction of each of those narratives, however, belongs to the viewer and suggests both the viewer's own fantasies and also the cultural narratives the media present every day. The women in the stills are frequently staring into mirrors, regarding themselves as they are regarded, acknowledging how they are specularly constructed in the visual field. Many are looking towards an off-screen other. While the images look composed the women themselves are rarely so; instead the poses are more often of women agitated or anxious, suggesting vulnerability and/or desperation to different viewers. Where the images are of women who could be called composed, their posture appears unrelaxed and the pose self-consciously 'struck'. Yet, to ascribe any characteristics to the staged figures in the photographs immediately involves the viewer in the personification of models whose only reality is Sherman's masquerade, aligning the formal genre as much with catalogue shots, glamour magazine images, or softcore pornography, as movie publicity stills.

Sherman has also said the stills were untitled because she didn't wish to 'spoil the ambiguity', and it was only the first gallery in which they were shown, Metro Pictures, that ascribed numbers to the photographs. She says: 'At first I wanted to do a group of imaginary stills all from the same actress's career . . . I didn't think about what each movie was about, I focused on the different ages and looks of the same character.'[12] Some of the shots were inspired by particular European actresses, such as Anna Magnani, Brigitte Bardot, Jeanne Moreau, Sophia Loren and Simone Signoret, and 'I definitely felt that the characters were questioning something – perhaps being forced into a certain role. At the same time, these roles are in a film: the women aren't being lifelike, they're acting. There are so many levels of artifice.'[13] Sherman says she was aiming at shots that looked as though they were in-between the action: after a confrontation, for example, or on their way to a rendezvous. Laura Mulvey agrees: 'The women in the photographs are almost always in stasis, halted by something more than photography, like surprise, reverie, decorum, anxiety, or just waiting.'[14] The implication, as will be discussed below, is that the photographs tap into the common representation of women as awaiting male activity and intervention.[15] This makes plain the formulation of gender differences across the range of representations in Western society:

> Woman then stands in patriarchal culture as a signifier of the male other, bound by a symbolic order in which man can live out his fantasies and obsessions through linguistic command by imposing them on the silent image of woman still tied to her place as bearer, not maker, of meaning . . . In a world ordered by sexual imbalance, pleasure in looking has been split between active/male and passive/female. The determining male gaze projects its fantasy onto the female figure, which is styled accordingly. In their traditional exhibitionist role women are simultaneously looked at and

displayed, with their appearance coded for strong visual and erotic impact so that they can be said to connote *to-be-looked-at-ness*.[16]

Mulvey therefore understands the visual presence of women in film as a break in the action: as a moment of erotic contemplation. And this is precisely how Sherman presents her photo-studies: as moments in-between action, before crisis or after confrontation.

What is partly so interesting about Sherman's work is her assembly of a lexicon of popular cultural images. Though the shots refer to nothing directly, their use of visual vocabulary is such that the audience is likely to think that they are stills from a film and that each has a particular kind of story behind them. They refer to the cinematic stereotypes of femininity, provoking a feeling of recognition in the viewer. For example, Judith Williamson writes that:

> In the Untitled Film Stills we are constantly forced to recognise a visual style (often you could name the director) simultaneously with a type of femininity . . . The image suggests that there is a particular kind of femininity in the *woman* we see, whereas in fact the femininity is in the image itself, it *is* the image.[17]

Yet the stills would convey a different meaning if they were from actual Hollywood movies. Therefore, for Jan Avgikos, the power of the stills is that they are on the border of the familiar and the unfamiliar: 'familiar enough to draw us in; unfamiliar enough to make us see in ways we have not seen before'.[18]

As well as positioning the woman as sexual (short skirt, parted legs, skin revealed) and vulnerable (crouching over spilled goods from a split bag), a shot such as #10 implies the presence in the room of another person (in addition to the camera lens mediating the eventual viewer of the photo), which cinematic conventions would lead the viewer to imagine as male.[19] Laura Mulvey argues that the construction of stills such as this position the camera as masculine, with the woman portrayed as the passive subject of a male gaze. The conclusion is that the nameless woman is 'fashioned' by her clothes, becoming whatever contemporary stylists and the media deem her to be, constructed not by selfhood (as a man might be) but by clothes and make-up. Sherman both makes plain the arrangement of woman as object before man as subject and undermines it by depicting the same woman in numerous stereotypical poses, from femme fatale to baby doll. Because the stills allude to an age of cinema that has passed (the 1940s and 1950s) they play nostalgically on a desire for a past time and for an eclipsed moment in sexual relationships, before second wave feminism.

Sherman elected to end the series in 1980 when she felt her photos were becoming repetitive and were in danger of becoming complicit with the images they revealed as stereotypical, raising questions of genre boundaries: when does a homage/parody/pastiche become a part of the type or category of texts it imitates? Thus Sherman became increasingly in danger of simply adding her works to those she aimed to critique and of providing the same visual pleasure, as

Doane points out: 'Spectatorial desire, in contemporary film theory, is generally delineated as either voyeurism or fetishism, as precisely a pleasure in seeing what is prohibited in relation to the female body.'[20] So for some critics, there is no distance between Hollywood publicity photos and Sherman's work, as her stills reproduce the stereotypes that other critics believe they subvert. Sherman herself gave up the series when she realised they were no longer being seen as challenging but as examples of the very images they sought to pastiche. Their appeal for some viewers has been in their sexual display, which is exacerbated by the stills' individual reproduction for hanging in the home, providing a very different private environment for their consumption away from the context of the gallery. Which raises the question of the series' impact as a whole in distinction from their meaning as isolated stills, where Sherman appears in one eroticised pose, rather than in one amongst many, where the force of the exercise is apparent.

Sherman's work contains at least three key elements: self-(re)fashioning, cultural performance or pastiche, and a stark awareness of the (male) gaze. Her photographs make manifest the usually hidden relationship between subject and object, between the person viewed and the person viewing. It is a knowing, highly self-conscious art of exhibitionism and implied voyeurism which reverses the common idea that the gaze follows on from the spectacle. The internalised understanding that the individual (woman) is being looked at creates a self-imposed passivity captured in the artform of the film still, a silent moment of stasis in deep contrast to the dynamics of the 'talkie' and the 'moving picture'. Sherman's use of multiple images of 'women' who are the same woman in the 'Untitled Film Stills' also makes plain the way in which femininised identity is aligned with 'make-up' and 'fancy dress': a masquerade in which multiple masks of desirability are donned to meet the expectations of the gaze. In this dynamic the camera-eye is a surrogate 'male gaze' composing, fixing and objectifying the 'model' for a hidden viewer.

In Sherman's stills the figures' awareness of being watched is apparent by the eye-line of their own gaze off-camera, observing an implied observer who is watching the pose they strike. Writing a few years before Sherman started her film stills series, John Berger, in his influential analysis of the history of art and advertising, *Ways of Seeing*, articulates the view that:

> men *act* and women *appear*. Men look at women. Women watch themselves being looked at. This determines not only most relations between men and women but also the relation of women to themselves. The surveyor of woman in herself is male: the surveyed female. Thus she turns herself into an object – and most particularly an object of vision: a sight.[21]

Sherman enacts this quite explicitly by repeatedly staging herself as an object of the gaze of others. For Berger women are split-subjects, continually watching themselves, always accompanied by their own image, surveying themselves whether they are 'walking or weeping'. Thus, while a man's actions are an end in themselves, a woman's actions for Berger are a demonstration of how she wishes to be treated. Consequently, he argues that a man will often treat a woman according to how she behaves, seeing this as an expression of how she views herself in relation to him.

Such arguments ought not to be universalised but historicised, yet Janey Place argues that most Western culture is predicated upon 'a male fantasy' inasmuch as it participates in a particular economy of gender identities:

> The dark lady, the spider woman, the evil seductress who tempts man and brings about his destruction is amongst the oldest themes of art, literature, mythology and religion in Western Culture . . . She and her sister (or alter ego), the virgin, the mother, the innocent, the redeemer, form the two poles of female archetype.[22]

Writing in 1980 at the time Sherman decided her work was in danger of becoming complicit with this tradition, Place sees women as defined by their sexuality, around which accretes two templates of the virgin and the whore, the light and the dark, the innocent and the experienced, child-bride and mother: Snow White and dark queen, both inquiring 'who is the fairest of them all' of the masculine mirror while simultaneously understanding that mirror to provide an indication of the reflection they provide to men of the male ego (as Virginia Woolf argued in *A Room of One's Own*).[23] These are not absolutes, or identities rooted in actuality, for the individual woman, but images and subject positions available for each woman constructing an appearance through clothes and make-up, pose and attitude, the styling of hair, face and body.

In patriarchal culture as in film noir, Frank Krutnik argues, '[W]omen tend to be subservient to the dramatic conflicts structured around men.'[24] Thus, in drawing on the imagery of film noir, Sherman constructs her black and white shots of femininity according to the binary of feminine representation, caught between situations in which men are agents and women acted-upon recipients simultaneously reflecting male egos and their own desires for self-construction. For David Harvey this reveals Sherman's representation of a wider aesthetics of flatness, helplessness and loss of autonomy in the depthlessness of contemporary cultural production: 'its fixation with appearances, surfaces and instant impacts'.[25] Harvey thinks the stills 'focus on masks without commenting directly on social meanings other than on the activity of masking itself'.[26] Thus the photographs are unaccompanied by title, commentary or the films they purport to be promoting.

Through the lens of Judith Butler's theory of sexual and gender performativity (in which gender is a mime of dominant characteristics conventionally attributed to gender through the naturalised categorisation of two different sexes – see Chapter 6), Sherman's film stills appear less an expression of the gap between authentic identity and fragmented appearance than a series of performances in which female identity is not obscured but constituted by role-play. Here, identity is akin to drag, with drag understood not as a veil behind which identity hides but the basis on which it is performed – a surface effect producing femininity through visual codes.[27]

Mulvey observes that in her use of dressing-up and make-up Sherman depicts femininity as a mask such that she 'makes visible the feminine as masquerade. And it is this homogenous culture of fifties-like appearance that Sherman uses to adopt such a variety of same, but different, figurations. Identity, she seems to say, lies in looks.'[28] One might notice the double-play of meaning in this last sentence: that identity both exists and dissembles in looks, unmasking through masquerade the cultural belief in singular, essential identity. The view of 'Womanliness as Masquerade' was proposed by Joan Rivière in a still-important essay of 1929. The essay concerns 'women who wish for masculinity [and] put on a mask of womanliness to avert anxiety and the retribution feared from men',[29] but has been most influential for critics and artists in its implication that womanliness is always a masquerade, a form of mimicry imitating a cultural and patriarchal template of femininity: 'The reader may now ask how I define womanliness or draw the line between genuine womanliness and the 'masquerade'. My suggestion is not, however, that there is any such difference . . . they are the same thing.'[30] This is accentuated in the dynamics of cinema, a formal masquerade where the signs of femininity, in terms of clothes, make-up, poses, looks and so on, circulate from film to film, or as in Sherman's work, are reproduced from film still to film still.

Finally, what Sherman's photographs illustrate is a position in gender theory drawn from Freud and Lacan:

> Hence one of the chief drives of an art which today addresses the presence of the sexual in representation – to expose the fixed nature of sexual identity as a fantasy and, in the same gesture, to trouble, break up, or rupture the visual field before our eyes.[31]

Sherman achieves this by the plurality of cinematic sexual poses and images drawn on in her photographs, which are nonetheless of one and the same physical woman, multiplied into the numerous but fixed images of sexual variety that the scopic male fantasy desires. Which is in part to say that it is the pose(s) that signify and attract desire and not the subject thought to precede and underlie them: sexuality is constructed through the image and responds to the staging of its own desire – and Sherman's photographs could be as effective if their subject were a man, also in drag.

REFERENCES AND BIBLIOGRAPHY

Avgikos, Jan, 'To Hell and Back Again', *Women's Art Magazine* 59, 1994, pp. 38–9.
Berger, John, *Ways of Seeing*, Harmondsworth: Penguin, 1972.
Coward, Ros, 'The Look', in Thomas (ed.), pp. 33–9.
Doane, Mary Ann, *Femme Fatales: Feminism, Film Theory, Psychoanalysis*, London: Routledge, 1991.
Harvey, David, *The Condition of Postmodernity*, Oxford: Blackwell, 1989.

Heath, Stephen, 'Joan Rivière and the Masquerade', in Victor Burgin, James Donald and Cora Kaplan (eds) *Formations of Fantasy*, London: Methuen, 1986, pp. 45–61.

Jones. Amelia, 'Tracing the Subject with Cindy Sherman', Museum of Contemporary Art, *Cindy Sherman: Retrospective*, London: Thames and Hudson, 1997, pp. 33–49.

Kaplan, E. Ann (ed.), *Women in Film Noir*, London: BFI, 1980.

Kaplan, E. Ann, *Looking for the Other: Feminism, Film and the Imperial Gaze*, London: Routledge, 1997.

Krutnik, Frank, *In a Lonely Street: Film Noir, Genre, Masculinity*, London: Routledge, 1991.

Lacan, Jacques, 'The Mirror Stage as Formative of the Function of the I as Revealed in Psychoanalytic Experience', in *Écrits: A Selection*, trans. Alan Sheridan, London: Routledge, 1977, pp. 1–7.

Lacan, Jacques, *The Four Fundamental Concepts of Psycho-Analysis*, trans. Alan Sheridan, Harmondsworth: Pelican, 1994.

Mulvey, Laura, *Visual and Other Pleasures*, London: Palgrave, 1989.

Mulvey, Laura, 'A Phantasmagoria of the Female Body: The Work of Cindy Sherman', *New Left Review* 188 (Jul.–Aug.) 1991, pp. 136–50.

Place, Janey, 'Women in Film Noir', in Kaplan (ed.), pp. 35–54.

Rivière, Joan, 'Womanliness as Masquerade', in Victor Burgin, James Donald and Cora Kaplan (eds), *Formations of Fantasy*, London: Methuen, 1986, pp. 35–44.

Rose, Jacqueline, *Sexuality in the Field of Vision*, London: Verso, 1986.

Sherman, Cindy, *The Complete Untitled Film Stills*, New York: Museum of Modern Art, 2003.

Thomas, Julia (ed.), *Reading Images*, Basingstoke: Palgrave, 2000.

Williamson, Judith, 'Images of Woman', *Screen* 24: 6 (Nov.–Dec.) 1983, pp. 102–6.

NOTES

1. Williamson, p. 104.
2. Luce Irigaray, quoted in Heath, p. 54.
3. Lacan places most importance on the 'mirror-stage', when the child sees and identifies (with) its reflected, specular image, whereas other psychoanalysts in the British tradition, especially D. W. Winnicott, argues that watching the mother's face as mirror was more important for the child's development.
4. Lacan terms this phase of the infant's development the 'Imaginary' order. See Jacques Lacan's 1936 paper (revised 1949), 'The Mirror-Stage as Formative of the Function of the I as Revealed in Psychoanalytic Experience'.
5. In this later phase the child is finding a place in the 'Symbolic' order in Lacan's terminology.
6. Coward, p. 34
7. Ibid., pp. 38–9; for a discussion of this in relation to 'race' see Kaplan (1997).
8. Sherman is one of a number of women working in the area of gender representations, voyeurism and the gaze. For example, Sophie Calle is a leading contemporary artist who acknowledges voyeurism, sensationalism and intrusion in her work. In *Suite Vénitienne* (1980) she arbitrarily follows a man to Venice, stalking him by the use of disguises. In *L'Homme au Carnet* (1993) she profiles an unknown man from his lost address book.
9. Sherman's work is sometimes bracketed with that of Richard Prince, Jenny Holze and Barbara Kruger.
10. Sherman's photographs are like paintings in that they are highly composed and imaginative images, and she later draws from historical portraiture in self-portraits that emphasise the sexualised role of the female subject in art. In more recent work, she no longer uses her body, which has been replaced by mutilated dolls, grotesque fragments or body parts, which suggest the anatomisations of pornography. Taken

as a whole, Sherman's work seeks to reveal how visual art displays women as sexualised, vulnerable, weak and hysterical.

11. Mulvey, 1991, pp. 146–7.
12. Sherman, p. 7.
13. Ibid., p. 9.
14. Mulvey, 1991, p. 142.
15. An illustration of this ideology occurs in Ian McEwan's *The Comfort of Strangers* (1981): 'A play with only women? I don't understand how that could work. I mean, what could *happen*?' (London: Vintage, p. 71).
16. Mulvey, 1989, pp. 15–19. For Mulvey, femininity is constructed by the male gaze, a fetishistic fantasy for patriarchal culture in which scopophilia is an act of projection and penetration.
17. Williamson, p. 102.
18. Avgikos, p. 39.
19. See Mulvey's essay, 'Visual Pleasure and Narrative Cinema' (1975) in Mulvey, 1989, pp. 14–26.
20. Doane, pp. 19–20; for a discussion of voyeurism and fetishism see Mulvey, 1989, pp. 21–2.
21. Berger, p. 47.
22. Place, p. 35.
23. '[W]omen have served all these centuries as looking-glasses possessing the magic and delicious power of reflecting the figure of man at twice its natural size. Without that power probably the Earth would be swamp and jungle. How is he to go on giving judgement . . . unless he can see himself at breakfast and at dinner at least twice the size he really is?' (Virginia Woolf, *A Room of One's Own*, London: Grafton, 1973, pp. 35–6).
24. Krutnik, p. 194.
25. Harvey, p. 58.
26. Ibid., p. 101.
27. Jones, p. 39
28. Mulvey, 1991, p. 142.
29. Rivière, p. 35.
30. Ibid., p. 38.
31. Rose, p. 229.

POLITICAL SPEECH: MARGARET THATCHER'S HYMN AT THE SERMON ON THE MOUND

Approach: Historicism

It is not the creation of wealth that is wrong but love of money for its own sake. The spiritual dimension comes in deciding what one does with the wealth. (Margaret Thatcher)[1]

The mission of this government is much more than the promotion of economic progress. It is to renew the spirit and solidarity of the nation. (Margaret Thatcher)[2]

In this chapter I want to consider the import of a political speech in the context of the relation between the ethical and the political, the spiritual and the material. To do this I want to play off the historical moment and its surrounding contextual discourses with the speech's invocation of a transhistorical and universal set of values. New Historicism evolved in the 1980s as in some ways a reaction to structuralism and formalism. Indebted to political, poststructuralist and reader-response theory, it has focused on the intertextuality of literary and non-literary texts and the presence of diverse culturally specific discourses within and around each particular text under examination. Which is to say that a text is partly of interest because of the discourses that feed into it. A political speech is an appropriate text for this approach because it is part of a dialogue with absent voices which may be invoked, but which are often praised or criticised implicitly. In this case, the text is a formal political address by a prime minister: Margaret Thatcher's speech to the General Assembly of the Church of Scotland, at the Assembly Hall, the Mound, Edinburgh, on 21 May 1988.[3] A transcript of Thatcher's speech, along with many others, is available at the Margaret Thatcher foundation website as one of her 'key documents', where it is included under the heading 'Reshaping Britain'.[4] In the speech, Thatcher uses her transcendental religious convictions to engage with history (one of her favourite words, often wrapped up with a sense of destiny) in particular circumstances at a concrete moment of social change. Her speeches have often become notorious for their historicist emphasis, championing 'the [Victorian] values when our country became great', and for the soundbites that newspaper editors have selected from them, such as 'the lady's not for turning' and 'As God once said, and I think rightly . . .'. In this particular speech, it was the phrase 'If a man will not work he shall not eat', from Paul's Second Epistle to the Thessalonians, that was most widely written down and remembered.

More than any other British head of state in the postwar period, Thatcher was a politician whose rhetoric was shaped by the discourse of religion. She also saw herself as far more than a political leader, believing in a set of spiritual values, culled from her reading of the Old Testament, that amounted to a vision of Britain as a chosen land. This was fundamentally a religious vision, and was forcibly outlined in a number of speeches she gave during her three terms of office as Prime Minister.[5] Her view of the Church within this was that it should support the state and promote law and order along with the need for personal morality and self-reliance. Consequently, when the Anglican Church refused to celebrate the war at the time of the Falklands Memorial Service in 1982, Thatcher set out on a course of evangelical Methodist instruction in which she would repeatedly tell the Church its function and assert her own interpretation of the Bible, which she studied throughout her period of office, while dismissing as 'Marxist rubbish' the Church of England's views on a range of subjects from nuclear disarmament to Britain's inner cities.[6] Consequently, the 1988 speech under consideration here, though delivered to the Church of Scotland, was, according to Henry Clark, 'Thatcher's interpretation of Christianity as an earnest cultivation of the bourgeois virtues', and its 'real target was the bishops of the Church of England'.[7]

The speech was made towards the beginning of Thatcher's third and final term of office in power, from 1987 to 1990. The key measures of this period of Conservative government were: reform of the education system (1988), including the creation of the national curriculum; the introduction of the Community Charge, or 'poll tax', as a new local government tax system (in Scotland in 1989; in England and Wales in 1990); and National Health Service legislation to strengthen management and introduce competition by separating purchasers and providers (1990). At the time of the address, the economy was booming but growing too quickly, such that interest rates doubled in 1988. This led to the resignation of the Chancellor of the Exchequer, Nigel Lawson, in the following year, as his desire to check growth by linking the pound to the Deutschmark through the European Exchange Rate Mechanism (ERM) was strongly opposed by Thatcher. In another move in 1988 that held Britain apart from Europe, Thatcher, who opposed any form of continental political or economic integration, also made her Euro-sceptic Bruges speech, which in some ways inaugurated the split in the Conservative Party over Europe that has still not healed twenty years later. In 1990, Foreign Secretary Sir Geoffrey Howe resigned over the European question, precipitating the decisive challenge to Thatcher's leadership that year by Michael Heseltine. Additionally, 1988 was the last year before the end of the Cold War, whose termination was marked by the dismantling of the Berlin Wall in 1989, in which Thatcher, dubbed 'the Iron Lady' by a Soviet newspaper, had sought to present herself as a tough leader who could successfully do business with Reagan and Gorbachev. In brief, 1988 was the year at which Thatcher's power seemed strongest, just before the introduction of the poll tax, opposition to which contributed significantly to her eventual overthrow in 1990, when the Tories saw her as more of a liability than an asset. These events provide one historical context to the values expounded in Thatcher's speech and the roles she defines for Church and State. They are all marked by her special vision of England (God's country, apart from Europe if a part of Britain) and the emphasis on individual responsibility that lay behind the poll tax.

Lamenting the rise of social Christianity, the government in the 1980s perceived the liberal Church as an over-comfortable bureaucratic section of the Establishment, internally pluralistic but narrowly focused, opposed to wealth creation and in need of reformation. For its own part, the Church of England, and particularly the Bishop of Durham, David Jenkins, accused the government of not caring about the disadvantaged members of society while preaching at them. Opponents to the Conservative government in 1988 quickly nicknamed Thatcher's speech 'the Sermon on the Mound' for its presumption and prescription.[8] According to Henry Clark in his 1993 book *The Church Under Thatcher*:

> [T]he Sermon on the Mound was a significant statement of the Prime Minister's social philosophy. It is an affirmation of faith in religious individualism which ignores everything that has been discerned and proclaimed by social Christianity in the past 120 years, and fits very nicely with Mrs Thatcher's notorious statement to the effect that 'there is no such thing as society, only individuals and families.'[9]

In the week after the address, the Bishop of Gloucester, John Yates, who was also the Chair of the General Synod's Board for Social Responsibility, co-wrote a rejoinder in which he condoned the emphasis on personal responsibility but condemned the idea that this could be understood separately from a sense of community and from the social character of human life that, he maintained, government had an obligation to promote. He thought that, by over-stressing individuals' obligations as well as rights to shape the economic conditions of their own lives, the speech effectively denied government's part in combating unemployment, distress and poverty.[10]

Yet, as in many of her speeches, Thatcher was speaking for herself more than for her government. She says she begins by 'speaking personally as a Christian, as well as a politician'[11] and what is in some ways most interesting in her speech is her attribution of transcendental status to her conviction politics as well as her religious convictions. An evangelical drive and discourse have been attributed to Thatcher(ism) by a range of commentators; for example, a materialist account such as Stuart Hall's still refers to Thatcher's ability to translate the 'gospel of the free market into the homespun idioms of the Tory householder' in the context of 'the mission of Thatcherism'.[12] However, few critics consider Thatcher's actual religious beliefs.

A critic who is an exception to this, Jonathan Raban, was so taken by the speech that he published its text along with his own 'counterblast' in 1989.[13] Raban was trained as a literary critic and so says that he tries 'to read Mrs Thatcher's address to the Church of Scotland as if it had the resonance and density of a poem – which, in a way, it does'.[14] Following a line-by-line retort to the philosophy and politics expressed in the speech, he concludes that Thatcher's text is of great interest because it indicates 'this language in which we are now governed'.[15] What Raban reluctantly admires about Thatcher is her 'integrity', in the sense that she has a whole and definite vision about which she is plain, direct and honest. This conviction is also apparent in her look, voice, clothes, manner and rhetoric, which appear 'more impressively all-of-a-piece than those of any British politician in recent history'.[16] Raban's analysis takes the speech paragraph by paragraph in an attempt to make clear the tenets of Thatcher's political philosophy but also to pick out its inconsistencies, heresies and sleights of hand. For Raban, Thatcher's speech is delivered in 'the language of power . . . bereft of all the usual strategies of persuasive argument',[17] such that he finds her language to be lacking rhetorical power while still full of linguistic coercion.

Raban summarises Thatcher's three 'distinctive marks of Christianity',[18] which he terms 'articles of faith', in the following way: 'the belief in the doctrine of Free Will; in the divinely created sovereignty of individual conscience; and in the Crucifixion and Redemption as the exemplary, supreme act of choice'.[19] Yet these ahistorical precepts have a specific significance in the historical context of the 1980s, and may be collectively summarised as: the Christian free will to choose (faith) is the basis for economic free choice. This echoes throughout the speech, from the assertion that the Church of Scotland sprang from the 'independence of mind' of the Scottish people to 'the responsibility that comes with freedom' being the responsibility of individuals to look after their own and their family's economic welfare.

The nub of this argument is the belief that spiritual redemption and social reforms should go together. Yet Thatcher's view of spiritual redemption is based on an Old Testament rather than Christian vision. Thus, she summarises the Old Testament as laying down the Ten Commandments, the injunction to love one's neighbour, and the importance of a strict code of laws (according to Paul Gilroy, this last had been central to Thatcher's rise to power)[20], but reduces the New Testament to the importance again of loving one's neighbour and doing as you would be done by.[21] Crucially, Thatcher interprets this last point not in terms of empathy but in terms of judging others according to your own standards. Thatcher's recasting of the New Testament is also evident in her atypical view of the parable of the Good Samaritan, who 'had to have the money to help, otherwise he too would have had to pass on the other side'.[22] It is wealth creation, not its redistribution, that secures the compassionate, charitable society. Again the interpretation she gives to the Ten Commandments is focused on the authority given to a legal framework in which the poor should not seek wealth redistribution because this is covetousness. Similarly, 'society' (the existence of which Thatcher denies) is never to blame if the individual breaks the law, whose purpose is to 'provide for health and education, pensions for the elderly, succour for the sick and disabled'. Which means the laws are there to provide only for the young and old and those who *cannot* physically work: 'intervention by the state must never become so great that it effectively removes personal responsibility'. In the context of the Edinburgh address, Thatcher's aim in the speech can be summarised as a separation of responsibilities: '*We* Parliamentarians can legislate for the rule of *law*. *You* the Church can teach the life of faith.' Which implies that the Church should know not to interfere in politics but tend to its flock and support the law.

Whether religion and politics can be separated was an issue raised in 2004 over the very text that Thatcher chose to praise at the end of her speech to illustrate the partition of the secular and the spiritual 'worlds'. This is the hymn 'I Vow to Thee, My Country', which was also sung at both the wedding and funeral of Diana, Princess of Wales and is increasingly being selected by couples for inclusion in their marriage ceremonies. It is a hymn that Thatcher 'love[d] to quote',[23] and clearly underpins her vision of Britain as a chosen land.

Echoing the conflict in 1988 between Thatcher's values and those of the Church, the furore in August 2004 began when the Bishop of Hulme, the Right Reverend Stephen Lowe, 'attacked English nationalism in a diocese newsletter' and compared the hymn with 'right-wing attitudes'.[24] He called for the banning of, at least, the first verse of the song. The Bishop thought the poem jingoistic, because it is a hymn to country above all else, and also 'heretical', because it suggests an individual Christian's first duty is to country not God. The contrary argument to this viewpoint is that the words recommend only that the country be placed above 'All earthly things'. The entire two verses are as follows:

> I vow to thee, my country – all earthly things above –
> Entire and whole and perfect, the service of my love;
> The love that asks no question, the love that stands the test,
> That lays upon the altar the dearest and the best;
> The love that never falters, the love that pays the price,
> The love that makes undaunted the final sacrifice.
>
> And there's another country, I've heard of long ago –
> Most dear to them that love her, most great to them that know;

We may not count her armies, we may not see her King;
Her fortress is a faithful heart, her pride is suffering;
And soul by soul and silently her shining bounds increase,
And her ways are ways of gentleness, and all her paths are peace.

Compounded by the title's foregrounding of the word 'vow', implying a sacred pledge, the second verse specifies patriotism as comparable to a love for God's kingdom, and this was at the heart of Thatcher's message. In quoting the hymn, she was speaking to both the Church and the people of Scotland,[25] as well as more widely to 'the country'. The lines quoted by Thatcher are: 'I vow to thee my country – all earthly things above – entire, whole and perfect the service of my love . . . another country I heard of long ago' whose king can't be seen and whose armies can't be counted, but 'soul by soul and silently her shining bounds increase'. The final message of gentleness and peace is elided.

The hymn, set to music from Gustav Holst's *The Planets* suite, was written by Sir Cecil Spring Rice, a diplomat and ambassador to Washington during the First World War.[26] Two versions of the hymn were composed; the first was written in Stockholm when he was British Ambassador to Sweden, and glorified war, speaking approvingly of helmeted warriors and the thunder of guns. Spring Rice's brother Gerald had just died in the war. David H. Burton, Spring Rice's biographer, considers the lyric a period piece about spirituality intertwining faith in God, belief in sacrifice and love of country in the context of an imperial war fought by the European nations. Thus, not only the message of patriotism and faith in the country's leadership are relevant, but the hymn's historical context of a divided Europe and Britain's ultimate victory seems pertinent to Thatcher's own anti-European stance.

Undoubtedly, the parallels and separations that inhere in the duality of the two-part structure of 'I Vow to Thee, my Country' were central to its appeal to Thatcher. The first speaks to the country's government and citizens; this is Thatcher's kingdom. The second speaks to the Church, whose country is God's kingdom. What unites the religious and the political in Thatcher's perspective are conviction, dogmatic moral values and charismatic leadership. Raban asserts that the hymn has never been sung in the Church of Scotland and that it is an English military song, and so he thinks 'this foreign hymn about young men dying' is included to bring to mind the Falklands. He also notes that the day after the speech, a senior Scottish theologian responded on Radio Forth to say that the gloss Thatcher had placed on the lines 'soul by soul' advocated an 'individualist's paradise' which the Church would never countenance.[27]

From one angle, what is most interesting in the hymn's first verse is two reflections it suggests on Thatcher's creed. On the one hand, 'The love that asks no question' represents Thatcher's belief in obedience to a code of laws and the relation between Church and State. The duty of the citizen is to support the law; the duty of the Church is to support the citizen, the law and the government. On the other hand, the abrogation of choice and responsibility implied by 'no question' sits uneasily with the emphasis on free will and personal responsibility throughout Thatcher's address. Yet this is at the heart of the political ideology denoted by Thatcherism, expressed as early as 1968 in the Conservative Political Centre lecture Thatcher gave as a member of Edward Heath's Shadow Cabinet. Entitled 'What's Wrong with Politics?' the speech declares: 'What we need now is a far greater degree of personal responsibility, and decision, far more independence from the government, and a comparative reduction in the role of government.'[28] Which is to say that the most authoritarian government in British postwar history stakes its rule on people's independence from government. Thatcherism relies on intense control of the public sector allied to deregulation of the private sector. The Welfare State consensus that had existed from 1945 was overthrown as Thatcher took on the unions, local government and the professions.

But for Thatcher, the place in the second verse deemed 'another country' is also Britain. It is the imperial Britain that has been in decline since the war, as she outlined in 1979 before her first-term election victory:

> Somewhere ahead lies greatness for our country again. This I know in my heart. Look at Britain today and you may think that an impossible dream. But there is another Britain of thoughtful people, tantalizingly slow to act, yet marvellously determined when they do.[29]

From a cultural perspective, 'Another Country' was a well-known phrase in the Thatcher period for another reason. Julian Mitchell's play of that name was first performed in 1981 in London and adapted in 1984 into a prominent film, part of the British new wave that followed in the wake of the 1981 Oscar success of *Chariots of Fire*. The film of *Another Country* featured several young British actors who became the best-known of their generation: Rupert Everett, Kenneth Branagh, Daniel Day Lewis and Colin Firth. Set in an English public boarding school in the early 1930s, its version of 'another country' refers to temporal and spatial alternatives: one other country is that of England between the wars, a second other country is Soviet Russia. The play's central protagonists are Guy Bennett, modelled on a student who would later become one of the notorious Cambridge Spies (Guy Burgess), and Tommy Judd, a committed Marxist. It is a play about ostracism and snobbery, class and socialism. The 'other Britain' suggested by the play is entirely different from the other Britain Thatcher locates in the imperial past, as she outlined in 1983: 'I want to see one nation, as you go back to Victorian times, but I want everyone to have their own potential property stake.'[30] Ironically, then, Thatcher's clearest relationship to 'another country' was best represented by her hand in reviving Disraeli's 'Two Nations' image of Victorian Britain, divided between 'haves' and 'have nots', especially the entrepreneurial self-employed, more fully supported than any other group by Thatcher, and the growing number of unemployed in Scotland, Wales, Northern Ireland and the north of England.[31]

Thatcher espoused 'I Vow to Thee, My Country' because it seemed to her to endorse personal responsibility in the context of her promotion of choice and free will, yet the counter-reading asserts that the hymn negates these things by advocating a blind faith in country, with its associations of nationalism. Hence, in terms of historical significance, Bishop Lowe in 2004 added he had noticed it was being sung at 'various national occasions' and was raising the issue in the wider context of the 'vilification' of migrants in the media. He argued: 'It's saying my country right or wrong. I don't think anybody could actually say they could adopt an approach whereby they said they would not ask any questions of their government and their policies and so on.' Lowe concluded that the rhetorical force of the hymn was its advocacy of unquestioning support for the government: 'The government under the Queen in this country is actually the representation of this country and it has all the . . . echoes of 1930s nationalism in Germany and some of the nastier aspects of right wing republicanism in the United States.'[32] The hymn thus finds a context across a century from the First World War, through the 1930s, Thatcher's speech in the 1980s, and Diana's wedding and funeral, to the controversy in 2004. The hymn's appeal to Thatcher, however, is not just in its sentiment but in its unwavering 'vision', for which individuals should fight to the death. There is no such thing as society, but there is such a thing as a country, whose representative is the government, to which the British have a patriotic duty.

In the new century, Thatcher's 'landmark speech' was also not forgotten. Under the title of the 'Inaugural Sermon on the Mound Dinner', Conservative Christians gathered to dine in 2002 at the New Club, Edinburgh in celebration of 'Prime Minster Margaret Thatcher's address to the General Assembly of the Church of Scotland delivered on 21st May 1988'.[33] The toast offered by the Tory MSP for Mid Scotland and Fife was pleased to point out that Christians could be on the right politically: 'It was assumed, he said, that to be a Christian one had to be left of centre in [one's] politics. Margaret Thatcher blew that notion out of the water and sent a seismic shock through the state-addicted Christians of the day. The Presbyterians present may not have agreed with her, but they would certainly not forget her.' Thus, another reading of the historical significance of the speech starts to emerge.

REFERENCES AND BIBLIOGRAPHY

Clark, Henry, *The Church Under Thatcher*, London: SPCK, 1993.

Gilroy, Paul, *There Ain't No Black in the Union Jack*, London: Routledge, 1992.

Hall, Stuart, 'The Toad in the Garden: Thatcherism among the Theorists', in Cary Nelson and Lawrence Grossberg (eds), *Marxism and the Interpretation of Culture*, Macmillan: Basingstoke, 1988, pp. 35–57.

Margaret Thatcher foundation: http://www.margaretthatcher.org/essential/keydocs.asp (accessed 4 Aug. 2005).

Media House International (with 'Highlights' of the speech): http://www. forerunner. com/forerunner/X0145_Margaret_Thatcher_Sp.html (accessed 4 Aug. 2005).

Milner, Andrew, *Cultural Materialism*, Melbourne: Melbourne University Press, 1993.

Raban, Jonathan, *God, Man and Mrs Thatcher*, Chatto Counterblasts No. 1, London: Chatto, 1989.

Riddell, Peter, *The Thatcher Era and its Legacy*, Oxford: Blackwell, 1991.

Today BBC website: http://www.bbc.co.uk/radio4/today/reports/ arts/vow_ 20040813. shtml (accessed 4 Aug. 2005).

NOTES

1. Margaret Thatcher, 'A Speech to the General Assembly of the Church of Scotland', 21 May 1988.
2. Margaret Thatcher, quoted in Riddell, p. 7.
3. Speech headings were: Introduction; Christianity – Spiritual and Social; Bible Principles – Relevance to Political Life; Political Action and Personal Responsibilities; Religious Education; Tolerance; Christians and Democracy; Conclusion.
4. Margaret Thatcher foundation: http://www.margaretthatcher.org/essential/keydocs.asp
5. This reign lasted between 1979 and 1990, during which time the top 10 per cent of earners enjoyed an average rise in earnings of 47 per cent; for the bottom 10 per cent that figure stood at just 2.9 per cent. And the period also was notable for the very high unemployment figures of up to 3.2 million people that persisted until 1986.
6. Clark, p. 10.
7. Clark, p. 11.
8. For discussion of the nickname, see *Interview for Scotland*, 31 October 1988.
9. Clark, p. 40.
10. Clark, pp. 40–1.
11. Raban, p. 9,
12. Hall, pp. 38–9.
13. Raban does not make reference to the title of the address, which was 'Christianity and Wealth' – 'perhaps the most forthright statement of Christian economic policy ever made by a national leader in many decades'. (Media House International)
14. Raban, p. 5.
15. Raban, p. 70.
16. Raban, p. 1.
17. Raban, p. 68.
18. Raban, pp. 9–10.
19. Raban, p. 32.
20. Gilroy, p. 74.
21. Thatcher subscribes to a 'Judaic-Christian tradition' but her understanding of religion, like her own values and philosophy, is wholly based on her approach to the Old Testament and not on Christ's teachings, which she ignores in her speech.
22. Quoted in Riddell, p. 2.
23. Clark, p. 10.
24. *Today* BBC Website: http://news.bbc.co.uk/1/hi/england/manchester/3557750.stm (accessed 30 Sept. 2005).
25. While the Church was not as supportive of the Conservatives' policies as Thatcher wished, Scotland was the area of Britain in which the Tories had least support.
26. Spring-Rice attended Eton and Balliol College, Oxford, and served in the War Office and Foreign Office, and as Earl Granville's private secretary. He became the British Chargé d'Affaires in Tehran in 1900, and British Commissioner of Public Debt in Cairo in 1901. He went on to serve in St Petersburg, Russia (1903), Persia (1906), Sweden (1908), and as Ambassador to the United States (1912–18).
27. Raban, p. 67.
28. Quoted in Riddell, p. 2

29. Quoted in Riddell, p. 7.
30. Quoted in Riddell, p. 3.
31. See Riddell, pp. 149–67.
32. *Today* BBC Website: http://news.bbc.co.uk/1/hi/england/manchester/3557750.stm (accessed 30 Sept. 2005).
33. 'One Lady – Many Toasts', Roland Watson Archive: http://www.lewrockwell.com/watson/watson41.html (accessed 4 Aug. 2005).

CRITICAL TEXT: ALAN SOKAL'S SHAM TRANSGRESSION

Approach: Reading Postmodernism

But how can one show that the emperor has no clothes? Satire is by far the best weapon; and the blow that can't be brushed off is the one that's self-inflicted. (Alan Sokal)[1]

In the domain of the natural sciences, where protocols of reading and knowing differ greatly, we must, of course, take very seriously the demand for a certain stability of knowledge. But, natural sciences aside, theoretical correctness seems subtly to defeat the process of conceptual work. (Homi Bhabha)[2]

The text I will look at in this chapter is critical in a number of senses. It is critical in the sense that a critical essay offers a viewpoint on a subject and debates it; it is also critical in the sense that it has been considered deeply, if not uniquely significant; and finally it is critical in the sense that it is an attack, albeit a camouflaged one. In terms of the reading of critical texts, it helps to raise important issues about the production, publication, provenance, partisanship and divided purposes of academic criticism. The approach taken is broadly that of a textual reading sympathetic to differences in critical methods in the natural and social sciences in the context of postmodernism.

In an article published in *Lingua Franca* entitled 'A Physicist Experiments with Cultural Studies', Alan Sokal, a professor of physics at New York University, announced that his article, 'Transgressing the Boundaries: Toward a Transformative Hermeneutics of Quantum Gravity', printed in a special 'Science Wars' edition of the social science journal *Social Text*, was a hoax. 'Transgressing the Boundaries' had claimed that Western science was ideology masquerading as objectivity, that 'scientific "knowledge" ' encodes a culture's power relations, and that 'physical "reality" ' is as much a socio-linguistic construct as is social reality. To prepare the ground for revealing his article as bogus, Sokal had peppered it with what he knew or believed to be preposterous assertions, scientific falsehoods and logical errors. In 'A Physicist Experiments', he therefore exposed his earlier article as, according to his intention, 'a melange of truths, half-truths, quarter-truths, falsehoods, and syntactically correct sentences that have no meaning whatsoever'. His aim was to reveal postmodernism, as he understood it, as itself an insidious ideology; one which a non-refereed journal like *Social Text*, published by an editorial collective, had accepted so fully that it was willing to publish an article that had no intellectual merit merely because it toed their party line. For Sokal, the serious exposure that the article was able to make was of the potential dangers of non-specialists using scientific concepts without understanding them, and consequently using them incorrectly but to an extent persuasively through the deployment of arcane, specious and obfuscatory language: much postmodernist theorising was wearing the emperor's new clothes. Two immediate effects of this were, first, to spark an attack in sections of the media on all recent critical theory, especially the French poststructuralists and postmodernists, and second, to provoke the response that Sokal was an example of his own argument because he understood little of the theory he was labelling a sham. The resulting debate included accusations, clarifications and refutations, all of which attempted to reclaim the high ground in something that soon resembled an intellectual brawl more than a discussion.

Sokal's intervention could be read as a plea for literary and social theory to obtain a better grasp of science or as an implicit reassertion of the 'two cultures' divide that had famously exercised C. P. Snow and F. R. Leavis at the turn of the 1950s.[3] In his later 'Afterword' (published in a third journal, *Dissent*) to 'Transgressing the Boundaries' Sokal says:

> One of my goals is to make a small contribution toward a dialogue on the Left between humanists and natural scientists – 'two cultures' which, contrary to some optimistic pronouncements (mostly by the former group), are probably farther apart in mentality than at any time in the past 50 years.

Yet, Sokal was in fact not making a 'small contribution toward a dialogue' but wheeling a Trojan horse into the social sciences by sending an intellectual offering that contained a concealed attack within – one that would be let loose after the article was accepted.

In his original article, Sokal takes Heisenberg's uncertainty principle and Einstein's relativity theory into a contemporary 'postmodernist' view of quantum gravity where, 'Now not only the observer, but the very concept of geometry, becomes relational and contextual.'[4] Sokal thus moves towards describing a nascent 'liberatory science':

> [T]he fundamental goal of any emancipatory movement must be to demystify and democratize the production of scientific knowledge, to break

down the artificial barriers that separate 'scientists' from 'the public'. Realistically, this task must start with the younger generation, through a profound reform of the educational system. The teaching of science and mathematics must be purged of its authoritarian and elitist characteristics, and the content of these subjects enriched by incorporating the insights of the feminist, queer, multiculturalist and ecological critiques.[5]

Given that Sokal is here talking of 'the production of scientific knowledge', his argument, though presumably insincere, is a fair one. Scientific knowledge may not be changed (as opposed to redirected) by these critiques, which I take is his actual contention in the later article that comes to refute this 'fundamental goal', but its 'production' and objectives certainly could be. The production of scientific knowledge is not apolitical in its focus because there is always the underlying question of what aspects of science are investigated and to what end? Institutional scientific investigation might certainly be open to the objection in several cases that its structures are authoritarian, patriarchal and interested, while its aims may be environmentally damaging or militaristic. The contention that 'knowledge is power' is not merely a comment on who possesses knowledge but an observation that knowledge and power are functions of each other: Foucault's concept of power/knowledge.[6] Knowledge, scientific or otherwise, is produced according to political priorities: technological, educational, medical, ecological, financial, and so forth. It therefore seems extremely important to bring a sociological perspective to the conditions under which scientific knowledge is produced.

However, the nub of Sokal's attack is suggested in his final paragraph:

> [T]he content of any science is profoundly constrained by the language within which its discourses are formulated; and mainstream Western physical science has, since Galileo, been formulated in the language of mathematics. But *whose* mathematics? . . . a liberatory science cannot be complete without a profound revision of the canon of mathematics. As yet no such emancipatory mathematics exists, and we can only speculate upon its eventual content. We can see hints of it in the multidimensional and nonlinear logic of fuzzy systems theory; but this approach is still heavily marked by its origins in the crisis of late-capitalist production relations. Catastrophe theory, with its dialectical emphases on smoothness/ discontinuity and metamorphosis/unfolding, will indubitably play a major role in the future mathematics; but much theoretical work remains to be done before this approach can become a concrete tool of progressive political praxis. Finally, chaos theory – which provides our deepest insights into the ubiquitous yet mysterious phenomenon of nonlinearity – will be central to all future mathematics.[7]

Of all the sciences, mathematics is the one that appears most disinterested, yet the distinction between pure and applied mathematics illustrates that it has two interrelated aspects: theory and praxis. Sokal is primarily concerned with theory in his article, but his points can have wider implications in terms of the ends to which mathematics is directed. An emancipatory pure mathematics may seem farcical but an emancipatory applied mathematics is not.

Aside from simple errors, where Sokal's article is intentionally most open to stricture is in its deeply naïve assertions, such as that chaos theory 'will be central to all future mathematics'. An 'emancipatory mathematics' at this level appears to the non-specialist hugely unlikely but that an eminent professor of physics asserts it cannot fail to be of interest; and Sokal risks his own reputation far more than that of *Social Text* in making the assertion, which the journal's editors are ethically obliged to assume is sincerely made.[8]

In his revelatory article 'A Physicist Experiments with Cultural Studies', Sokal describes the essay as a 'parody'. He explains in this article that:

> [T]o test the prevailing intellectual standards, I decided to try a modest (though admittedly uncontrolled) experiment: Would a leading North American journal of cultural studies . . . publish an article liberally salted with nonsense if (a) it sounded good and (b) it flattered the editors' ideological preconceptions?[9]

This question is cast in particular terms which seem to characterise Sokal's standpoint: that those working in the natural sciences are exercised by tests, experiments and intellectual standards, while those in the social sciences are susceptible to superficiality, flattery and ideological bias. Yet, from another perspective, what his experiment shows is the importance of other kinds of difference between the social and natural sciences. From such a perspective, it also implicitly asks the *relativistic* question of whether context matters: does an article *mean* something different when published in a social science journal from what it would mean in a natural science journal? Most theoretical positions, on the one hand, and common-sensical perspectives, on the other hand, would suggest widely differing answers.

Partly, what I want to do here is playfully hypothetical: to ask what happens when the two articles are put into dialogue with each other. To an extent, this is a matter of conjecturing on how the 'insincere' Sokal of the first text might respond to the 'ingenuous' Sokal of the second. Out of many initial points and questions that might be introduced here, it is immediately interesting to ponder whether the 'faults' ascribed to the insincere Sokal are absent in the article by the ingenuous. The second text accuses the first of lacking 'the slightest evidence or argument', of employing 'scientific and mathematical concepts in ways that few scientists or mathematicians could possibly take seriously', of giving 'no reasoned argument to support' links in its assertions, and of having 'a fundamental silliness'. Above all, the first article is said by the ingenuous Sokal to be based not on argument and evidence but on 'assertion' and fatuous reasoning: 'Nowhere in all of this is there anything resembling a logical sequence of thought; one finds only citations of authority, plays on words, strained analogies, and bald assertions.' In this way the first article is a parody, both belonging to and sitting outside of the genre it is critiquing – the 'faults' ascribed to it by the second article are rhetorical strategies that the ingenuous Sokal laments in much postmodernist theorising in the social sciences and humanities.

In 'A Physicist Experiments', Sokal is bemused and dismayed by how readily the editors of *Social Text* 'accepted my implication that the search for truth in science must be subordinated to a political agenda'. Sokal's position here appears to be that science is at present apolitical in its search for 'truth'. That he conducts his argument in terms of 'truth' (not 'facts') immediately signals a difficulty to many a scholar in the social sciences and humanities, for whom 'truth' is more an embattled discursive cul-de-sac than something easily verifiable (for example, one might recall here Nietzsche's well-known view of truth: 'A moveable host of metaphors . . . which, after long usage, seem to a people to be fixed, canonical, binding. Truths are illusions we have forgotten are illusions.'[10]).

Sokal's essay very deliberately asserts the disparities between the natural sciences and the humanities, but his subsequent article shows no understanding of those differences. It is still worth restating I. A. Richards's argument that what is required of scientific language (that is, lucidity) is not necessarily demanded in poetry, where ambiguity may be valued more highly (modernist criticism turned it into a virtue, equivalent roughly to 'richness' or 'wit'). If 'ambiguity' were simply opposed to 'clarity', as it might be in many branches of the sciences, it would need to be considered a fault, but in the arts, where postmodernist theory sits, it need not. There is also a crucial point to make if we subscribe to the American philosopher Richard Rorty's view of the major difference between those scholars working in the sciences and those in the arts. Rorty defines the difference in terms of agreement (see Introduction). In the sciences, he argues, there is an agreed terminology, but in the arts there is not. Rorty thus proposes a model in which 'science' is an area where a vocabulary is shared and argumentation is comparatively minimal, while 'art' is an area in which even terminology itself is a site of argumentation – creating a case of what the postmodernist Jean-François Lyotard calls 'paralogy', putting terms into play that various specialist groups in fact understand very differently.

What Sokal most objects to is 'a particular kind of nonsense and sloppy thinking: one that denies the existence of objective realities'. Though this is an attack echoed in critiques of postmodernism by others such as Christopher Norris,[11] it is a misreading of most 'postmodernist' thinking, which is concerned with a scepticism towards 'objective realities' in terms of the human access to and representation of reality (see, for example, Chapter 7 on Baudrillard and the Gulf War). This indeed can apply to science: 'paradigm shifts' denote moves between key understandings of the fundamentals of physical reality, and while science might be broadly thought of as moving between paradigm shifts over time, the arts move between synchronous conceptual paradigms. This is the context in which any claim that there is no 'objective reality' has to be understood, because it asserts that subjective beings cannot achieve a final objectivity and much postmodernist writing seeks 'less a representation of reality than its transfiguration'.[12]

Yet, this is a philosophical question that highlights a fundamental difference found repeatedly in the Western tradition's arguments between idealism and materialism. For Sokal: 'There *is* a real world; its properties are *not* merely social constructions; facts and evidence *do* matter. What sane person would contend otherwise?' A sane person would be unlikely to dispute that scientific *facts* enable innumerable predictable and quantifiable material measurements and changes, such that they *matter* in myriad ways. Yet a sane person might argue that understandings of reality are conditioned by, amongst other things, technological development: indeed even a scientifically understood 'truth' is a proposition that has been repeatedly demonstrated and never yet disproven, which is not to say that it never will be, and this is at least a theoretical point. The argument from many in the arts and social sciences is also precisely that facts and evidence *do matter* because of the ends to which they are put. This is when facts acquire meaning for subjects and societies more than they do for science.

In his article exposing the hoax, Sokal points out that: 'Theorizing about "the social construction of reality" won't help us find an effective treatment for AIDS or devise strategies for preventing global warming. Nor can we combat false ideas in history, sociology, economics and politics if we reject the notions of truth and falsity.' In the context of Sokal's argument, the first point is a spurious one, which seems to be claiming a greater importance for the natural sciences because finding an effective treatment for AIDS is not the goal of theory in the humanities and social sciences – unlike the social and political forces and discourses that impinge on people with AIDS. The second point is again, in the context of Sokal's argument, a spurious if not a moot one for social theory in that it implies that in the social disciplinary spheres political agency is more a matter of truth/falsity than power/knowledge or ethics.

Sokal's intervention has two further aspects to it that will be mentioned here. One is that he draws attention to what he sees as the misuse or misappropriation of scientific terminology in 'theorizing'. This is the most effective part of his attack (chiefly in the later co-authored book *Intellectual Impostures*), where he can reveal non-scientists to be erroneously claiming that concepts mean particular things to scientists. But this does not mean that a theorist is wrong to use a concept from science to mean something other than what it would mean to a scientist. Yet this is largely the basis of Sokal's criticism of what he sees as postmodernism: that it uses scientific concepts in ways that scientists would not agree with (as did modernist and pre-modernist theorists). Another aspect to his intervention is his own *level* of engagement with postmodernism. Sokal shows little understanding of the debates over postmodernism and fails to define, identify or engage with postmodernist theorising. Which is to say that there is a sleight of hand performed whereby postmodernism is defined not by a consideration of the body of work that falls under this umbrella term but by the abuses, errors and intellectual solecisms to which Sokal objects. His polemical premise appears more to be that poor scholarship is postmodernism than vice versa.

It also impinges on Sokal's argument that theorising is not based on the hall-marks of empirical scientific investigation: hypothesis, experiment, evidence and proof. Instead, theorising is often necessarily conjectural and in many cases metaphorical (a point Sokal later admits in further articles). Sokal's counter-argument against postmodernist arguments to a noteworthy extent relies on pointing out that the vehicle used in the metaphor is poorly understood by the theorist, yet it can be questioned whether this invalidates, or significantly coun-ters the theory. Theorising in the humanities and social sciences has more in common with literature than science (or scientific theorising) in that it is often creative, connotative and illustrative, and concerned with affective power. To point out that the modernists did not understand relativity theory may be just as fruitless in critiquing their representation of society and human interaction as pointing out that postmodernists do not understand the scientific concepts they draw upon.

Consequently, we might ask whether the naïve theorising of 'Transgressing the Boundaries' is, first, completely invalidated by its own scientific shortcom-ings, and second, at all helpful in terms of contemporary cultural critique. To take the first question, there are theoretical assertions in the essay that are based on conclusions wrongly drawn from scientific concepts, and the conclusions therefore could be considered erroneous in their use of evidence. From an empirically-based scientific perspective this would invalidate them, but from a humanities perspective, for example, this is not necessarily the case, because the concepts are being used for their illustrative power – such that to consider the arguments to have empirical evidence as such is often a false start. More import-antly, to (over-)emphasise Sokal's point that postmodernists do not understand the scientific concepts they use, leads to one of two conclusions. The first is that the two cultures should not employ each other's concepts because those concepts will not be well understood and deployed (as Sokal perhaps misunderstands much of postmodernist theorising). The second is that the 'two cultures' would benefit from a more profitable if not necessarily rigorous understanding of each other, which is not something that Sokal appears to support in his fundamental hostility to postmodernism.[13] Which raises the question as to whether the 'two cultures' have different intellectual priorities, rather than, in Sokal's terms, stan-dards. There is also a slippage in Sokal's language between 'postmodern science' and 'postmodernist science', which prompts two other queries: one over the lack of appreciation of the significant difference between the period term and the the-oretical, the other over the usefulness of a postmodernist science – an argument over whether science and postmodernism are productively compatible could have been a helpful one for Sokal to stage.

The second question I raised above is whether 'Transgressing the Boundaries', taken at face value, might be helpful in terms of its contemporary cultural critique (the context of the publication) rather than in its use of science. Certainly, the editors of *Social Text* thought so, and published the article in a special issue of their journal that was concerned with debates over the place of science in culture and society, prompted by Gross and Levitt's book *Higher Superstition: The Academic Left and its Quarrels with Science*.[14] Sokal contends that the editors were unprofessional in not sending the article to a natural scientist for comment, and as this is based on his own intellectual *priorities*, it is a self-sustaining argument. Yet, from another perspective, what it in fact implies is that the editors did not place a priority on the article's scientific rigour – bizarre and unacceptable as that may seem to Sokal and others – and were more interested in the socio-political conclusions to be drawn from its argument, partly because they see the journal's lineage in the independent Left 'little magazine' tradition as much as in that of academic scholarship.[15] In Sokal's terms, of course, this means something different: simply publishing the article for *ideological* reasons irrespective of its (scientific) worthiness.

An example of what Sokal takes to be this ideological appeal of 'Transgressing the Boundaries' for *Social Text* might be the sentence in which the text states:

> [I]t is imperative to restructure and redefine the institutional loci in which scientific labor takes place – universities, government labs, and corporations – and reframe the reward system that pushes scientists to become, often against their own better instincts, the hired guns of capitalists and the military.[16]

Sokal's bogus article makes other points about the need to reform the language in which science is conducted and bring about a 'progressive science' as part of the 'radical democratization of all aspects of social, economic, political and cultural life'.[17] These are different – political – points from the ones made in the largely historical and contextual scientific explorations throughout the earlier sections of the article. It is clear that the erroneous science that surrounds these political points does not invalidate them; but Sokal's argument is that the vociferous assertion of this ideological position by a physicist is insufficiently significant alongside the importance of the scientific or factual weakness of the article. From the position of a social science journal interested in cultural studies it is less straightforward precisely because of the journal's aims and the untransgressed boundaries between the natural and social sciences. *Social Text* is likely to have been most interested in the supposed political agenda behind the article: to liberate the *production* of science from the ideology of its paymasters. What remains is the 'truth', in Sokal's terms, of the 'hoax' and the equally fraught as well as contentious questions of ideological conviction and intellectual integrity that it involves.

'Transgressing the Boundaries' begins with the statement that:

> There are many natural scientists, and especially physicists, who continue to reject the notion that the disciplines concerned with social and cultural

criticism can have anything to contribute, except perhaps peripherally, to their research.[18]

Once the sham has been exposed, it appears that this is the most straightforward statement in Sokal's article, and Sokal himself evidently epitomises such a will to rejection (though in a 'hoax' article everything is suspect/undecidable). It is worth noting, though, that the opening statement refers not to postmodernism but to all criticism on the other side of the 'two cultures' (Sokal later embraced a less dismissive position). The fact that the editors of *Social Text* trusted that Sokal was not one of these many scientists dismissive of social criticism, and indeed did not themselves take the equal but opposite view of natural science, is not something Sokal wishes to engage, such that his intervention appears finally to settle on two possible positions: natural scientists are correct (to an unspecified degree) to 'reject' the theory and criticism of the social sciences, and the social theorists are wrong to try to engage at all with the concepts of the natural sciences, because they do not seem to understand them (Sokal doesn't dwell on examples of correct usage). This is mirrored in Sokal's lack of engagement with the contexts in which his chosen social theorists operate, but Sokal sees fit to disparage them in any case. With such a standpoint it may be little wonder that the 'two cultures', as Sokal later says, 'are probably farther apart in mentality than at any time in the past 50 years'.

After the initial debate over the 'Transgressing the Boundaries' article, Sokal went on to write a book with Jean Bricmont entitled *Impostures Intellectuelles*, in which Sokal's original criticisms were elucidated and expounded at length with reference to American and particularly French theorists (one argument mounted against Sokal has been that he is writing from an empirically dominated US culture about a French intellectual tradition that draws more on style and interpretation), such as Baudrillard, Kristeva Lacan and Deleuze. Here, Sokal and Bricmont point out four abuses: the use of 'terminology without bothering much about what the words actually *mean*'; importing concepts without justification; 'throwing around technical terms in a context where they are completely irrelevant'; and '[m]anipulating phrases and sentences that are, in fact, meaningless'.[19] Though in the book few of the authors critiqued are usually seen as postmodernists, the last 'abuse' is glossed in terms of postmodernist theorists' 'veritable intoxication with words'. This perhaps begins to lead us to the fundamental difference between Sokal and those under attack, who are for the most part poststructuralists. One dictionary definition of poststructuralism runs:

> a school of thought . . . reacting against structuralist pretensions to scientific objectivity and comprehensiveness . . . These thinkers emphasized the instability of meanings and intellectual categories . . . and sought to undermine any theoretical system that claimed to have universal validity . . . They sought to dissolve the fixed binary oppositions of structuralist

thought, including that between language and metalanguage – and thus between literature and criticism. Instead they favoured a non-hierarchical plurality or 'free play' of meanings, stressing the indeterminacy of texts.[20]

From even this brief outline of the poststructuralist agenda it is evident that many of Sokal's accusations embody precisely the position that the theorists he is criticising sought to challenge. Sokal's belief that poststructuralism is not logical, rigorous or meaningful exposes a particular understanding of what scholarship, theory and critique should aspire to in ways reminiscent of the objections in fine art to cubism or in poetry to the Dadaists.

In an essay published in the *Times Literary Supplement*, Sokal and Bricmont further explained the aims of their book, which had provoked a debate as fierce as Sokal's first article:

> Note that we do not criticise the mere use of words like 'chaos' (which, after all, goes back to the Bible) outside of their scientific context. Rather, we concentrate on the arbitrary invocation of technical notions such as Gödel's theorem or compact sets or non-commuting operators. Also, we have nothing against metaphors; we merely remark that the role of a metaphor is usually to clarify an unfamiliar concept by relating it to a more familiar one, not the reverse. Suppose, for example, that in a theoretical physics seminar we were to explain a very technical concept in quantum field theory by comparing it to the concept of aporia in Derridean literary theory. Our audience of physicists would wonder, quite reasonably, what purpose such a metaphor served (whether or not it was apposite), if not merely to display our own erudition. In the same way, we fail to see the advantage of invoking, even metaphorically, scientific concepts that one oneself understands only shakily when addressing a non-specialist audience. Might the goal be to pass off as profound a rather banal philosophical or sociological observation, by dressing it up in fancy scientific jargon?[21]

Though literary critics would balk at saying the purpose of a metaphor was simply or even primarily to clarify, the fault criticised here of directionless self-serving erudition might indeed be censured but such a charge needs, of course, to be proven, not just stated (self-promotion has in turn been a charge levelled against Sokal with regard to the ends of his 'experiment'). Then there is the question of relativism:

> A secondary target of our book is epistemic relativism, namely the idea – which is much more widespread in the Anglo-Saxon world than in France – that modern science is nothing more than a 'myth', a 'narration' or a 'social construction' among many others.[22]

Here Sokal and Bricmont mistake methodological relativism, the view that the researcher should suspend or bracket their own cultural bias when seeking to understand objects of inquiry in unknown or local contexts, for epistemic relativism, the view that all truths are relative to a social group and so all knowledges are equal.

Finally, Sokal and Bricmont's aims are to warn scholars, especially students, against charlatanism and to ' "deconstruct" the reputation that certain texts have of being difficult'.[23] Adopting the perspective of their own critique, it is at least intriguing to wonder what Sokal and Bricmont understand by 'deconstruct' here: apparently, this is equivalent to demonstrating that texts 'mean precisely nothing'.[24] Leaving aside the complex question of how meaning is made in the nexus of culture, writer, text, reader and language, one might at least point out one opening statement in a definition of deconstruction: 'a philosophically sceptical approach to the possibility of coherent meaning in language'.[25] To deconstruct a text is always a move to open up, multiply and complicate meaning, but it appears to Sokal and Bricmont that this is to expose the text as meaningless. A conclusion might therefore be that the Sokal affair illustrates what happens when an approach that sees texts as either meaningful or meaningless collides with a more pluralistic set of theories about linguistic complexity and instability. This is not a case of 'two cultures' but it is an example of antithetical ways of thinking for which Sokal has perhaps done little to provide the basis for points of synthesis, except inasmuch as he has introduced science to satire and satire into science.

REFERENCES AND BIBLIOGRAPHY

Baldick, Chris, *Oxford Concise Dictionary of Literary Terms*, 2nd edn, Oxford: Oxford University Press, 2004.

Davis, Colin, *After Poststructuralism: Reading, Stories and Theory*, London: Routledge, 2004.

Kuroki, Gen, 'After the Sokal Affair and *Impostures Intellectuelles*', at http://www.math.tohoku.ac.jp/~kuroki/Sokal/ (accessed 4 Aug. 2005).

Lingua Franca (eds), *The Sokal Hoax: The Sham that Shook the Academy*, Lincoln: University of Nebraska Press, 2000.

Norris, Christopher, *Uncritical Theory*, London: Lawrence and Wishart, 1992.

Patai, Daphne and Will H. Corral (eds), *Theory's Empire: An Anthology of Dissent*, New York: Columbia University Press, 2005.

Singh, Simon, 'Bang, Bang, you're Matrixed', *The Sunday Times*, News Review Section (5), 21 November 2004, p. 6.

Snow, C. P., *The Two Cultures*, Cambridge: Cambridge University Press, 1993.

Sokal, Alan, 'Transgressing the Boundaries: Toward a Transformative Hermeneutics of Quantum Gravity', *Social Text* 46: 47 (spring–summer) 1996, pp. 217–52. (Available as an Appendix to Sokal and Bricmont's *Intellectual Impostures*, in *Lingua Franca et al.* (eds), pp. 11–45 and at http://www.physics.nyu.edu/faculty/sokal/#papers (accessed 4 Aug. 2005).)

Sokal, Alan, 'A Physicist Experiments with Cultural Studies', *Lingua Franca* 6: 4 (May–June) 1996, pp. 62–4. (Available in *Lingua Franca et al* (eds), pp. 49–53 and at http://www.physics.nyu.edu/faculty/sokal/#papers (accessed 4 Aug. 2005).)

Sokal, Alan, 'Transgressing the Boundaries: An Afterword' *Dissent* 43: 4 (fall) 1996, pp. 93–9. (Available at http://www.physics.nyu.edu/faculty/sokal/#papers (accessed 4 Aug. 2005).)

Sokal, Alan and Jean Bricmont, 'What is all the fuss about?', in the *Times Literary Supplement* (London), 17 October 1997, p. 17. (Available as 'The Furor over *Impostures Intellectuelles*: What is the fuss all about?' at http://www.physics.nyu.edu/~as2/tls.html (accessed 4 Aug. 2005).)

Sokal, Alan and Jean Bricmont, *Intellectual Impostures: Postmodern Philosophers' Abuse of Science*, London: Profile, 1998. (Originally published in French as *Impostures Intellectuelles*).

NOTES

1. 'A Physicist Experiments'. See the bibliography for references and weblinks to this and other essays by Sokal.
2. Seshadri-Crooks, Kalpana, 'Surviving Theory: A Conversation with Homi K. Bhabha', in *The Pre-occupation of Post-Colonial Studies*, Fawzia Afzal-Khan and Kalpana Seshadri-Crooks (eds), London: Duke University Press, 2000, pp. 369–80; p. 377.
3. C. P. Snow, *The Two Cultures and the Scientific Revolution*, Cambridge: Cambridge University Press, 1959, debated and responded to in F. R. Leavis, *Two Cultures: The Significance of C. P. Snow*, London: Chatto, 1962. Also see F. R. Leavis, 'Two Cultures? The Significance of Lord Snow', in *Nor Shall My Sword: Discourses on Pluralism, Compassion and Social Hope*, New York: Barnes and Noble, 1972. Snow's argument proceeds from this observation:

   > A good many times I have been present at gatherings of people who, by the standards of the traditional culture, are thought highly educated and who have with considerable gusto been expressing their incredulity at the illiteracy of scientists. Once or twice I have been provoked and have asked the company how many of them could describe the Second Law of Thermodynamics. The response was cold: it was also negative. Yet I was asking something which is about the scientific equivalent of: *Have you read a work of Shakespeare's?* (pp. 50–1)

4. Sokal and Bricmont, 1998, p. 210.
5. Ibid., pp. 225–6.
6. See Michel Foucault, *Power/Knowledge: Selected Interviews and Other Writings, 1972–1977*, ed. Colin Gordon, New York: Pantheon, 1980.
7. Sokal and Bricmont, 1998, pp. 226–9.
8. It might be added that scientists have often made equally baffling conjectural assertions, such as that the Earth may be a computer in a machine-created universe. See Singh.
9. Because there are a number of different publications of Sokal's articles and the ones available through Sokal's website (See References and Bibliography) are the most likely to be consulted, page references have not been given here or for subsequent quotations.
10. Nietzsche, Friedrich, *Philosophy and Truth*, ed. and trans. Daniel Breazeale, Brighton: Harvester, 1979, p. 84.
11. See Norris.
12. Patton, Paul, 'Introduction', in *The Gulf War Did Not Take Place*, Bloomington: Indiana University Press, 1995, pp. 1–21, p. 6.
13. A more fruitful approach might be to engage from a scientific perspective with the cultural critique offered by postmodernism, but this is something Sokal appears to feel unable to do despite his willingness to attack postmodernism from a scholarly perspective.
14. Paul. R. Gross and Norman Levitt, *Higher Superstition: The Academic Left and its Quarrels with Science*, Baltimore and London: The Johns Hopkins University Press, 1994.

15. For a response by two of the co-editors of the journal, which is published by Duke University Press, see Bruce Robbins and Andrew Ross, 'Response: Mystery Science Theater', *Lingua Franca* (July–Aug. 1996, reprinted in *Lingua Franca et al.* (eds), pp. 54–8).
16. Sokal and Bricmont, 1998, p. 225.
17. Ibid., p. 24.
18. Ibid., p. 199.
19. Ibid., p. 4.
20. Baldick, p. 202.
21. Bricmont and Sokal, 1997.
22. Ibid.
23. Sokal and Bricmont, 1998, p. 5.
24. Ibid.
25. Baldick, p. 59.

CHAPTER

11

POPULAR NOVEL: THE ETHICS OF HARRY POTTER

Approach: Ethical Criticism

[T]he power of the stories is in Harry's moral and spiritual strength, given to him by a dead mother's love. And this, surely, is what is so good about the books – that without being 'preachy', they have a firm underlying ethic. I suppose you could define it as the humanism which is the highest ethical ideal of most Potter-purchasers. (A. N. Wilson)[1]

In Chapter 3, I noted John Fiske's view that the difference between literary and popular texts lies in the latter's reliance on its contemporary social relevance for its popularity and significance. For Fiske, popular texts are evaluated according to their social values, not their universal or aesthetic ones. This may be true in literature departments in many cases, but it is not necessarily true in the context of wider cultural discussion. In this chapter, I will therefore look at a popular novel in the context of debates over questions of good and evil. These are concerned with readers' ethical ideals, as Wilson notes above, though it is debatable to what extent such ideals are ever universal, as will be discussed below.

J. K. Rowling's extraordinarily successful series of children's stories has inspired an unprecedented reaction across the world, in terms of devotion and denunciation. Celebrated in conventions in Bangalore, vilified in southern American schools, the Potter novels seem to present a straightforward binaristic world of good and evil, mixing the sub-genres of Victorian orphan fiction, medieval romance, Tolkein fantasy, public school Bildungsroman and children's adventure story.

Various communities have received the novels very differently from the adulation that has greeted each volume at its launch. Some have condemned the books for promoting magic and the occult: the Seventh Day Adventists banned the novels in sixty of their schools in Australia. The Catholic Church in Poland put pressure on their government to remove them from the national literacy drive. In the UK and the US, Christian fundamentalists have roundly decried the novels and protested against them in print and on film. One Christian commentator, Richard Abanes, argues that while the novels set up a simple dichotomy between good and evil, someone like Harry Potter who lies, deceives, cheats and flouts school rules is the opposite of a good role model.[2] As has been noted elsewhere, the 1990s saw a change in Christian concerns over children's fiction from issues of the body to those of the mind or the soul, especially in fantasy novels that ignore the prohibition against sorcerers and wizards in the Book of the Law, Deuteronomy 18: 9–12.[3] While religions consider art heterogeneously, Christian fundamentalists have aligned fantasy with deceit and lying – raising an issue of make-believe that is in fact central to any work of fiction.[4] From one perspective, this can be said to point up a distinction between belief and the suspension of disbelief, between deep convictions about 'the truth' and the uses of the imagination as well as enchantment. Such debates in 1989 famously surrounded Salman Rushdie's *The Satanic Verses* and its relation to blasphemy, and in 1993, the murder of Jamie Bulger in Bootle, Merseyside by two children who had supposedly been influenced by watching a fantasy horror video, *Child's Play 2*.

The moral case against the Harry Potter novels has not been concerned with blasphemy but has rested on their possible influence on the young:

> Christian censors around the world see the books as diabolic stories encouraging occult practices, magic, and witchcraft. Some parents, who may not be concerned about magic and witchcraft, see the books as yet another example of overly scary and violent media that children should not be exposed to.[5]

The first perspective concerns belief and sees (diabolism and) witchcraft as part of a belief-system that both has its adherents and is antithetical to Christianity; it also understands a sharp distinction between what is real (God's creation) and what is false (the devil's temptation), in the sense of evil as well as illusory; and it perceives a worrying, even competitive, rise in pagan/Satanic religion in the 1990s, blurring any significant distinction between Satanism, Wicca, New Age religious philosophies and the Occult. The second perspective concerns the inability to suspend disbelief and worries that either children will not be able to distinguish the true from the fantastical and so be filled with fear or they will not be able to distinguish the value systems of made-up worlds from that of their parents' society and so will themselves act in ways that harm or create fear in others. What both perspectives share is an understanding of the child – almost irrespective of age – as open to influence, as having a developing mind that can be shaped in different ways by culture and fantasy. What both also evince is a concern with what is fantastical rather than what is socially descriptive in the novels, seemingly less interested in matters of class, gender and ethnic representation than in the books' suggestion that there is another, but contra-Christian order of 'reality' alongside the muggle world of the Dursleys. This order of analysis and objection is thus exercised by the books' presentation of ethics in relation to fantasy and the immaterial, not society and the material. To other critics of the novels, the elements of elitism, playground culture, class snobbery, inherited characteristics, gender and national stereotypes, and ethnic focus are more important in terms of the influence Rowling's texts may have on readers.

Such debates and verdicts concern the relation between art and morality, representation and ethics. Succinctly put, morality is concerned with rules, principles and judgements of conduct but in ways that are different from, if overlapping with, for example, the theological, the legalistic or the aesthetic. Morals are cultural and historical but discussion of them frequently tends towards the universal. They are fraught with uneasy convergences of the rational and the emotive, encumbered with prohibitions and imperatives, and liable to systematisation but when put into practice tied to specific circumstances that almost always exceed the generalities of theoretical formulation. However, critics that seek to define the ethical in distinction from morality, construct the former as disinterested and undetermined, while the latter is the discourse concerned with duties, obligations, codes and norms of correct behaviour. While morality attempts to prescribe and prohibit, ethics seeks out excess, exception and estrangement.

In this chapter I aim to explore the relation to ethical imperatives implied in the different receptions of stories that have a near-universal appeal but which have been read to imply vastly divergent subject positions for different readers. The nub of the discussion is the question of whether the wide appeal of this literature is based on shared moral absolutes, or on different ethical perspectives that the books are able to represent, or whether ethical questions are not central to the appeal of fiction.

Ethics has only returned as a prominent subject in literary criticism in the 1990s. The reasons for its retreat among liberal critics prior to this decade, and the rise in political criticism is key, are explained by Cristina Mejia: while social discourse may still espouse universalist claims, modern criticism

> discarded the notion of a shared humanity as naïve, spurious, and worse: totalising, oppressive, and offensive to the liberal commitment to personal and aesthetic autonomy – the final obstacle to a sort of gentle invasion of the ethical field by aesthetics, a scenario in which the good or worthy life will no longer be held hostage to truth-seeking, reasoning, and judgement about human relations, but require only that we take a properly aesthetic attitude towards others.[6]

Another perspective is offered by Wayne Booth in his 1988 essay 'Why Ethical Criticism Fell on Hard Times' where he ascribes the 'deplored role' of ethical criticism to four dogmas: the rejection of questions of value in theory; the orthodoxy that credible reason proceeds through critical doubt and not assent or faith; the cultural, historical and personal instability of value judgements; and the dominance of formal aesthetic theories.[7]

Though there are now claims for a return to a rationalist universalism, the reason for the resurgence of ethics is best understood in terms of the refashioning of ethical inquiry away from universalism towards difference, from issues of normativity to ones of alterity rooted in historical and cultural relativity. According to one study, 'The famous question on which Aristotle based his ethical philosophy, how shall we live life, has been transformed into the question, how can we respect the other? What responsibilities do we owe to our fellows?'[8]

I

I want now to move to a consideration of the three parts of the question outlined above (p. 120). The argument for the (near) universal appeal of the Harry Potter novels most confidently rests on the stories' re-enactment of some staple ingredients of much older narrative forms, particularly the folk tale, the romance quest and religious narrative. The Potter stories sketch a world in which imaginative engagement with the force of good to overcome evil (broadly understood as that which opposes the good) merely necessitates identification with the books' hero. If to see oneself as the other is to sympathise with Harry Potter, then this is a subject position easily adopted by readers, irrespective of gender, ethnicity or even current age, because the character is largely a blank if not a cipher: Harry Potter is an orphan with few anchors in social or familial reality, his life before going to Hogwarts limited to domestic abuse and friendlessness, such that he is as 'alone' and 'apart' as the solitary reader immersed in the dialogue between fantasy and the self. Harry is a gifted child who embodies the hopes of the individual whose unique self-perception engenders a feeling of specialness, and whose trials and tribulations may be aggrandised as the interventions of the merely jealous and the plainly wicked: he is oppressed by conventional life (the Dursleys), nurtured by a beneficent elite (Hogwarts), and opposed by various dark forces (from the Malfoys to Voldemort). Only the petit-bourgeois Dursleys and their maltreatment of Harry are rooted in a quotidian environment: one that represents the inequalities of mundane reality as much as the below-stairs drudgery of Cinderella, so easily contrasted with the ethereal and magical but detached and apolitical world of the ball. Thus, if *Harry Potter* has a particular ethical angle that engenders a universal appeal it is through a championing of the oppressed, alongside gestures towards cultural plurality. So, the novels support the lower middle-class Weasleys against the superior Malfoys – championing 'mudblood' over claims of 'Pureblood'. They also introduce a number of ethnic 'others' to imply, in opposition to most people's social reality, the inclusiveness of the Hogwart's world: Parvati and Padma Patil (Indian), Cho Chang (East Asian), Seamus Finnigan (Irish), Lee Jordan and Angelina Johnson (black). They have been accused of gender stereotypes but are written by a woman (whose initials on the book cover were at first supposed to render her genderless) and arguably feature a near-central, strong-willed, ratio-nal heroine in the character of Hermione. The argument for universal appeal, however, has little to do with ethics, as the issue of the other is addressed mono-chromatically by the presentation of a Manichean world of good and evil people, with suspense primarily created by the problem of their identification.

II

For Andrew Blake, Harry Potter's appeal emerges in between the crises in faith over religion, politics and science, reminding readers of a pre-Enlightenment, largely pre-colonial period of enchantment, when belief was not made sub-servient to orthodoxies and institutions:

> [A]ll these investments in the non-rational add up to a weight of popular knowledges which refute brute common sense and its refusal to ask the big questions, and which have no truck with a state-sponsored religion that seems to be part of the problem. Add to this the much-trumpeted dis-appearance of grand narratives of historical explanation (such as Marxism), and the increasingly controversial status of scientific work on biotechnology and genetics, and we have a general crisis of faith in both Christianity and scientific rationality, the forces that in and after the seventeenth century suppressed and then superseded magical practices both in Europe and in the American colonies. Enter Harry Potter, who is white and English, but not a White Anglo-Saxon Protestant. All of which is one reason why it is easy to read the Harry Potter stories as universal rather than Anglo-American.[9]

It is thus the absence of religion – alongside the absence of politics or history – that enables a global appeal. The religions of the world have few shared moral absolutes but a plethora of beliefs that encode 'good' and 'evil' into systems, none of which (and therefore simultaneously all of which) is present in the novels. The books' depiction of right and wrong is not hampered by a recog-nisable socio-cultural reality, thus allowing the reader to indulge in easy virtue. Siding with good over evil is not in itself an ethical position but a self-perception (rather than a choice) that precedes ethics and interaction.

For example, the books are concerned throughout with the exercise of power and powers, but have been said to avoid the question of the relationship between ethics and power:

> Acocella develops a fascinating analysis of power in Rowling's books: arguing that 'Each of the novels approaches the problem from a different angle': the first is heroic; the second is 'secular, topical, political'; the third is psychological; the fourth is more ambitious in its politics, introducing new topics (such as sex) but not yet answering the question of whether power is 'reconcilable with goodness'.[10]

The books allow multiple cultural groups to identify with the values ins-cribed in the texts not because they are culturally pluralistic but because they avoid the complexities of life that might be experienced by the reader. According to Richard Rorty, the special ethical claim of the novel is that it allows the subtle and multiperspectival description of specific moral practices though narrative. Fiction can move between perspectives and explore contin-gencies, aiming not at a universal ethic but a commentary on the moral choices made in a particular, richly described situation. As Andrew Gibson explains:

> The novelist presents us with individuality and diversity alike without any attempt to reduce either to the terms of a singular scheme or totality. The novel thereby becomes the form for and expression of an ethics of free, democratic pluralism.[11]

In the Harry Potter novels an ethics of pluralism is avoided through eschewal of the 'real world', or at best by proceeding through analogy. One critic explains this in terms of an absence of complex decision-making:

> Like fairy-tale heroes, [Harry Potter] never has any ethical dilemmas or moral choices . . . As a true hero, Harry takes the right side in the strug-gle between good and evil, leaving no doubt to the readers as to where their sympathies should lie. Even though some of the adults in Harry's immediate surroundings prove the opposite of what they initially seem to be, the basic distinction between right and wrong is still there, and Harry's choice does not present any serious moral dilemmas.[12]

So, if the ethical dilemmas of readers of the Harry Potter novels are rooted in specific and complex situations and are created by the near-absence of straightforwardly 'good' or 'evil' agencies, compounded by the existence of multiple personal responsibilities and social circumstances, then the pleasure of such fantasy fictions is more likely to arise from the simplicity of the ethical action they portray than from their ability to represent different ethical per-spectives. Also, if it is a central tenet of Christian doctrine that humans have been granted by God the fundamental right to choose between good and evil, Harry Potter is to this extent a fine role model for children because, in his eth-ically monochrome world, he virtually always chooses good.

III

Thus, it is arguable that the ethical decisions in the novel are between simple good and evil, posed in such ways that neither characters nor readers are sig-nificantly challenged:

> Hogwarts confronts the ethics of magic and science directly. Its purpose is to help its students harness and focus their powers. These powers might be called magic or they might be called technology; but in this case they

are called magic. The problem for the educators in the books is that they cannot be certain that people (wizards) will use these powers for the common good. It boils down to a choice between the common good and the dark arts.[13]

In this regard, the novels do not involve ethical questions, but allow the reader to participate, or indulge, in a morally black and white world where contemplation of the other moves no further than identifying whether they are on the side of right – here presented as the use of magic, money or anything else in ways that do not (intend) harm – or wrong.

While there are various ways to explain the appeal of Rowling's novels, contemporary ethical questions are hardly confronted by them at all. What the Harry Potter novels do not do well is address questions of sensitivity towards others – and in this they do not engage with the capacity that the novel has to consider the position of the other. As Richard Rorty explains, the

> process of coming to see other human beings as 'one of us' rather than as 'them' is a matter of detailed description of what unfamiliar sorts of people are like and of the redescription of what we ourselves are like. This is a task not for theory but for genres such as ethnography, the journalist's report, the comic book, the docudrama, and, especially, the novel.[14]

The appeal of the Potter books is arguably outside, or aside from, such considerations. Ethical questions raised by the books are not complex, but instead rest on deciding how best to identify and oppose wrongdoers. These are not dilemmas but choices of action reliant upon the correct distinction between the false and the true, and while the books involve detective work aimed towards establishing who is on the side of 'right' and who on the side of 'evil', these are not themselves complex categories, or ones that involve seeing through the eyes of the other let alone seeing oneself as another.

The ethical relationship between self and other has been most prominently discussed by Emmanuel Levinas, for whom the ethical power of the other lies in destabilising subjective categories. Andrew Gibson helpfully outlines five aspects to Levinas's discussion of the ethical relation.[15] First, it does not seek to establish objective foundations. Second, it is not reliant on principles that precede the encounter with the other – it does not look back to previous or prior experience and comprehension for prescriptive guidance about, or a frame in which to situate, the other. Third, it does not include a theory of being – it does not subscribe to categories or essences of identity, and the other is not there to be 'grasped', but the self is there to be presented. Fourth, the ethical relation is particular – bound up with responsibility and with responsiveness in concrete situations. Fifth, it is not a matter of prior knowledge or understanding, of intuition or cognition – to perceive the other in relation to one's own terms of reference is in itself unethical.

One way in which *Harry Potter*, and much other fantasy fiction, could be considered ethical is precisely in its lack of pretence to verisimilitude. Levinas maintains that ethics, because it concerns itself with what should be rather than with what is, involves the Utopian. It is arguably in the fantastical world of Hogwarts that we see the ethical valuing of Harry, in stark distinction from the unethical treatment of him as an 'other' (nephew) in the Dursley family in the 'real' world. Which is to say that he is understood in the world beyond platform 9¾ as both a 'wizard' and a force for good, whereas in the Dursleys' household he is seen as both bad and backward. The fantasy world is one that Harry enters through a Levinasian 'flight from being' in that he has to slough off the sense of self he has grown up with, and understand himself differently, and one sense of identity collapses in order to grasp a new sense of difference in the world. In this, Harry's discovery that there are wizards, and that he is one of them, can be considered in some ways analogous to other discoveries that can be made about the 'other' that are also discoveries about the self, for example, in terms of ethnicity or sexual orientation. The novels are thus placed in a long line of fictional texts for children that posit other worlds, behind the wardrobe-door or down the rabbit-hole, in which the child pro-tagonist comes to a new sense of self through the encounter with the other. Transformations of the self and the world are fundamental to a new reality of spells and potions that employs magic as the primary signifier of otherness, or re-presenting objects and people in other guises, as in excess of the ontologies and epistemologies thought to contain them in advance. The fantasy world also implies an infinity of otherness, a sense in which one's understanding of the world will always be false as each new other cannot be pre-known but has to be experienced in its indeterminacy and its potentially radical alterity. As Colin Davis writes, for Levinas, with its reliance on narrative and the author's sole perspective, '[L]iterature *qua* literature is obscure, absurd, selfish, cut off from lucidity; and crucially, in moral terms it is pernicious because it fails to acknowledge the priority of the relation to the Other.'[16] Though Levinas believes that art is to be treated with suspicion because it both is illusory and inevitably deals with the representation of, rather than a face-to-face dialogue with, the other, the limitlessness of fantasy also tends inevitably towards uncertainty and excess, overflowing the boundaries of representation and identity, emphasising difference over sameness. Levinas is more concerned with representations of history, where it is unethical to misrepresent an event – such as the Holocaust – in any way whatsoever, rather than with imaginative fiction which posits worlds and people which are not attempting to depict his-torical events. Levinas's viewpoint can also be contrasted with that of Paul Ricoeur:

> In the unreal sphere of fiction we never tire of exploring new ways of evaluating actions and characters. The thought experiments we conduct in the great laboratory of the imaginary are also experiments in the realm

of good and evil . . . Moral judgment has not been abolished; it is rather itself subjected to the imaginative variations in fiction.[17]

For Ricoeur, fiction enables that imaginative leap which allows the self not just to contemplate the other but also to see the other in the self. In this Ricoeur tries to negotiate Levinas's position, seeing that life is composed of narratives, and 'it is the encounter of our narrative identity with the other that brings out the fuller ethical dimensions of the self' in 'the constant effort to place the narrative self in relation to the face of the "other" '.[18]

The Harry Potter novels might be said not to contain ethical dilemmas or to approach the ethics of representation that Rorty believes the novel to be capable of, in, say, *Middlemarch* or *The Golden Bowl*. But if Levinas provides a pejorative critique of art precisely because it is bound up with the representation of others, then the flights of fancy contained in fantasy fiction are perhaps arguably and certainly surprisingly less unethical than a text such as *Middlemarch* precisely in their eschewal of mimetic representation of the world of readers. The attempt to represent the other in the novel, or to present a plurality of subject positions, may always be doomed to ethical failure because the fictional encounter with the other is always with an absent other, who cannot (re)present themselves. But the unethical in fiction is not synonymous with the immoral, however readers might wish to condemn a text for inadequately representing the codes of behaviour and the cultural beliefs to which they subscribe.

Finally, one might note the preponderance of male theorists in this debate over ethics. Many feminists have instead turned towards an Aristotelian emphasis on 'virtue theory' as an alternative to moral philosophy. Carol Gilligan, for example, argues in her 1982 book *In a Different Voice* that women more often consider morality as a matter of relationships rather than rules. Where men emphasise duty, obligations, laws, rights and doctrines, women may stress the fulfilment of needs and desires alongside the cultivation of desirable emotions. Therefore, narrative in the Harry Potter novels, like much children's fiction, could be said to have as one of its aims the cultivation of good ethical action in its readers. Other philosophers such as Elizabeth Anscombe and Mary Midgley have also suggested alternative perspectives rooted in virtue theory, while Martha Nussbaum in *Love's Knowledge* (1992) explores literature as a form of ethical inquiry, concluding that it is essential to ethics because it provides a testing-ground for moral theory.

REFERENCES AND BIBLIOGRAPHY

Applebaum, Peter, 'Harry Potter's World: Magic, Technoculture and Becoming Human', in Heilman (ed.), pp. 25–51.

Blake, Andrew, *The Irresistible Rise of Harry Potter*, London: Verso, 2002.

Booth, Wayne, *The Company We Keep: An Ethics of Fiction*, Berkeley: University of California Press, 1988.

Davis, Colin, *After Poststructuralism: Reading, Stories and Theory*, London: Routledge, 2004.

Gibson, Andrew, *Postmodernity, Ethics and the Novel*, London: Routledge, 1999.

Hadfield, Andrew, Dominic Rainsford and Tim Woods (eds), *The Ethics in Literature*, London: Palgrave, 1999.

Heilman, Elizabeth E. (ed.), *Harry Potter's World: Multidisciplinary Critical Perspectives*, London: Routledge, 2003.

Levinas, Emmanuel, *The Levinas Reader*, ed. Sean Hand, Oxford: Blackwell, 1989.

Mejia, Cristina, 'Moral Capacities and Other Constraints', in Hadfield et al. (eds), pp. 212–28.

Nel, Philip, *J. K. Rowling's Harry Potter Novels*, London: Continuum, 2001.

Nikolajeva, Maria, '*Harry Potter* – A Return to the Romantic Hero', in Heilman (ed.), pp. 125–40.

Noel-Smith, Kelly, 'Harry Potter's Oedipal Issues', *Psychoanalytic Studies* 3, 2001, pp. 199–207.

Ricoeur, Paul, *Oneself as Another*, trans. K. Blamey, Chicago: University of Chicago Press, 1992.

Rorty, Richard, *Contingency, Irony and Solidarity*, Cambridge: Cambridge University Press, 1989.

Sweeney, Robert D., 'Ricoeur on Ethics and Narrative', Morny Joy (ed.), in *Paul Ricoeur and Narrative*, Alberta: University of Calgary Press, 1997, pp. 197–206.

Taub, Deborah J. and Heather L. Servaty, 'Controversial Content in Children's Literature: Is Harry Potter Harmful to Children?', in Heilman (ed.), pp. 53–72.

NOTES

1. A. N. Wilson, 'Why I believe in Harry Potter', *The Daily Telegraph*, 16 July 2005, Main Section, p. 21.
2. Blake, pp. 94–7.
3. Taub and Servaty, p. 54.
4. Historians such as Hayden White have argued that the features of novels, such as metaphor and emplotment, are common to all narratives, questioning simple generic divisions between fact and fiction.
5. Heilman, p. 3.
6. Mejia, p. 213.
7. Booth, pp. 25–46.
8. Hadfield et al., p. 9.
9. Blake, pp. 101–2.
10. Nel, p. 41; Nel is writing on Joan Acocella, 'Under the Spell', *New Yorker*, 31 July 2000, pp. 74–8.
11. Gibson, p. 8.
12. Nikolajeva, pp. 134–5.
13. Applebaum, p. 48.
14. Rorty, pp. xvi.
15. Gibson, pp. 16–17.
16. Davis, p. 91.
17. Ricoeur, p. 164.
18. Sweeney, p. 203.

CHAPTER 12

SHORT STORY: BARTHELME'S BALLOON AND THE RHIZOME

Approach: Deleuzian Criticism

Has unity been sacrificed for a sprawling quality? (Barthelme)[1]

[T]here is no social system that does not leak from all directions. (Deleuze and Guattari)[2]

The short story is unfairly named. Shortness is only a quality in relation to something else, and so this epithet 'short' epitomises the way in which the novel has been taken as the standard for modern fiction.[3] Such bias was long ago lampooned by Ambrose Bierce in his 1911 satirical compendium *The Devil's Dictionary*:

> *Novel*: A short story padded. A species of composition bearing the same relation to literature that the panorama bears to art. As it is too long to be read at a sitting the impressions made by its successive parts are successively effaced, as in the panorama. Unity, totality of effect, is impossible; for besides the few pages last read all that is carried in mind is the mere plot of what has gone before.[4]

If Barthelme were familiar with this definition it might be argued that his story's observation at the head of this chapter, that the expanding balloon sacrifices unity for a sprawling quality, might be a comment on the novel's relation to the short story form that Barthelme specialised in and excelled at.

However, there are many ways in which critics have tried to distinguish between the novel and the short story, for example seeing the story as a snapshot: as a photo to the novel's film. In terms of the representation of individuals, it has been argued that the novel develops character whereas the short story is only able to show it, as in the 'slice of life' story perfected by Anton Chekhov.

It was Edgar Allan Poe's criticism in the early to mid-nineteenth century that first offered influential theories about the qualities and characteristics of short-story writing (to the extent that, combined with his stories, Poe's criticism is sometimes credited with originating the modern short story form).[5] Anticipating Bierce's points about the novel above, Poe emphasised that the story usually concentrates on a single character or relationship and has the following qualities: unity of plot; the expression of a single idea; aesthetic wholeness; a 'unity of effect or impression' and 'one pre-established design'. Poe thought the first thing for the writer to do was to establish a 'desired effect' and that the story differed from the novel in that it could be read at one sitting, and so the reader's experience could be tightly controlled.

Since the early twentieth century, critics have generally outlined two types of short story: the plot-based (for example, those of Guy de Maupassant or Robert Louis Stevenson) against the plotless, often open-ended, psychological story associated with the modernists (such as Virginia Woolf and Katherine Mansfield). According to Dominic Head, the twentieth-century modernist short story is not founded on unity (or simple revelation rather than complex epiphany) but on ambiguity and disunity. It is also true of modernist fiction that paradox is a major component of many short stories, and there can frequently be a tension between the control of the form/structure and the ambiguity of the content/meaning.

Looking at a postmodernist short story in this chapter, we need to consider the fact that different principles are at work again. The notion of character starts to dissolve, and plot is replaced by parable. In terms of story-narrative, where modernism has a paradoxical aesthetic unity in its emphasis on disunity, or fragmentation, as though art could contain life's chaos, postmodernist writing often mocks this pretension to pursue order through language and shows language either breaking down or going into overdrive. In terms of character, modernist 'alienation' is no longer tenable because there is no coherent 'self' to be alienated. Individuals are 'schizophrenic' in the sense that each person is many subjects – not because of urban experience, but because the individual is only the site of, a meeting-place for, competing and diverse discourses – different languages and groups constantly competing for our 'identification'.[6] There is no attempt to represent an identity let alone a stable transcendent ego, only a series of different roles the individual (mostly unconsciously) aspires to or at least thinks in terms of.

Donald Barthelme's 'The Balloon' is originally from his volume *Unspeakable Practices, Unnatural Acts* (1968), but is also included in his more readily available collection *Sixty Stories*. Barthelme's enigmatic short story can be summarised quite easily in terms of its narrative, but not its meaning(s). The story is often taken as an exemplary postmodernist text because it is concerned with not depth but surfaces, and resists both rationalisation and interpretation. It is usually taken by critics to be a self-reflexive text and so, in relation to Poe's conception of the story, 'The Balloon' perhaps seems not to comment on anything but itself when it asks, 'Has unity been sacrificed for a sprawling quality?', because the story signifies so much.

The narration begins with the simple fact that a balloon has expanded one night over forty-five blocks of a city. At first there are 'reactions' to the balloon from various people, some of whom argue about 'the meaning'. But it is soon decided that argumentation over the meaning of the balloon is fruitless and there are more practical uses to which it can be put. Children play on the balloon, but, the narrator says: 'The purpose of the balloon was not to amuse children.' To the adults, the balloon's 'purposelessness' is 'vexing' but they are unable to destroy it and 'a public warmth' towards the balloon arises. The narrator then considers what a number of citizens might feel about the balloon, and offers a range of examples of the divided 'critical opinion'. It is then said that the balloon is used to provide orientation points for citizens negotiating the city, and that its expanding and contracting shape is the reason it is most 'admired'. After twenty-two days the balloon is dismantled when the narrator's lover returns from Bergen to be told that the balloon belongs to the narrator and that it is 'a spontaneous autobiographical disclosure' that will not be needed again until 'some other time of unhappiness'.

Barthelme's story can be read in numerous ways and is itself concerned with a multiplicity of critical interpretations – those that greet the appearance of the balloon. It is one of the most striking aspects of the story that it resists interpretation, but Barthelme constructs the story as though it concerns an art work: a city-wide installation that garners 'reactions' and interpretations. The balloon thus has parallels with 'The Balloon' and can be considered as a metafictional exploration of the responses that might greet the story itself. The story's end suggests that the balloon is a personal artefact, whose origin in private unhappiness cannot be appreciated by the public or by critics, who are at liberty to find their own uses and meanings for this overnight manifestation.

Because the 'apparent purposelessness of the balloon was vexing' to the people of the city, the balloon can also be seen as an example of an autotelic work of art, one which has no purpose beyond itself. To some citizens, it is worse than that: it is an artificial construct that detracts from the natural, 'something inferior to the sky that had formerly been there, something interposed between the people and their "sky" '. It could also be argued that the story reveals art as a product because in Western 'over-developed' countries, the power of the market in late capitalism is recognised to extend over the entire range of cultural production where everything is a commodity (including education, health, morality and information).

Some citizens respond to the balloon as one might to something creative, rather than functional; others consider it pointless to conjecture over a meaning and so do make practical use of *the* balloon by hanging balloons or writing public messages on it. Children climb over it, unconcerned with its meaning, while adults respond with warmth or hostility, suspicion or pleasure, needing to know what its purpose is. The effect Barthelme achieves is somewhat akin to reactions to much conceptual art, which vary from incomprehension to hatred, tolerance to fascination. Thus, some see the balloon as a benefit in their lives, others as a blight on the city.

The story is unusual in that it implicitly includes the reactions it might provoke in readers. 'Critical opinion', 'concepts', 'dreams', 'fantasies' and 'feelings' are all brought to bear on the balloon, each suggesting a different theoretical emphasis or view of art and experience. If 'The Balloon' is a baffling, though intriguing short story, this may itself signal a problem with the way the reader approaches the text, searching for a meaning on which to hang an interpretation. The story itself seems to include such attempts to make sense of the balloon, and shows them to be frustrated. A text, like any other work of art, may not have a message and the critic need not analyse it in terms of intention; as explored in the Introduction, this is a part of what is recognised in the shift from 'work' to 'text'. Abstract art, more easily and clearly than prose writing, eschews representation and concentrates instead on form – Brancusi,[7] for example, was one of the first sculptors to want the beauty of materials and smooth shapes to be art in themselves, while minimalists, at the time Barthelme was writing, occupied themselves with strict geometrical forms. For a culture that looks for degrees of verisimilitude in art this can be testing.

Nonetheless, Barthelme's story can be considered in part a survey of responses and reactions to experimentalism and the unexpected – particularly in art and architecture. The balloon provokes an adult lay response (it is 'interesting'), a modern intellectual response ('we have learned not to insist on meanings'), an affective response ('what was important was what you felt') and a utilitarian response ('activities' on the balloon). It provokes feelings of jouissance ('pleasure in being able to run down an incline'), disappointment (it is 'inferior to the sky', which is nature/reality), and identification ('People began, in a curious way, to locate themselves in relation to aspects of the balloon'). From one perspective, the balloon suggests how under postmodernity aesthetics are reduced to spectacle, in which there are no immutable standards of judgement, only pleasurable responses to the spectacle, the pleasure of the text.

Before the balloon's relationship to its owner is revealed at the end of the story, there is this penultimate paragraph:

> It was suggested that what was admired about the balloon was finally this: that it was not limited, or defined. Sometimes a bulge, blister, or subsection would carry all the way east to the river on its own initiative, in the manner of an army's movements on a map, as seen in a headquarters remote from the fighting. Then that part would be, as it were, thrown back again, or would withdraw into new dispositions, the next morning, that part would have made another sortie, or disappeared altogether. This ability of the balloon to shift its shape, to change, was very pleasing, especially to people whose lives were rather rigidly patterned, persons to whom change, although desired, was not available. The balloon, for the

twenty-two days of its existence, offered the possibility, in its randomness, of mislocation of the self, in contradistinction to the grid of precise, rectangular pathways under our feet. The amount of specialized training currently needed, and the consequent desirability of long-term commitments, has been occasioned by the steadily growing importance of complex machinery, in virtually all kinds of operations; as this tendency increases, more and more people will turn, in bewildered inadequacy, to solutions for which the balloon may stand as a prototype, or 'rough draft'.

That the balloon exceeds limitations and definitions is seen as the most likely reason for its attraction, and its protean shape-shifting represents an alternative to the rigid patterning of the city and to regularised urban living. This aspect to the story can be likened to the work of Deleuze and Guattari in its emphasis on 'nomadic movements or processes of ongoing re- and de-territorialization'.[8] In *A Thousand Plateaus,* Deleuze and Guattari in effect mount an assault on traditional Western thinking, which uses an 'arborescent' model of thought. Such a model is everywhere in science and philosophy, where consciousness 'mirrors' or reflects reality and where knowledge of reality is hierarchically arranged according to tree-structures: branches of knowledge with foundations/roots, centred on a mainstream (or trunk) of thought.

I want to suggest that, like the challenge posed by Deleuze and Guattari to the arborescent basis of Western philosophy, Barthelme's story can be considered as a postmodern gloss on *the history of interpretation*. 'The Balloon' ranges over the spectrum of responses only to dissipate into the postmodernist eschewal of meaning itself: 'There was a certain amount of initial argumentation about the "meaning" of the balloon; this subsided, because we have learned not to insist on meanings, and they are rarely looked for now.' So, this short story, that finally presents itself as being about a balloon spreading over a city as the narrator awaits the return of a lover, resists interpretation. The balloon seems to be a symbol of something, because that is the way criticism responds to the artwork, but emerges as a signifier without a signified, tempting but escaping critical readings. The approach that can best accommodate the multiple meanings of the text is arguably a poststructuralist one in which meaning is deferred and disseminated along the chain of other signifiers the reader can associate with the 'balloon'. A Derridean approach through theories of différance and dissemination can be fruitful, but so can a reading that draws on Deleuze and Guattari's *A Thousand Plateaus*, which emphasises the deterritorialised path of the 'vari-shaped' balloon's expansion throughout the city as an image of desire without centre and without containment or limits.

In his translator's introduction, Brain Massumi likens *A Thousand Plateaus* to a record rather than a conventional book – because it is an assembly of varied pieces that can be enjoyed or not, repeat played or skipped, attended to in a different order, and so on. An art form that Massumi could have turned to instead of an album is the short-story collection. This is also an 'assemblage' that has favourites and minor pieces, works in different registers and styles, isolated images and linked themes. Another way to look at this is in terms of the concept of the rhizome that Deleuze and Guattari explain in the Introduction to *A Thousand Plateaus*. The rhizome is a web or network put forward in opposition to the traditional philosophical model for thought of the tree. The work of art thus, too, is thought of differently by Deleuze and Guattari from the root-book with its leaves and branches, central trunk, flowering and deep rootedness. An example of tree-thought in science (and one which could be said to expose an inability to understand poststructuralist approaches) is given in the final sentence of Alan Sokal's article 'Transgressing the Boundaries', discussed in Chapter 10:

> And yet, these images of the future mathematics must remain but the haziest glimmer: for, alongside these three young branches in the tree of science, there will arise new trunks and branches – entire new theoretical frameworks – of which we, with our present ideological blinders, cannot yet even conceive.

The metaphor of the tree is centred on structure, genealogy, singularity, but, as Niall Lucy explains, a rhizome 'is any plant (like ivy or grass) whose root-system is co-extensive with the plant itself, as the plant grows ever outwards and across'.[9]

Deleuze and Guattari write of the 'principal characteristics' of the rhizome in terms that recall Barthelme's growing and contracting multidirectional balloon:

> [U]nlike trees or their roots, the rhizome connects any point to any other point, and its traits are not necessarily linked to traits of the same nature; it brings into play very different regimes of signs, and even nonsign states . . . It is composed not of units but of dimensions, or rather directions in motion. It has neither beginning nor end, but always a middle (milieu) from which it grows and which it overspills . . . The rhizome operates by variation, expansion, conquest, capture, offshoots.[10]

This is reminiscent of the polymorphous, overspilling and multi-connecting balloon spreading over society, challenging and resisting containment or interpretation. Like the balloon, rhizomes 'combat totalizing modes of thought and social regulation' as they map the flows of desire.[11]

In terms of art, the rhizome is a philosophical concept for Deleuze and Guattari: one that opposes the pursuit of realism in the tree-book, which structures the narrative on the root-and-branch arborescent model. While the tree-book aims to reflect the world, the rhizomatic text is usually metafictional, aiming not at mimesis but self-reflexivity. The rhizome is made up of lines, not points, positions and hierarchies. It has multiple entry and exit points, and represents a logic that is not centred but 'nomadic'. Like Barthelme's balloon, the rhizome is also associated with impulse and desire (seen not as an individual's desire but as a flow across bodies) for Deleuze and Guattari, as Edith Wyschogrod explains: '[Desire is] transformed into an economic resource like hydroelectric or nuclear power, and its modus operandi decided by those who possess sufficient force to control its circulation.'[12] The rhizome is a way of mapping the flows of desire for Deleuze and Guattari, just as the balloon is seemingly positioned as a manifestation of desire at the end of Barthelme's story.

More importantly, like the challenges posed by postmodernist fiction to realism, the logic of the rhizome is inclusive and multiple, exchanging the either/or binary of the tree-book for the associative conjunctions of 'and/also' thinking, which is also built into the form and implied argument of Barthelme's story. For Deleuze and Guattari 'literature is *productive*, not representative. Literature has the power to mobilise desire, to create new pre-personal investments, and enables thought and affects that extend beyond the human.'[13] Desire is a productive force that Deleuze and Guattari oppose to the model of Freudian repression. For Lucy, unlike traditional Western philosophy, which sifts and fixes, literature 'spreads' – is associative, experimental, and disseminatory. Thus 'The Balloon' could be considered as an assertion of this understanding of literature in opposition to the realist model of verisimilitude and mimesis: it is closer to the metaphor of the lamp than the mirror. Literature's significance partly lies in its characterising ability to imagine otherwise, to configure alternatives and different logics. The importance of literature to Deleuze and Guattari is that '[I]n its disseminatory (rhizomatic) extensions, [it] is allowed to go on imagining ever more (im)possible worlds that defy philosophical truth, and of course that defy scientific truth as well.'[14]

Because literature is rhizomatic, in opposition to philosophy, it has the capacity to make the world afresh rather than the obligation to attempt to describe it mimetically. Thus they are in part summarising the characteristics of literature when Deleuze and Guattari summarise the characteristics of the rhizome as: espousing principles of connection and heterogeneity, multiplicity, de- and reterritorialization, cartography and decalcomania – to transfer by tracing.[15] As a metaphor for the organisation of human experience, the rhizome advances by way of leaps and linkages between different parts of the system. Chaotic and metamorphic, it forges temporary associations between different discourses and categories only for them to disintegrate as new pathways are mapped and new connections forged. This suggests not just 'The Balloon' but the network of intertextual reference that constitutes 'literature' – a vast inter-connecting web of narratives and characters which may be entered or exited at any point, and in which critical interventions at one point will set off vibrations throughout the web.

The rhizome is only one of the concepts Deleuze and Guattari outline in *A Thousand Plateaus* and it is not to be taken as a central or overarching concept, which would in itself contradict the logic of the rhizome. Similarly, the balloon is not a defining image in Barthelme's work, but one way of imaging his thought about art. The rhizome can helpfully illuminate a perspective on the story, but is not an explanation of it. Both the rhizome and the balloon map lines of desire, free-flowing, expanding and amorphous in their fluctuating movements.

Deleuze and Guattari develop the idea of the rhizome in their book on Kafka. Here they argue for a category of 'minor literature', which it could be argued fits very well with much short story writing, and in particular with a disruptive text like 'The Balloon'. They argue that, first, minor literature turns against established or traditional principles and forms, using a 'withered vocabulary, an incorrect syntax'. Secondly, it places individuals in political situations rather than, as major literature does, examining the relationships between individuals. Lastly, minor literature furnishes a platform for a new conception of community: takes on a collective value.[16]

The junior status, in terms of genre, that the short story inherits makes it eminently suitable for the expressions of minor literature. However, minor literature is not itself generic but is writing that subverts major literature from within, which is what Barthelme does repeatedly with the short story by eschewing the pre-existing models of the 'slice of life' or 'moment in time' templates, compounded by his toying with both typography and story. Also, Deleuze and Guattari aver that '[T]he first characteristic of minor literature in any case is that in it language is affected with a high coefficient of deterritorialisation.'[17] Everything in Barthelme's story spreads – language, meaning, desire – resisting containment as the narrator inflates, or perhaps tumesces, a balloon spontaneously in response to a lover's absence. The most fundamental slippage and spillage, however, is beyond the boundaries of form as the 'story' transgresses its generic parameters.

At the close of her book on Deleuze, Claire Colebrook says that '[T]he challenge of "Deleuzism" is not to repeat what Deleuze *said* but to look at literature as productive of new ways of saying and seeing'; and this has to be how a concept like the rhizome is best applied to literature, seeing in a story a web of alternative readings and oppositional practices.[18]

A final paragraph here might suggest a different way of looking at 'The Balloon'. The narrator claims the balloon as a personal expression or manifestation of private emotion reminiscent of Wordsworth's view of a poem as a 'spontaneous overflow of powerful feelings', but this need not be considered to resolve the matter in terms of text or world. Barthelme is merely introducing the perspective of authorial intention, which ascribes one individual private meaning to an artwork that has become a public text. The balloon may also be a metaphor for the world (in which the positing of a creator provides one approach to meaning) and for its contemporary operation. Arjun Appadurai describes the global community in this way: 'The world we live in now seems rhizomic, even schizophrenic, calling for theories of rootlessness, alienation and psychological distance between individuals and groups.'[19] This provides one further perspective on 'The Balloon' as a story concerned with the movements, meanings and flows of culture and capital where multiple viewpoints understand the world in vastly different ways. The balloon expands over the cityscape like the economic and informational flows of capitalism and globalisation, spreading in multiple directions and meeting with divergent understandings and local uses, connecting people in terms of its reach and spread, but meeting with reactions of alienation and perplexity as it extends over every aspect of people's lives.

REFERENCES AND BIBLIOGRAPHY

Appadurai, Arjun, 'Disjuncture and Difference in the Global Cultural Economy,' in Patrick Williams and Laura Chrisman (eds), *Colonial Discourse and Post-Colonial Theory*, Hemel Hempstead: Harvester, 1993, pp. 324–39.
Barthelme, Donald, 'The Balloon,' in *Sixty Stories*, London: Minerva, 1991, pp. 53–8.
Best, Steven and Douglas Kellner, *Postmodern Theory: Critical Investigations*, Basingstoke: Macmillan, 1991.
Colebrook, Claire, *Gilles Deleuze*, London: Routledge, 2002.
Deleuze, Gilles and Félix Guattari, *Kafka: Toward a Minor Literature*, trans. Dana Polan, London: University of Minnesota Press, 1986.
Deleuze, Gilles and Félix Guattari, *A Thousand Plateaus*, trans. Brian Massumi, London: Athlone, 1988.
Head, Dominic, *The Modernist Short Story*, Cambridge: Cambridge University Press, 1992.
Lucy, Niall, *Postmodern Literary Theory*, Oxford: Blackwell, 1997.
May, Charles E., *The Short Story: The Reality of Artifice*, London: Routledge, 2002.

NOTES

1. Barthelme, p. 57. The opening paragraphs of the story are also reprinted at http://www.eskimo.com/%7Ejassamyn/barth.
2. Deleuze and Guattari, 1988, p. 204.
3. In the twenty-first century, with the continued rise of the novel's comparative popularity, the short story is thought to be under threat. See http://www.saveourshortstory.org.uk/ (accessed 4 Aug. 2005).
4. Ambrose Bierce, *The Devil's Dictionary*, London: Folio, 2004, pp. 217–18.
5. Of particular importance is Poe's review of Hawthorne's *Twice-Told Tales* in which he makes a series of points about the nature of 'the brief prose tale'.
6. In this sense, advertisements and poster campaigns have parallels with all uses of language as each one allocates subject-positions that the individual is asked to slot herself or himself into: '*You* need this product' or '*Your* country/church/party/ family/school needs *you!*'
7. Constantin Brancusi, Romanian abstract sculptor, 1876–1957.
8. Lucy, p. 195.
9. Ibid., p. 186.
10. Deleuze and Guattari, 1988, p. 21.
11. Best and Kellner, p. 103.
12. Quoted in Lucy, p. 186.
13. Colebrook, p. 145.
14. Lucy, p. 200.
15. Deleuze and Guattari, 1988, pp. 7–12.
16. Deleuze and Guattari, 1986, pp. 15–16.
17. Ibid., p. 16.
18. Colebrook, p. 151.
19. Appadurai, p. 325. For a discussion of globalisation see Chapter 15.

CHAPTER 3

LYRIC: 'WHERE'S MY SNARE?':
EMINEM AND SYLVIA PLATH

Approach: Psychoanalytic Criticism

Released on 16 September 2002, Eminem's song 'Cleanin' Out My Closet' signals itself as a child's rebellion in its title by alluding to the common parental demand to clean up private space in the family home and using this as a metaphor for emotionally and mentally exorcising past traumas inflicted by the parent.[1] Presented as an image of the repository for the clutter and 'skeletons' of the past, the closet is also both the psyche of the singer and a representation of the child's space in relation to the mother, ultimately the womb.[2]

In Ian McEwan's Kafkaesque short story 'Conversations with a Cupboard Man' in *First Love, Last Rites* (1975), the narrative stages a monologue delivered to a social worker by a man who repeatedly shuts himself in a cupboard to escape the world. One of the first things the narrator says is: 'I never saw my father because he died before I was born. I think problems started right there – it was my mother who brought me up and no one else . . . She was twisted up, you know, that's where I got it from.'[3] The cupboard man says he has never learned to be an adult, that his mother infantilised him and was obsessed with him remaining a child, 'busy trying to push me back up her womb' until he was 17: 'That's why I spit on the memory of my mother because she made me this way.'[4] When his mother then marries the cupboard man feels neglected and leaves for an institution, until he is 21, where he tells the social worker he painted a picture of his mother: 'I made large red mouths all over the paper – that was her lipstick – and in the mouths I painted it black. That was because I hated her. Though I didn't really.'[5] After leaving the home, the narrator is abused at work, leaves and takes to stealing, for which he is imprisoned. Now, released from jail:

> I want to be contained. I want to be small . . . I go in [that cupboard], I lock the door behind me and sit in the darkness for hours . . . I envy these babies I see in the street being bundled and carried about by their mothers . . . I want to be one year old again. But it won't happen. I know it won't.[6]

In addition to elements of violence and maltreatment, McEwan's story and Eminem's song have similarities of abandonment by the father and ambivalence towards the mother, whom the child hates and loves, resents and implores, loathes and desires. Above all, each text suggests the importance of the speaker's relationship with the mother, in the significance attaching to the womb-like closet/cupboard. In the second verse of the song, Eminem sings 'I got some skeletons in my closet' which he wants to expose, 'before they thrown me inside my coffin and close it', thus completing the womb-to-womb imagery that, by the association of death and birth, takes him back to the first year of his life: 'I'll take you back to '73 . . . I was a baby, maybe I was just a couple of months', when his father left home: 'I just fuckin wished he would die.' The use of the past tense ('wished') associates a desire for the death of the father with a very early childhood wish, an Oedipal desire. Eminem then avers that he would never leave his own child, even if he hated his wife – a significant comment because the lyric is a song of hatred against his mother: his father's wife. This is asserted in distinction from his own father and is underlined by the reference to recent events in Eminem's life when in response to his wife's infidelity he chose violence over desertion: 'What I did was stupid, no doubt it was dumb, But the smartest shit I did was take them bullets outta that gun, 'Cuz I'da killed em; shit I woulda shot Kim and them both.'[7] Notably, the assertion that he will not leave his child does not mean Eminem will not leave his wife, which in turn could mean that he is not allowed to see his child by a court (especially given the intimations of violence and the possibility of murder suggested by the song). The implication, by the direct juxtaposition and implied comparison, is that his father should have left his wife, Eminem's mother, but not the child, Eminem.

The lyric is in large measure a denunciation of Eminem's mother Debbie Mathers-Briggs, who had recorded a rap CD entitled 'Why Are You Doing Me Like You Are' to tell her side of the story of their dispute in Eminem's medium. She explained in interviews that she had sued her son on advice from her lawyer (she eventually was awarded $1,600), because Eminem needed to understand the seriousness of his actions when he spoke publicly against her. As noted in the song, his mother herself has been accused of suffering from Munchausen's syndrome: harming her children to gain attention for herself (by contrast, Eminem says, 'I would never diss my own momma just to get recognition'). In 1996 Mathers-Briggs was taken to court by school officials for allegedly abusing Eminem's half-brother Nathan. She later pleaded 'no contest' to reduced charges.[8]

Though Eminem in the song says that he would not leave his own child the way that his father left him, there is a parallel and a displacement involved here. The person he would abandon is his mother, and in this abandonment he, the father, would also take away her granddaughter. Though the specific action of his father, abandoning his child, is vehemently refused, the general action of rejecting family members (as long as they are adults) is accepted.[9] Indeed

Eminem re-enacts one behavioural aspect of the father from whom he asserts his difference by repudiating his mother – the woman his father deserted. Also, his rejection of his mother is portrayed in terms of completing and healing the pain caused by the father's abandonment of *him*.

Eminem had earlier acted in a similar way – making private matters public before they were known privately – by taking his daughter from her mother to the recording studio to contribute some vocals to a song aimed against Eminem's wife. Which is to say that as much as a response to his mother's actions, the recording of the song acts like a snare: a device that traps or entangles someone unawares. A snare is itself a double-sided device in its operation: it both attacks and holds, harms and domesticates the other. So, Eminem's reference to the snare drum at the start of the song illuminates his intentions towards his mother,[10] to catch her out and cause harm but also to exercise control and stop her fleeing (Eminem muses as the song begins: 'Where's my snare? I have no snare in my headphones – there you go. Yeah . . . yo, yo').

Music lyrics are not the same as poetry; but this is a statement that is worth examining. Before the novelist Giles Foden compared Eminem to Robert Browning in 2001,[11] a debate in the 1980s concerned the relative merits of the lyrics of Bob Dylan and the poetry of John Keats – an ultimately futile discussion inasmuch as Dylan's lyrics are specifically written to accompany music and Keats's poetry is not. They are thus different art forms and comparing them in certain respects is little more edifying than comparing a novel and a film. However, in other respects, comparisons may be profitable, for example with regard to theme, intertextuality and uses of language such as rhyme and enjambement. A lyric can be considered separately from the music it accompanies in a performance or recording, but to do so is not to discuss the song, it is to discuss the words as a separate text, as critics may do with a playscript in isolation from its dramatic performance(s).

His stage name being itself a pseudonym taken from the initials of his real name Marshall Mathers, Eminem's earlier lyrics adopted personae, most obviously Slim Shady, the alter ego on his first album. 'The Eminem Show', the title of his third album, is mentioned in 'Cleanin Out My Closet' to reference the way in which a life in the glare of publicity is a life lived publicly, permanently on show. Yet, 'Cleanin Out My Closet' appears to have little or no assumed identity – it is as close to an uncensored lyric of self-expression as poems by Wordsworth or Heaney. The chorus's repeated assertion of self through the repetition of 'I' at the start of every line emphasises the aspect of confession. The lines of the lyric are self-reflexive to the extent that they argue the singer would not launch a tirade against his mother in public 'just to get recognition', while implying that this is precisely what she did in relation to her son. The lyric is also repeatedly ambiguous in terms of its use of the second person, and shifts its apparent address in each of the first and third verses. Listeners are liable to believe that they are being addressed by such lines as 'Have you ever been hated or discriminated against?' or 'put yourself in my position', but by the end of each of these verses the lines are being addressed directly to the singer's mother. The second verse is also ambiguous when it declares 'I'll take you back to '73', while there seems to be a direct statement to the audience in the line, 'I'd like to welcome y'all to "The Eminem Show" ', though this may be rhetoric or a simple idiomatic expression rather than an address to the listener.

Either way it is read, this final line is a reference to modern-day TV culture and the ways in which celebrities' lives are not just performed but constructed in public, though it may also allude to confessional talk shows like those hosted by Oprah Winfrey and Jerry Springer. Indebted to the spiritual and the confession, the contemporary music lyric frequently offers to reveal, to declare and to testify. In doing so, once the artist has become famous, it often critiques or promises exposure of the celebrity. As Mick Jagger sings on 'It's Only Rock n Roll' (1974):

> If I could stick a knife in my heart
> Suicide right on stage
> Would it be enough for your teenage lust
> Would it help to ease the pain? . . .
> If I could dig down deep in my heart
> Feelings would flood on the page
> Would it satisfy ya . . .

Such a lyric acknowledges the messianic aspect to rock musicians' personae but also the psychical investments fan(atic)s have in the emotional revelations of performers, which can be expressed in terms of a desire for physical, even visceral exposure. As Jacques Lacan argues, the motivation behind the voyeur's 'passive' act is to see everything because of the sense that something is always hidden.[12] There is no end to the striptease until the stripper is stripped of everything and nothing remains to be revealed – all that remains is no-body. This is echoed in the video accompanying Robbie Williams's song 'Rock DJ' (2001) in which, standing in the centre of a recording studio that has become a miniature roller-skate rink, he tears off his clothes and then his flesh to throw to the women circling him – until he is only a skeleton. The fan's or the media's desire for (the possession of) celebrities is an aggressive act that wishes to tear away layers to reveal what is(n't) hidden. To an extent, critical analysis is characterised by a similar desire for revelation.

While acknowledging the formal difference between poetry and music lyrics, from a literary perspective it is worth considering how 'Cleanin' Out My Closet' has several facets in common thematically with a poem that has undergone considerable critical analysis: Sylvia Plath's 'Daddy'. In her guise as confessional poet, Plath has had some direct and indirect influence on popular music. For example, a closer immediate comparison for Plath's poem would be Madonna's song 'Oh Father' from her album *Like a Prayer*. Madonna has named Plath, whom she read as a teenager, as one of her inspirations, and in some respects the lyrics to her song bear direct comparison with 'Daddy'.[13]

This is also true of 'Daddy' and 'Cleanin' Out My closet'. For example, in addition to the sustained address to the parents, there are the profane, vituperative attacks: 'You selfish bitch; I hope you fuckin burn in hell for this shit' (Eminem) and 'Daddy, I have had to kill you . . . Daddy, daddy, you bastard, I'm through' (Plath). Plath has said that 'Daddy' is about a girl with an Elektra complex and it would be possible to read Eminem's lyric as Oedipal in its wish to kill the father as well as control the mother as a ' "motherfuckin" kid'. Given that he was raised without a father at home, his mother also occupies a double position as both parents simultaneously.

Points of comparison between Plath's poem and Eminem's lyric must also include the way in which they are principally interested in matters of psychical transference and performance: in both poem and lyric we find the appeal of confessional texts that engage the listener by seeming to offer understanding and catharsis.[14] The following two observations are drawn from Anne Stevenson's critical biography of Plath:

> 'Daddy' operates by generating a duplicate of Plath's presumed psychic state in the reader, so that we reexperience her grief, rage, masochism and revenge, whether or not these fit the 'facts'.[15]

> Anyone who has heard the recording of 'Daddy' that Sylvia made for the British Council that October will remember the shock of pure fury in her articulation, the smouldering rage with which she is declaring herself free . . . The implication is that after this exorcism her life can begin again, that she will be reborn.[16]

In the last four stanzas of the poem, like Eminem's equal disgust at his mother and his wife, Plath shifts her venom towards her husband, whom she sees as 'a model' of her father: 'A man in black with a Meinkampf look'. Similarly, Eminem sees his wife as an image of his mother, and his daughter as a representation of himself when a child. This is the child (his daughter and his young self) he wants to protect, while he vows he will refuse the male parental role model with which he has grown up (all of the lyric pitches good children against bad parents, in which Eminem sees himself as one of the former determined not to become one of the latter)[17]. This intimates how the family triad creates a template for the child's adult relationship. Plath is explicit about this, as she seeks replication of the father while rejecting childhood relationships, and Eminem creates the paradox in which he can declare 'I'm not sick' while claiming he is reflecting society's sickness, thus projecting his 'badness' onto society in order to see his actions as a symptom of that society.

Elizabeth Bronfen notes that Plath's poem deals with familiar childhood fantasies, embracing the parental loss that denies a traditional happy family. Like Eminem, she seeks to become self-sufficient through self-assertion:

> As she declares 'Daddy, daddy, you bastard, I'm through,' she embarks upon yet another family romance, the fantasy of the orphan, no longer

suffering from the reminiscence of a lost seaside childhood and its parental representative but rather fully innocent of the traces of the past – indeed so self-reliant is this utter dislocation from any family root as not to need any paternal addressee at all.[18]

This is similar to the ambiguity of address in Eminem's lyric, in which he also strives for a transcendent position free from both the parent and the past. Where Eminem differs from Plath, however, is in deciding, in the last line, to stage his death rhetorically to a living parent, rather than bury a dead one ('I am dead – dead to you as can be'). In both texts, however, death is not an emotional release; instead the speakers endeavour to persuade themselves of a psychical ending by declaring and asserting the finality of death. In their different ways both texts insist upon a final breaking free from the parent. In 'Daddy', Plath asserts that she has finally killed in her psyche the father who died when she was a girl ('You do not do, you do not do / Any more, black shoe / In which I have lived like a foot / For thirty years, poor and white'). Eminem's lyric also aims to expunge once and for all the negative influence of a parent on the eve of his 30th birthday.[19]

In terms of affect, what the poem and the lyric have in common is rage (and this is not just from the speakers, for example, 'emotions run deep as ocean's exploding/Tempers flarin from parents'). In Eminem's lyric this is most strongly expressed in terms of death. Aside from explaining that he would have killed his wife Kim and her lover if he had had bullets in a gun he was carrying, Eminem's lyric envisages his mother's funeral, states a wish that his father was dead (echoed in the mother who 'wished' Eminem had died), and declares himself dead to his mother. These are aspects of the act of 'cleaning out my closet': expelling the skeletons of the 'dead', expressing the mind's aggression to clean it out, and projecting the bad parts of the self onto the mother.

Melanie Klein explains this in terms of object-relations theory in which the infant develops through the psychic interaction between external and internal (mental) objects and in which relationships with important objects (of which the most important is the mother) contain a mixture of love and hate.[20] In this psychodynamic view, the infant's ego-development requires defences such as splitting the object and creative/destructive impulses, idealisation, introjection and projection, and the denial of inner and outer reality. Klein says that projection is used as an ego defence-mechanism and it originates from the deflection of the death instinct outwards.[21] Here, whereby the bad parts of the ego are split off and projected into the mother, the mother is felt to be the bad self:

> Much of the hatred against parts of the self is now directed towards the mother. This leads to a particular form of identification which establishes the prototype of an aggressive object relation. I suggest for these processes the term 'projective identification'. When projection is mainly derived from the infant's impulse to harm or to control the mother, he feels her to

be a persecutor. In psychotic disorders this identification of an object with the hated parts of the self contributes to the intensity of the hatred directed against other people.[22]

Aspects of this view are present in Eminem's lyric, not least in the aggressive portrayal of his mother as the one who should be hated, not himself. The verses also shift between Eminem's position as someone who is 'hated', 'discriminated against', 'protested and demonstrated against' to someone who hates: 'give 'em hell long as I'm breathin'. However, the climax of the song is a specific attack on the mother who is seen as the bad object trying to portray herself as the good: 'See what hurts me the most is you won't admit you was wrong/Bitch do your song – keep tellin yourself that you was a mom!' In terms of the psychical development of the child, early feelings of overpowering rage aimed at not just the physical mother but also her internalised image make it impossible for the child to synthesise 'good' and 'bad' parental images. Thus, for Eminem the split occurs between the 'good' parent (here seemingly a role taken by himself in relation to his daughter) and the 'bad' parent, his mother.

Lastly, if one were to look at the lyric differently, it might be said that Eminem's song foregrounds a disturbing portrayal of a contemporary Western crisis of masculinity in its indirect attack on not mothers but husbands and fathers. Both the singer and his father are portrayed as delinquent: the father through abandonment, the singer through violence and armed assault. Yet Eminem is content to blame his behaviour on his environment: on his parents and society more generally – he sees himself as a sign of the times. It is also clear that the racial politics of contemporary music involves broader questions of collective identity running alongside personal, psychological factors. In the chapter on Michael Jackson, that singer's complex relationship to chromatism was broached, but the elements of passing, mimicry and cultural appropriation operate in many directions. In some profiles of Jackson, the singer is considered to be a black man who wishes to be white, yet the history of postwar mainstream white popular music is frequently characterised in terms of the appropriation of black musical forms. The most recent of these are rap and hip-hop, black street styles that have entered the mainstream after and perhaps only through the fame of Eminem, the first global rap superstar because the first significantly successful white rapper.[23]

REFERENCES AND BIBLIOGRAPHY

Bronfen, Elisabeth, *Sylvia Plath*, Plymouth: Northcote House, 1998.

Klein, Melanie, 'Notes on Some Schizoid Mechanisms', in Paul Du Gay, Jessica Evans and Peter Redman (eds), *Identity: A Reader*, London: Sage, 2000, pp. 130–143.

Krims, Adam, *Rap Music and the Poetics of Identity*, Cambridge: Cambridge University Press, 2000.

McEwan, Ian, 'Conversations with a Cupboard Man', in *First Love, Last Rites*, London: Picador, 1976, pp. 75–87.

Stevenson, Anne, *Bitter Fame: A Life of Sylvia Plath*, London: Viking, 1989.
Stubbs, David, *Cleaning Out My Closet*, London: Carlton, 2003.
Thompson, Ben, *Ways of Hearing*, London: Orion, 2001.

NOTES

1. Though also widely reprinted on the web (e.g. see http://www.eminem.net/), the lyrics to all the songs are reproduced in Eminem, *Angry Blonde*, London: Harper Collins, 2002.
2. In terms of its relation to his life, Eminem uses the song as a way to catch his mother unawares through an attack that will be made publicly before it is known privately. His third album, on which the song appears, is a confessional one in which he places his public identity, 'Eminem', at the centre of the lyrics. This device itself appears as an extended response to his mother's record, in which she took up his medium to speak to him, by using a song to frame a response to her song – setting up a call and response.
3. McEwan, p. 75.
4. Ibid., p. 76.
5. Ibid., p. 79
6. Ibid., pp. 86–7.
7. Eminem started going out with his future wife Kim when she was 12 and he was 15. Their daughter Hailie was born in 1996. They married in June 1999 and were divorced in October 2001. In June 2000, Eminem had been arrested twice in one weekend for carrying a concealed weapon, the first time in a dispute with one of his entourage, the second when he discovered his wife kissing another man. Eminem might have been sent to jail but was eventually given a suspended sentence for assault and carrying an unlicensed gun. His wife, who became involved in both incidents, was fined and ordered to attend Alcoholics Anonymous.
8. Evident in the song and reported by Stubbs, when her much younger brother Ronnie had committed suicide, Mathers-Briggs had supposedly told her son that she wished he had been the one who died. Ronnie was roughly the same age as Eminem and introduced him to hip hop.
9. Eminem's father left when he was a baby. A poor, minority white child in Detroit's violent neighbourhoods, Eminem's real name is Marshall Bruce Mathers III. In his early childhood, Eminem and his mother moved from city to city, rarely staying more than a few months in one place before they settled in Detroit. An attack in Detroit, when he was aged 10, left him in coma. According to David Stubbs, Eminem at this time perceived his mother as contributory to the family's problems:

   > As for her paranoia, Mrs Mathers-Briggs was, it seems, constantly involved in ructions with her neighbours, one of whom, according to school officials, she accused of killing her dog in a satanic ritual. She also suggested that her house was being monitored by video cameras and that an un-named enemy had sent her a tarantula in the mail. Police from St Clair Shores confirmed that she often called them out on what turned out to be unsubstantiated complaints against her neighbours. (Stubbs, p. 102)

10. Eminem is ostensibly talking to the drum programmer in the studio, DJ Head.
11. Giles Foden, 'Just how good is he?', *The Guardian* G2, 5 February, 2001.
12. See Slavoj Žižek, 'Two Ways to Avoid the Real of Desire', in *Looking Awry: An Introduction to Jacques Lacan through Popular Culture*, Cambridge: MIT Press, 1992, pp. 48–66. Cf. Roland Barthes on the 'Striptease': 'Striptease is based on a contradiction: Woman is desexualized at the very moment when she is stripped naked', *Mythologies*, trans. Annette Lavers, Hill and Wang: New York, 1984. Available on-line at http://xroads.virginia.edu/~DRBR/strip.html (accessed 10 Aug. 2005).

13. From Madonna's 'Oh Father': 'I got away from you, I never thought I would/You can't make me cry, you once had the power . . . Seems like yesterday/I lay down next to your boots and I prayed/For your anger to end.'

14. This is itself expressed in Roberta Flack's song about seeing Kris Kristofferson perform: 'Strumming my pain with his fingers/Singing my life with his words' ('Killing Me Softly'). As suggested by the title, this can be felt to be an extremely intense emotional experience, bonding singer and listener, though the experience is an internal one for the listener, and so can only be communicated back to the singer. This can lead to identifications of the kind explored in Eminem's own song about fans who over-invest in their identification with him: 'Stan'.

15. Quoted in Stevenson, p. 265.

16. Ibid. Otto Plath died from a diabetes-related illness when Plath was still a girl.

17. In accordance with his desire to be the 'good' father, and in line with his lyric's claim that he would wish to be with his child's mother, in January 2006 Eminem remarried Kim, stating that he wished to build a stable home for Hailie, his niece Alaina and his stepdaughter Whitney.

18. Bronfen, p. 84.

19. Eminem was born in October 1972.

20. Object-relations theory is a strand of post-Freudian psychoanalysis that focuses particularly on the relation between mother and child. Taking her term from Freud, Melanie Klein arrived through extensive work with children at her theory of the good and bad 'object', the first of which encountered by the infant being the breast. The breast is alternatively seen as giver and denier of food and so split between good and bad object. Subsequent to this, the child projects onto the mother (and then other objects) this ambivalent love (like that for the 'good' breast) and hate (for the 'bad'), which are at root expressions of the life and death drives. Successful child development is characterised by the integration or synthesis of the good and bad objects into one.

21. Klein, p. 133.

22. Ibid., p. 135.

23. See Bakari Kitwana, *Why White Kids Love Hip Hop: Wankstas, Wiggas, Wannabes, and the New Reality of Race in America*, Civitas Books: 2005.

CHAPTER 4

AUTOBIOGRAPHY: MARTIN AMIS'S *EXPERIENCE*

Approach: Self-Life-Writing

[W]e assume that life *produces* the autobiography as an act produces its consequences, but can we not suggest, with equal justice, that the autobiographical project may itself produce and determine the life. (Paul de Man)[1]

[E]ach new attempt at autobiography will tell a different story since the story has changed in the course of its telling and as a result of it. (Brian Finney)[2]

The study of autobiography has been resurgent in recent decades, and the genre is now often discussed by historians, literary critics and others alongside biographies, memoirs, letters, diaries and reminiscences – as well as works more conventionally considered 'history' or 'fiction' – under the banner of life writing (the term 'self-life-writing' is Avrom Fleishman's). One reason for this is the rise of interdisciplinary areas of study that have found autobiography to be a particularly useful form of writing, and so have accorded it a distinctive place in the study of both authenticity and alterity. In the 1970s, women's studies, American studies, ethnic and black studies all started to turn to autobiography for voices of 'experience' from within, as James Olney sees it.[3] Or, as Martin Amis puts it in his own *Experience*:

> [W]hat everyone has in them, these days, is not a novel but a memoir. We live in an age of mass loquacity. We are all writing it or at any rate talking it: the memoir, the apologia, the c.v., the *cri de Coeur*. Nothing, for now, can compete with experience – so unanswerably authentic, and so liberally and democratically dispensed.[4]

Couser and Fichtelberg decide: 'It is the claim that my past matters, my history has meaning, that still distinguishes autobiography as a mode of truth.'[5]

Yet, this is at odds with the view expressed by Brian Finney and also Amis about the literary worth of autobiography, emphasising the different values, ethical or aesthetic, that may be placed on self-life-writing. Finney in 1985 lamented the fact that there had been no literary study of 'English' autobiography. In correcting that, he concluded that 'successful autobiographies' depend more on their literary quality than on the incidents in the life story.[6] Similarly, for Amis the problem with autobiography is its subject's artlessness:

> The trouble with life (the novelist will feel) is its amorphousness, its ridiculous fluidity. Look at it: thinly plotted, largely themeless, sentimental and ineluctably trite. The dialogue is poor, or at least violently uneven. The twists are either predictable or sensationalist. And it's always the same beginning; and the same ending.[7]

In line with this, from a literary historical perspective in 1968, Stephen Shapiro explains the chief reason why he thought the stock of autobiographies had fallen in the mid-twentieth century:

> I suspect that critics of literature avoid autobiography, despite its distinguished tradition and undeniable importance to readers, because, like their colleagues in philosophy and the social sciences, literary critics are indulging in the currently prestigious 'professional' scorn for merely human problems, preferring to research the mysteries of methodology.[8]

Thus the critical concerns of New Criticism and formalism seemed to relegate the autobiography to the margins of literary criticism, from where it has been rescued by phenomenology, feminism, postcolonialism, New Historicism, and (post) structuralism. The last, and in particular the essays 'The Death of the Author' (1968) by Roland Barthes, mentioned in the Introduction, and 'What is an Author?' (1969) by Michel Foucault, took discussion in a significantly new direction by declaring 'the author' not a unified subject and source of meaning but a functional construct, an effect of the text rather than the anterior referential self that previous critics had taken it to be.

One way of dealing with this knot of self-referentiality is to cut it. Paul Ricoeur, in his books *The Rule of Metaphor* and *Time and Narrative* considers human experience primarily to have a pre-narrative quality. Which is to say that life is nothing more nor less than a biological phenomenon until it is interpreted, made into narrative and configured rather than represented. So, autobiography, like all narrative, is not referential (except to time for Ricoeur) and does not describe a prior life of the author, having only the world of the text as its reference. Autobiography does not put the story of a life into words but creates a life story.

Martin Amis's autobiography *Experience* was published in 2000. The book is in two parts, with a postscript, an appendix and an addendum; it is also interspersed with contemporaneous letters. Amis's book is particularly interesting for its use of 'timebends', in Arthur Miller's phrase,[9] its copious footnotes, and its self-conscious portrayal of Oedipal conflict. It is also, as the above might suggest, notable for portraying the development of a writer rather than fashioning a portrait of either an individual or an individual life.[10]

Experience begins with Amis's 'Dad', and Part One, entitled 'Unawakened', to an extent concerns Amis's emergence from his father Kingsley's shadow.[11] The first chapter is called 'Introductory: My Missing' and recalls Kingsley Amis and Lucy Partington, but also Delilah Seale, Amis's daughter raised by another family. The three chapters of the much shorter Part Two of the book, 'The Main Events', return to Delilah Seale and Kingsley Amis, and specifically to Amis's reacquaintance with the former when she was 18, in 1995, and the death of the latter in the same year. The book in some ways organises itself as a reinscription of these 'missing' around the author, and so seems to be a coming-to-terms with past loss. An ethical issue that arose in Amis's writing of *Experience* was his portrayal of his relationship with Lucy Partington, who disappeared in 1973 and was discovered two decades later to have been one of the serial-murderer Fred West's victims when her body was exhumed from his garden. The general question here concerns the autobiographer's obligation to others who appear in his or her life-story, particularly those unable to speak for or represent themselves.[12] As G. Thomas Couser notes, it 'is now a critical commonplace that all *auto*biography is necessarily *hetero*biography as well because one can rarely if ever represent one's self without representing others . . . Where does the right to express and represent oneself begin to infringe on another's right to privacy?'[13]

The index of an autobiography, if present, can also be of interest because of what it signals about the author's self-presentation or self-narrativisation. In the case of *Experience* the index is almost exclusively composed of the names of people and places. Under Amis's own entry, divided into two parts, one for the life and one for the works, there is a list of events, such as 'marriage to Antonia Phillips', and place references, such as 'in Chicago'. Under his father's entry, also divided into the life and the works, there is a slightly richer flavour of references as it includes such subjects as 'ageing process, and gaining weight' and 'phobias of'. Though mention is made of 'education' and 'first love', the nearest subjects to these in Martin Amis's own entry is the sore subject of 'dental problems'.

Amis constructs himself as a writer rather than a character because that is the reason for interest in his autobiography, but also partly because he is a particular kind of novelist, one that has little interest in the traditional concept of characters. As Laura Marcus explains: 'Cultural postmodernism, while endorsing fictionalism and conventionalism, has to an extent relativised the sphere of the "literary" and thus troubled the concept of literary identity.'[14] This is as much a comment on the form and focus of autobiography as of fiction because it raises the question of the degree to which literary autobiography's model is the introspective novel or (in the case of an artist) the *Künstlerroman*, as contended in such works as Northrop Frye's *Anatomy of Criticism* (1957) and

Robert Kellogg and Robert Scholes's *The Nature of Narrative* (1966). For example, Marcus writes of Wayne Shumaker's *English Autobiography: Its Emergence, Materials and Forms* (1954):

> Subjective autobiography, Shumaker asserts, finds its apotheosis in novelised form. Modern autobiography emerged alongside, although independently of, the eighteenth-century novel, but its development from the late eighteenth century onwards involved a borrowing of novelistic techniques. In the nineteenth century, subjective autobiography became primarily concerned with charting psychic and intellectual development; the philosophical determinism and naturalistic accounts of individuality and society underlying the autobiographies of the period are also locatable.[15]

In the modernist writing of the early twentieth century this develops into the fictionalised autobiographies of D. H. Lawrence's *Sons and Lovers* (1913) or James Joyce's *A Portrait of the Artist as a Young Man* (1916) (see Nalbantian for a discussion of modernist self-fictionalisation). Such a perspective develops a hierarchical and developmental view of literary history in which the introspective literary autobiography succeeds the less self-reflective memoirs, diary-entries, reminiscences and anecdotal forms of earlier models.

However, for all its experimental and fragmented presentation of the individual, modernism adheres to the principle of individual identity wrapped up with the life coherently narrated, as Pierre Bourdieu writes:

> To produce a life history or to consider life as a history, that is, as a coherent narrative of a significant and directed sequence of events, is perhaps to conform to a rhetorical illusion, to the common representation of existence that a whole literary tradition has always and still continues to reinforce.[16]

From a postmodernist perspective, identity is alternatively 'a signifying practice, infinitely variable not only because experience is variable but because language is composed of "plural" discourses'.[17] Additionally, the autobiographer is inevitably a split subject, divided between the self writing in the present and the past self being written, the effect of which is similar to the conceit of a first-person novel such as *Great Expectations* in which Pip is simultaneously narrating voice and narrated protagonist: the same person but also quite different 'characters'. There is additionally a temporal rupture in the autobiographical text as the speaking subject narrates a past spoken subject from a continuous present. For Couser and Fichtelberg, this suggests that autobiographical practice is a convergence of dismemberment and re-membering:

> As a figure for the autobiographical act, dismemberment suggests the autobiographer's radical separation from the dead selves borne down by time . . . he or she is forced to construct the text from the fragments so characteristic of postmodern experience and yet to proclaim that experience unified.[18]

That construction of a unity from fragments is achieved through re-membering, the assertion of wholeness implicit in the recounting of *a* life: one that is particular and deeply personal. Playing on another important term, this is a process of recollection, bringing together the parts of a self that has been fractured by time.

Most importantly for some, the peculiar claims of autobiography rest on self-knowledge, the willingness with which we invest in the individual a true, deep or intimate knowledge of their own experience, self or life. This is a matter of the relationship between being and knowing, ontology and epistemology: do we know ourselves better or worse than others do, or do we just know ourselves differently? It is primarily a matter of a life seen from the inside or the outside: the biographer can explain how another person lived but cannot describe the inner life: how it felt. Which prompts the further point that biographers and autobiographers usually have different motives for wanting to narrate a life, and the autobiographer's reason may well involve matters of coming to terms with or intervening in the past. Self-life-writing is often as much about feeling as fact, affect as much as effects. In other words, autobiography necessarily concerns the memory and memories of the subject, whereas biography does not, and 'the privileging of memory . . . is haunted by its post-romantic promise of authenticity, community, lived experience and identity.'[19] In contrast to this, a poststructuralist perspective would argue that the subject is not reflected but constructed in the autobiography; there is no self prior to the text, and the author does not express a self through language but is constituted in it. Some recent critics – especially feminists for whom life-writing is of particular importance for documenting the lives of (particularly working-class) women – have also interrogated the divide between autobiography and biography, arguing on the one hand that the autobiographer usually also writes about the lives of others (an allography, like Kingsley Amis's *Memoirs* (1991)) and on the other hand that the biographer must write about the self, not least because of a probable sense of identification with the subject.[20]

However, the subject of autobiography for some critics is arguably not an 'I' of any kind but the proper name of the writer, which is the autobiographer's 'marker of personal or authorial identity'.[21] For Philippe Lejeune, while the first person pronoun is a shifting signifier employed by nearly all autobiographers, the proper name of the subject is the basis of the 'contract of identity' between author and reader as well as a matter of self-identification for the writer, comparable to the Lacanian mirror stage, when the child perceives and so apprehends a difference between itself and everything else.[22] The mirror stage involves an act of misrecognition rather than recognition and the act of autobiography also may inevitably participate in a misrecognition of the self. This can be for conscious reasons of self-presentation, but there are also unconscious reasons, to do with psychic self-defence, narcissism and, in Freud's second model of the mind, the pressures of the superego and id on the ego. This does not lessen the interest of autobiographies but throws into a different light the truth-claims made on their behalf individually or as a genre.

For Lejeune, (auto)biography remains a distinct genre because the pact or contract entered into by author and reader includes the stipulation that the events and information are actual rather than just life-like or probable. However, for other critics it is questionable whether autobiography can be understood in generic terms. For example, Paul de Man argues that writing the self should be understood in terms of rhetorical and tropological structures because genre criticism seems merely to point up the fact that almost every autobiography is an exception to the norm.[23] For de Man 'autobiography' is 'a figure of reading and understanding' that works across the categorisations of 'genre': whenever authors use themselves in their understanding they are writing autobiographically. But to write about the self is also to disfigure it as the inscription of the self in writing has to be through linguistic figures and metaphors: autobiographical writing results not in self-knowledge or -disclosure but in a kind of tropical personification of a past (de Man would say 'dead') self that both produces and de-faces the subject in writing.

The arguments of historians such as Hayden White also question traditional divisions between texts concerned with 'fact' or 'fiction'. Unlike those of the sciences, the writings of fiction, history and (auto)biography are all narrative-based, and are all 'verbal fictions' in that they are all (not 'found' but) structured, selected, invented and shot through with kinds of literariness, such as metaphor, allusion and juxtaposition. This arguably outweighs in importance the degrees of 'referentiality' that supposedly distinguishes genres like history, fiction and biography.

However, a complete resistance to notions of genre runs the risk of misunderstanding the significance of generic modes, which may importantly impinge on writers' constructions of narrative as much as deflect critics from cross-generic aspects that are shared by all 'verbal fictions'. Turning back to Amis's *Experience*, we find that the dustjacket describes the book as a 'memoir' and a 'remarkable work of autobiography'. The traditional distinction between these two genres has been that the former offers anecdotal accounts of people and their actions while the latter is the drawing of a life as a whole. Though the term was only coined in the early nineteenth century, the model for autobiography is often taken to be Augustine's *Confessions* (c. AD 400), creating an expectation that such a work will be characterised by time, memory, reflection, introspection and a frank account of the subject's personal and professional life. According to James Olney criticism sees modern autobiography beginning in those 'moments when secular autobiography was slowly developing out of spiritual autobiography and when autobiography as a literary mode was emerging out of autobiography as a confessional mode'.[24] But Olney also points out that the first autobiography could be considered to be Plato's letters, Montaigne's *Essays*, Augustine's or Rousseau's *Confessions*, or, the first publication to use the term, W. P. Scargill's *The Autobiography of a Dissenting Minister* (1834).[25] It is autobiography's blessing and curse that it has few parameters or formal guidelines, only precedents and examples. Many popular autobiographies are written with or even by other people (scribes, ghostwriters, collaborators), while many fictions, from at least *Robinson Crusoe* onwards, are written in the autobiographical vein (all first-person narratives arguably have a family resemblance to autobiography).[26]

That *Experience* is a novelist's self-portrait is important as a life made significant by writing is (re)made in writing. Amis's book is additionally a reflection on his father Kingsley's movement from maturity towards death, an Oedipal story of the son's assumption of the father's familial role but also of his mantle of accomplished or famous novelist. *Experience* is presented at times as Kingsley's thanatography as well as Martin's autobiography – in this, the book has something in common with Carolyn Steedman's innovative autobiography *Landscapes for a Good Woman: A Study of Two Lives* (1986), which examines Steedman's mother's life as much as her own in the context of a wider sociological framework (as Amis uses a context of literary history and influence for his writers' lives). With fiction, the author is expected to use life to inform the artifice of imaginative writing: frequently novels are identified as 'thinly veiled' autobiographical stories. When a novelist turns to autobiography the reader may similarly expect artifice to inform self-life-writing, but may also expect the author's imagination to be put on hold while a recognisable prose-style remains. The novelist is expected to fabricate; the autobiographer is expected not to. The literary autobiography can also be distinguished from other kinds in terms of its reception because the writer is usually someone whose life is primarily valued by others because of their writing, which is often regarded as something apart from 'life' in the sense that it is ostensibly a solitary not a social act. The autobiography of politicians (such as Bill Clinton's) or entrepreneurs (such as Richard Branson's) is of interest to many readers because of the light it throws on their actions, but a writer's autobiography is not necessarily of this kind, as the reader will often be more interested in the subject's creative processes and reflective thoughts, or, as importantly, the (quality of the) writing of the autobiography itself.

Autobiography is a hybrid form of writing that has often been used to question generic boundaries because it both bridges and falls between psychology, history, literature and essay. As a study of the life of a writer (and the death of another), *Experience* contains a significant degree of literary criticism and reflection, accentuated by Amis's inclusion of copious footnotes. These create a sense of commentary and sometimes dialogue *within* the text as Amis's asides introduce a second authorial voice adding details and dimensions to the body of the text. The footnotes are intriguing because they add an extra layer of reflection but also because they are at the borders of the text, arguably a part of it and arguably supplementary to it. It is possible that for the critic, Amis's less-guarded sense of self appears far more in these interruptions, reflections and asides than in the main narrative: for example, the first of them, on the first page, notes that he is one of the dedicatees of his father's 'worst novel', *I Like it Here* (1958). Detailing references, explaining names, offering relevant quotations, Amis's footnotes stretch as far as discussing his editor's queries (p. 87) and fore-grounding the notes' composition after the main text: 'I have since read . . .' (p. 155). Like his own postmodernist fictions, in one of which 'Martin Amis' appears as a character, these footnotes also serve to create different levels from the 'Martin Amis' of the autobiography: the life and person who is the subject of the book, the self-writer composing the narrative, and the self-reader commenting in footnotes: 'I didn't notice, while writing this book (I only noticed while *reading* it . . .)' (p. 5).

According to Roy Pascal, autobiography is subjective writing where attention is focused on the self.[27] I think it is therefore questionable, given this definition, whether much of *Experience* is autobiography by traditional lights. In a commonsensical way the book as a whole undoubtedly is autobiography (and if autobiography is a self-defining genre, as some critics have argued, then the dustjacket resolves the question unequivocally), but the focus of the text is often away from the author to a greater degree than in a poem such as Wordsworth's *The Prelude* or even a novel with its god-like fingernail-paring author such as *A Portrait of the Artist as a Young Man*. It is possible to argue that *Experience* is a book with a missing centre, as the development of Amis as writer or person does not appear to be the focus of the text, which is to say that at this stage of literary history we may no longer want to maintain that literary autobiography need delineate (a) self any more than the novel is limited by the attempt to provide the 'well-rounded' characters of realism, or the introspective subjectivity of modernism.

REFERENCES AND BIBLIOGRAPHY

Amis, Martin, *Experience*, Jonathan Cape: London, 2000.

Anderson, Linda, *Autobiography*, London: Routledge, 2001.

Benveniste, Émile, *Problems in General Linguistics*, Florida: University of Miami Press, 1971.

Bourdieu, Pierre, 'The Biographical Illusion', in Paul du Gay, Jessica Evans and Peter Redman (eds), *Identity: A Reader*, London: Sage, 2000, pp. 297–303.

Couser, G. Thomas, *Vulnerable Subjects: Ethics and Life-Writing*, Ithaca and London: Cornell University Press, 2004.

Couser, G. Thomas, and Joseph Fichtelberg (eds), *True Relations: Essays on Autobiography and the Postmodern*, Westport: Greenwood Press, 1998.

de Man, Paul, 'Autobiography as De-Facement', *The Rhetoric of Romanticism*, New York: Columbia University Press, 1984, pp. 67–82.

Finney, Brian, *The Inner I: British Literary Autobiography of the Twentieth Century*, London: Faber, 1985.

Fleishman, Avrom, *Figures of Autobiography*, Berkeley: University of California Press, 1983.

Huyssen, Andreas, 'Trauma and Memory: A New Imaginary of Temporality', in Jill Bennett and Rosanne Kennedy (eds), *World Memory: Personal Trajectories in Global Time*, London: Palgrave, 2003, pp. 16–29.

Lejeune, Philippe, *Le Pacte Autobiographique*, Paris: Seuil, 1975.

Marcus, Laura, *Auto/Biographical Discourses*, Manchester: Manchester University Press, 1994.

Nalbantian, Suzanne, *Aesthetic Autobiography: From Life to Art in Marcel Proust, James Joyce, Virginia Woolf and Anaïs Nin*, London: Macmillan, 1997.

Olney, James, 'Autobiography and the Cultural Moment', in James Olney (ed.), *Autobiography: Essays Theoretical and Critical*, Princeton: Princeton University Press, 1980, pp. 3–27.

Ricoeur, Paul, *Time and Narrative*, trans. K. McLaughlin and D. Pellaeur, vol. 1, Chicago: University of Chicago Press, 1984.

Ricoeur, Paul, *Oneself as Another*, trans. K. Blamey, Chicago: University of Chicago Press, 1992.

Ricoeur, Paul, *The Rule of Metaphor: The Creation of Meaning in Language*, trans. R. Czerny, London: Routledge, 2003.

Shapiro, Stephen, 'The Dark Continent of Literature: Autobiography', *Comparative Literature Studies 5*, 1968, pp. 421–54.

NOTES

1. de Man, p. 69.
2. Finney, p. 13.
3. Olney, p. 13.
4. Amis, p. 6.
5. Couser and Fichtelberg, p. 3.
6. Finney, pp. 11–12.
7. Amis, p. 7.
8. Shapiro, p. 424.
9. Amis says his organisational principles derive from 'the novelist's addiction to seeing parallels and making connections' (Amis, p. 7).
10. Other writers have been accused of largely leaving themselves out of their own autobiographies. One example is Muriel Spark, whose *Curriculum Vitae* (1992) was criticised for telling too little about her own feelings and thoughts: for being too factual and for placing its focus on the lives surrounding Spark. This raises the question of the subject in both senses: subjectivity and the centre or focus of an autobiography.
11. Kingsley's equivalent to this is the essay 'A Memoir of My Father', in *What Became of Jane Austen? and Other Questions*, London: Panther, 1972, pp. 204–12, in which he says: '[M]y father inevitably failed to turn me into the sort of person he wanted me to be. That sort of person was, of course, a version of himself; a more successful version' (pp. 209–10).
12. Amis was criticised by family members in the press for 'exploiting' Lucy Partington.
13. Couser, p. x.
14. Marcus, p. 239.
15. Ibid., p. 237.
16. Bourdieu, p. 298.
17. Couser and Fichtelberg, p. 2.
18. Ibid., p. 3.
19. Huyssen, p. 17.
20. Marcus, p. 273.
21. See Lejeune, and Marcus, p. 192.
22. Lacan calls the mirror stage the first point at which the infant *misrecognises itself* as a unified, separate and autonomous individual, which is an earlier equivalent to the linguistic coherence provided by the proper name and the signifier 'I' in the symbolic order. The subject will always be striving to achieve this coherent self-identity.
23. See de Man, p. 68 and Marcus, pp. 229–72. Nalbantian concludes that de Man believes 'so-called autobiographical texts offer an illusion of reference rather than any referential truth.' (Nalbantian, p. 33).

24. Olney, p. 13.
25. Ibid., pp. 5–6.
26. Jamaica Kincaid has written a novel entitled *An Autobiography of My Mother*, which raises numerous questions of 'authenticity', representation and perspective as well as genre.
27. See Finney, p. 14.

15

VIRTUAL TEXT: AMAZONIAN DEMOCRACY

Approach: Globalization Studies

[T]he pioneer site Amazon.com has official editorial reviews of books, CDs and other products. However they also provide a mechanism for readers to contribute their own thoughts on the same products, listed together with the 'official' materials. They also allow individuals to create their lists of favourite items for others to read and rate. Other sites such as Slashdot.org, are almost entirely created by registered users, including new stories, comments on stories, reviews, etc. These can form real communities around shared interests and have the potential to be used as a basis for political activity. (Alinta Thornton)[1]

In his 1909 story 'The Machine Stops', E. M. Forster imagines a future underground world in which a vast mechanised web connects together all of its isolated, enervated citizens. In this society, all communication is undertaken through the machine, but its vast network can connect two people anywhere around the globe. Forster's story, though less well-known than the later Dystopian visions of Huxley's *Brave New World* or Orwell's *1984*, envisions one technological aspect of contemporary life more fully than either.

This is of course the Internet, which has enabled a new and different kind of cultural production to develop over the last ten years, combining graphic and system design, consumer sales and marketing strategy. The socioeconomic equivalent to the world wide web that has become the dominant software on the Internet is globalisation. Globalisation operates at local and international levels, producing both cultural fragmentation and homogenisation, connection and interaction, dispersal and dislocation in one connective and unifying but highly differentiated system. Anthony Giddens sees globalisation as 'the intensification of worldwide social relations which link distant localities in such a way that local happenings are shaped by events occurring many miles away and vice versa.'[2] Similarly, Roland Robertson emphasises connectedness: 'Globalisation as a concept refers both to the compression of the world and the intensification of consciousness of the world as a whole.'[3] This compression and consciousness has a significance in terms of migration and markets, production and destruction, culture and the media, politics and postnationalism.

The influential account by Giddens charts four dimensions to this new world order: the nation-state system; the world capitalist economy; the international division of labour; and the world military order. On and through these dimensions global relations are influenced by governments, corporations and financiers, the UN, NATO, technology, regional industrial specialists and raw materials producers. Also, in Giddens' system, behind all of these institutional dimensions lie the global media. However, such forces do not simply unfold over the globe, but negotiate particular cultures and places, arrange and market themselves differently to activate different identities. While Giddens sees globalisation as the result of modernity (a process which, once again, many would regard as fuelled by capitalism), Robertson's model locates the start of globalisation prior to the emergence of either capitalism or modernity, and sees it progressing via a series of stages, the first of which lasted for three and a half centuries, culminating in a 'take-off' stage from 1870 to 1925. As the quotation above indicates, however, for Robertson, the mental aspect of the globalising process, especially the ability to conceptualise the world as such, is vital. Benedict Anderson's well-known influential formulation of national identity as an 'imagined community' is therefore an important step in the movement towards being able to – in the over-used words of the current slogan – 'think global.'[4] A different use of Benedict Anderson's theory, though one which continues Robertson's emphasis on the mental aspect of globalisation, is made by Arjun Appadurai, who posits 'imagined worlds' constituted by 'the imagination as social practice' (rather than as individual fantasy). The complex topographies of these multiple states are structured by a series of 'scapes' (ethnoscape, technoscape, mediascape, finanscape, ideoscape), but against the stability which the geographical metaphor might suggest, Appadurai argues that the contemporary world is in fact constituted by global flows – movements of populations, money, ideologies, images and information – which work in and through the disjunctures between the scapes. Even that does not fully account for current complexity, however, and he suggests that the forms of the global cultural economy are overlapping (rather than distinct) and fractal (that is, they have no fixed or regular boundaries).

In globalisation, where the fact that 80 per cent of world capital circulates among just twenty-four countries indicates the profoundly unequal levels of insertion into the capitalist system on a world scale, but the highlighting of this problem is also inevitably pointing towards the solution (which may be no less 'equal') through the eventual redistribution of wealth that will be brought about by diaspora and global markets. As Arif Dirlik says:

> The situation created by global capitalism helps explain certain phenomena that have become apparent over the last two or three decades, but especially since the eighties: global motions of people (and, therefore, cultures), the weakening of boundaries (among societies, as well as among social categories) . . . Some of these phenomena have also contributed to an appearance of equalization of differences within and among societies. What is ironic is that the managers of this world situation themselves concede that they (or their organizations) now have the power to appropriate the local for the global, to admit different cultures into the realm of capital (only to break them down and remake them in accordance with the requirements of production and consumption) and even to reconstitute subjectivities across national boundaries to create producers and consumers more responsive to the operations of capital.[5]

In this developing world order it appears that multinationals will increasingly usurp the positions of nations, in terms of economic power but also in terms of identity (brand loyalty instead of patriotism):

> [C]orporations are the dominant agents within the world economy. In their trading relations, with one another, and with states and consumers, companies . . . depend upon production for profit. Hence the spread of their influence brings in its train a global extension of commodity markets.[6]

Another way of looking at this is through the lens of a possible future kind of democracy that may emerge within the new empire of capitalism.

This is the reverse logic of the global spread of capitalist connections and media communications across the world. Globalisation is in effect the process of the world becoming a single place, and so inevitably there are widely different ways in which it is perceived and understood. While some reject it as simply a form of domination by 'First World' countries over 'Third World' ones, in which local economies are more firmly incorporated into a system of global capital structured to serve the interests of corporations and the wealthiest nations, other critics embrace it enthusiastically as a positive feature of a changing world in which access to technology, information, services and markets will be of benefit to local communities, where dominant forms of social organisation will lead to universal prosperity, peace and freedom, and in which a perception of a shared environment will lead to global ecological concern. For this group, 'globalism' is a positive term for an engagement with world issues. As some recent studies have argued, such as Michael Hardt and Antonio Negri's *Empire*, the key to the link between classical imperialism and contemporary globalisation in the twentieth century has been the role of the United States and its control of global economic relations. Most importantly, the US during and after its early expansionist phase initiated those features of social life and social relations that today may be considered to characterise the global: mass production, mass communication and mass consumption. During the twentieth century, these spread transnationally provoking centre-and-margin studies of the new corporate imperialism.

However, the focus of much recent discussion of the phenomenon is on how globalisation is engaged locally. In this frame of reference the responses of local communities become critical. For example, some critics argue that globalisation must now engage everyone whether they oppose or support its forces. Several go further and suggest that the only means of resisting the negative effects of globalisation is to engage with and reorganise these forces themselves to a more just and equitable goal.[7] In their second book, *Multitude*, Hardt and Negri go on to argue that the power to resist capitalist oppression can be found in the exertions of democracy, which is to say the individual actions of millions asserting their collective preference. They liken this in one way to *The Matrix* films examined in Chapter 1:

> The circuits of social producers are the lifeblood of Empire, and if they were to refuse the relationship of power, to subtract themselves from the relationship, it would simply collapse in a lifeless heap. The film trilogy *The Matrix* interprets this dependence of power. The Matrix survives not only by sucking the energy from millions of incubated humans but also by responding to the creative attacks of Neo, Morpheus, and the partisans of Zion. The Matrix needs us to survive.[8]

Hardt and Negri argue that 'we need to rethink the concept of democracy [that of the multitude] in light of the new challenges and possibilities presented by our world.'[9] They note that in the past it has been possible for sovereign rulers (monarchs or governments) to ostracise and cast aside specific groups while maintaining a good relationship with the general population. But Hardt and Negri see a crucial shift occurring as groups of individuals establish their own social and cultural networks in ways that are quite different from the forms of economic production; and they argue that this implies a new kind of politics also – a politics that is operated by the democratic interactions of the many and not the decisions of the sovereign individual. Increasingly, no group in the future will be disposable because the entire global population will become producer and consumer, 'as users or participants in the interactive circuits of the network'.[10] The importance of the multitude is to operate this socio-cultural power, and such a response seems to Hardt and Negri the most likely to produce effective forms of resistance to the negative impact of globalisation as well as to constitute the most hopeful sign that there may emerge a positive global polity.

Technology will play a crucial part in this development and, as Douglas Schuler points out: 'For the first time in human history, the possibility exists to establish a communication network that spans the globe, is affordable, and is open to all comers and points of view: in short, a democratic communication infrastructure.'[11] Yet, Schuler notes, there is no necessity for the world wide web to develop in ways beneficial to the majority, and most of the Internet is already deployed for private financial gain. It is certain that politics will be changed greatly by on-line digital culture, but what is less clear is the direction that change will take in a connected world dominated by *consumer* democrcies.

To take something familiar to most Internet users, and perhaps the most well-known set of URLs, Amazon is a telling example of consumer culture in which a near-universal web of isolated voices meet in a global marketplace arranged into sections by country. Amazon arguably represents a kind of hyperreal consumer democracy in which anyone can, largely anonymously, pronounce with impunity in a world-forum a verdict on almost any cultural product available for purchase.

Though it varies according to governmental structures, a democracy is most simply defined as a system in which the enfranchised rule, if only by proxy. In ancient democracies, all citizens (which is not the same as all people) could speak and vote in assemblies that resembled town meetings. Amazon provides an inclusive forum for the 'demos', the people. Everyone is equal providing they are a consumer with Internet access: this defines them as 'netizens' who can actively participate in the debate over the pros and cons of consumer goods. Anyone can speak on behalf of any product, can praise or damn it. These voices enter into an ongoing conversation with others who've commented before or who comment after. The author of a book, for example, has a privileged position, in that he or she can advocate their book as a special voice, but only as one amongst the many. The voice is not privileged as the truth about the book, but simply as the author's perspective. At present, there are of course millions who are excluded from the Internet and from Amazon by technology and economics, but this is in no way incompatible with the principles of ancient democracies where the majority of the population, including women and slaves, had no political rights. Across the many modern day representative democracies, there is also a spectrum of systems, in some of which it is compulsory to vote, and in all of which the electorate is significantly limited to those who are accorded political rights – thus excluding at least those who are not officially registered, because they are migrants, asylum workers or simply homeless.

Amazon effectively operates along similar lines to a consumer democracy: one in which any opinion can be expressed, any book or other product can be rated, while reviewers (voters) are themselves rated. In its Z Shops, Amazon introduces goods that the company does not itself stock but which are available from other commercial sellers. It also has 'The Marketplace', a worldwide car boot sale: secondhand goods that often Amazon stocks new. Amazon ranks all its items from 1 to 1,000,000 in terms of popularity: in the sense of number of sales.

Amazon is comparable to other democracies in many ways, and it has more voters – netizens – than some countries because it has more actively participating members; it operates equal rights and promotes customer loyalty. It is a consumer democracy that as yet makes no profit, but just gets bigger, moving from regional to national to international to global proportions. A key aspect to Amazon is the fact that though it is worth billions of dollars, it is not profitable. The annual losses the company accrues are almost a source of pride to the founder, Jeff Bezos, a Princeton graduate in electrical engineering and computer science. Bezos has, of course, amassed a huge private fortune, but his investors have yet to receive a return. The company's medium-term aim is still growth. Amazon ultimately aims to make significant profits, but so do all democracies. Of course, it panders to its customers' wishes only to give them a better service so that they stick with them – as do all politicians. Amazon was not created by a large company but began, very deliberately for publicity purposes, in a garage – run by one person. Contrary to many perceptions, almost anyone with limited funds can set up in competition. There is, of course, also a range of other e-retailers, or etailers, for the consumer to choose from. It is only consumer choice – and huge investment in branding of a kind that political parties also indulge in; which is to say that while trading companies are becoming more like political parties or systems, politicians are becoming more like operators in a market, concentrating on image, brand and customer relations.

There are many different angles on Amazon that could be emphasised to illustrate how the company is far removed from a political democracy, but as examples of consumer participation, sites like Amazon suggest the future politics of the multitude envisaged by Hardt and Negri that will eclipse older forms of democracy. The Internet originated as a free means of information dissemination, communication and interaction but it has been increasingly taken over by private interests where commercial benefits can be accrued (for example, the collapse of Napster as a means of distributing music freely between 60 million people and its subsequent re-emergence as a for-profits company). The democratic force of cyberspace lies in the fact that it is dispersed, decentralised and as yet largely unregulated and borderless, but the immense power it represents means that many vested interests wish to control and police its operation. The potential of new technology to impinge on party politics is already very clear: e-voting is increasing dramatically year on year (Arizona was the first US state to allow on-line voting in the 2000 elections); the web is now used for political announcements, fund raising, debates, webcasts, and e-buttals critiquing opponents' performance; computer modelling of polling data is employed to optimise effective use of campaign funds; and donations to presidential candidates' campaigns were possible via Amazon in the run-up to the 2004 US elections.

Despite all the reasons to be sceptical of the rigour of many websites, the Internet remains one of the truest sources of political as well as cultural information, and there are many thousands of non-commercial websites and news-groups operating independently of commercial considerations. Weblogs give personal viewpoints during media political blackouts and the Internet generally provides unprecedented opportunities for direct access to politically relevant information, for unmediated communication between political organisations, and for interactive discourse among citizens. While the potential for e-voting to transform the scope and operation of elections is currently under widespread review, non-governmental organisations (NGOs) are using Internet technologies as a major tool of political leverage. Also, e-petitions and e-lobbying are now a widespread aspect to activist practice.[12] As the extract that heads this chapter notes, Amazon is a company run on the same basis as other private concerns, and so its accent is on 'consumer' rather than 'democracy', meaning that it simply illustrates a way in which technology can be used to facilitate democratic participation, and as such it merely marks a point of transition from sovereignty to Hardt and Negri's democracy, from technology-enabled capitalism to the network of the multitude. In a way it could be argued that with a URL such as Amazon, the system is in place, but, unlike slashdot.org, the impulse against sovereignty is as yet not. A similar democratic impulse to that of slashdot.org informs the editorial policy of the on-line encyclopedia Wikipedia: 'Wikipedia – anyone can edit, and we encourage users to be bold! Find something that can be improved, either in content, grammar or formatting, then fix it . . . So go ahead, edit an article and help make Wikipedia the best source for information on the Internet!'[13] For other commentators this constitutes anarchy rather than democracy: many experts meet with scepticism the belief that thousands of self-selected contributors can collectively arrive at truth, but the administrators of the site argue that: '[F]ree discussion and cooperation will tend, over time, to create more accurate and comprehensive articles.'[14] However individual sites and the motives behind them can be critiqued, what the Internet can indicate better than any other modern means of political communication is the potential for democratic mass participation of the kind advocated by Hardt and Negri. Yet, the overwhelming majority of the Internet is dominated by e-commerce, most websites concentrate on the leisure industries, and the poorest sections of the most affluent societies still have extremely little presence on the web. The web is unlikely to be used for democratic purposes in the sense that deliberation and decision are accorded to the majority but sites like Amazon are illustrative of the *consumer* power that is arguably the most prevalent form of political participation in the West, while the global reach of the Internet means that, if it is clearly a method of extending markets, it is also potentially a means to co-ordinate collective action on an unprecedented level by the multitude.

REFERENCES AND BIBLIOGRAPHY

Anderson, Benedict, *Imagined Communities: Reflections on the Origin and Spread of Nationalism*, London: Verso, 1983.
Appadurai, Arjun, 'Disjuncture and Difference in the Global Cultural Economy', *Public Culture*, 2: 2 (spring) 1990. Reprinted in Patrick Williams and Laura Chrisman (eds), pp. 324–39.

Giddens, Anthony, *The Consequences of Modernity*, Cambridge: Polity Press, 1990. Excerpted in Patrick Williams and Laura Chrisman (eds), pp. 18–19.

Hardt, Michael and Antonio Negri, *Empire*, Cambridge and London: Harvard University Press, 2000.

Hardt, Michael and Antonio Negri, *Multitude: War and Democracy in the Age of Empire*, New York: Penguin, 2004.

Hoogvelt, Ankie, *Globalisation and the Postcolonial World: The New Political Economy of Development*, London: Macmillan, 1996.

Jenkins, Henry and David Thorburn (eds), *Democracy and the New Media*, London: MIT Press, 2004.

Robertson, Roland, *Globalization: Social Theory and Global Culture*, London: Sage, 1992.

Turner, Bryan S., *Orientalism, Postmodernism, and Globalism*, London: Routledge, 1994.

Waters, Malcolm, *Globalization*, London: Routledge, 1995

Williams, Patrick and Laura Chrisman (eds), *Colonial Discourse and Post-Colonial Theory*, Hemel Hempstead: Harvester, 1993.

NOTES

1. Alinta Thornton, 'Does Internet Create Democracy', unpublished Masters thesis, revised 2002, University of Sydney, http://www.zip.com.au/~athornto/thesis7.htm#cont (accessed 4 Aug. 2005).
2. Giddens, p. 181.
3. Robertson, p. 8.
4. It is simultaneously ironic and altogether typical of the way capitalism works that a slogan – 'Think global; act local' – originally coined within the radical environmental movement should be appropriated as a maxim for business enterprises.
5. Arif Dirlik, 'The Postcolonial Aura: Third World Criticism in the Age of Global Capitalism', *Critical Inquiry* 20 (winter) 1994, p. 356.
6. Giddens, p. 185.
7. See Hardt and Negri, 2000, p. xv.
8. Hardt and Negri, 2004, p. 335.
9. Ibid., p. 328.
10. Ibid., p. 335.
11. Douglas Schuler, 'Reports of the Close Relationship between Democracy and the Internet May Have Been Exaggerated', in Jenkins and Thorburn, pp. 69–83; p. 69.
12. Jayne Rodgers, 'NGOs and E-Activism: Institutionalizing or Extending the Political Potential of the Internet?', http://www.isanet.org/archive/rodgers.html (accessed 4 Aug. 2005). With regard to e-voting it is a strange irony that people can if they wish vote almost constantly, on-line and through their TVs, and yet almost exclusively on trivial or non-political matters such as the best pop song from a certain decade.
13. Wikipedia can be found at http://en.wikipedia.org/wiki/Main_Page (accessed 4 Aug. 2005).
14. See Chris Bunting, 'Trust me, this is the last word. No this is', *Times Higher Educational Supplement*, 13 May 2005, p. 16.

CHAPTER 16

WORLD MEDIA EVENT: IT'S ABOUT TIME: CULTURAL HISTORY AT THE MILLENNIUM

Approach: Cultural Studies

For most of us, the millennium's future is all used up. It's redundant. Too much emotion had already been invested in a spectacle that hadn't been pre-sold, serialised in advance. It simply occurred one drowsy Sunday morning as the public picked at their bundles of newsprint. There were images that managed to shock, a black metal tangle reduced to vegetable pulp. Flashbulbs in the underpass. After Ballard and Cronenberg, after the hagiographies of Jackson Pollock, James Dean, Jayne Mansfield, Princess Grace, here was the symbol that the dying century, with its auto-sex, man/machine hybrids, required. Diana's death was not so much an intimation of mortality for newsbyte junkies as a reality fax. Large sections of the population (especially those from Essex and the Estuary) took to the streets, laying siege to swathes of Whitehall, Secret State holdings, privileged real estate. They produced an unprecedented tide of folk art, hand-printed cards, gaudy Xerox tributes, silver balloons, teddy bears, plantations of forced blooms. A glittering cellophane moat around the railings of the royal barracks. The heady perfume of dying wreaths and tissue-wrapped lilies, carnations, roses, chrysanthemums, heaped against the chapel where the body was lying in state. That's how it happens. Then it's over and we can all get back to the usual small strategies of survival. (Iain Sinclair)[1]

According to Iain Sinclair, writing in 1999, the millennium had no future because it had already happened. The millennial moment in Britain and beyond, was not the dawn of the year 2000 but the death of the Princess of Wales – discussed in Chapter 5. Sinclair is here working with the idea of affect and with an emotional moment; one that expresses the finality, transition and mourning that might be associated with an endpoint, even though the media mood for the millennial shift itself was unremittingly celebratory. Yet Sinclair's view that 'the millennium' happened somewhere or sometime else points up many aspects of the material absence but spectacular presence the turn of the third millennium proved to be, compounded by the simple fact that there was little agreement about when exactly 'the millennium' occurred – in terms of religious history, accepted chronology, planetary movement and brute logic. In this chapter I will discuss aspects to the broad cultural production and reception of the year 2000 as a significant 'global' cultural happening, hemmed in by apocalypse, fin-de-siècle prophesying, and fears of the millennium bug, alongside visions of a new dawn. Particularly interesting are the circuits of religious, social and political activity, and sometimes frenzy, concentrated on an artificial 'event' imbued with cultural meaning but lacking any significance outside of its representations: a sublime postmodern moment in which celebration became its own spectacle. The approach adopted here is thus broadly that of cultural studies, in which an event that is nominally deemed natural is considered in the light of its actual construction within the nexus of media, culture and society.

In *The Sense of an Ending* Frank Kermode writes that: 'Our sense of epoch is gratified above all by the ends of centuries. Sometimes, indeed, it appears that we induce events to occur in accordance with this secular habit of mind.'[2] In the context of the subject of the present end-chapter, it is fair to say that Kermode's emphasis on *centuries* is helpful on both these points: first, because a millennium, unlike a century, is too long and insufficiently distinctive either to constitute an epoch in the sense of an era or to be meaningful on an individual human scale (unlike Diana's death); and second because the year 2000 was an 'induced' event: one that in an era of mass media was celebrated as a 'birth' as much as it was religiously observed as an actual or potential 'ending'. The calendrical second thousand years *anno domini* was not epochal and over its course the significance of millennial thinking had both waxed and waned, or rather it had risen to the apogee of a frenzied fear of divine destruction and sunk to the nadir of a do(o)med tent in Greenwich, ostentatiously marking to a largely indifferent public the point in geopolitical space from which time has come to be measured.

The evolutionary biologist and science historian Stephen Jay Gould interrogates the ascription of particular significance to the dates 1000 and 2000 in his book *Questioning the Millennium* (1997). Gould concludes that though the advantages of decimal mathematics suggest an aesthetic attraction to the round numbers, it is only the metaphysical dimension that fascinates people: the number mysticism that supports a sublime belief that the date of the millennium may mean something important to superhuman powers as well as humans. Otherwise, the cultural significance of the millennium is as a media event: a huge Hogmanay party and also a chance to reflect on the past and future at a time that will be arbitrarily used, because of decimal mathematics, as defining in many cultural areas, such as history, literature and sport. Yet, while the opportunity to do anything in the twentieth century has passed, and the opportunity to (be the first to) achieve something in the twenty-first century has arrived, centuries are not the same as millennia. There have been too few millennia to use them as meaningful cultural markers.

Gould points out that, unlike the day, the month and the year, the period of the millennium has no connection with the movement of the Earth and the Moon and so is, in his terms, 'precisely arbitrary'. The word 'millennium' originally denoted a future 'thousand-year' Christian reign but its significance has transferred in the media to a global cultural secular event (some comparisons could be made with changing attitudes to the meaning and significance of Christmas). The perceived twin-movements of human time – cyclical and linear – meet at the millennium, however arbitrarily fixed, with such a mathematical elegance that the cultural inclination towards custom and ceremony, now most evident in media spectacle and self-promotion, is inevitably attracted towards it.

From a religious and cultural point of view, it is also crucially important that the millennium at 2000 is part of the Gregorian calendar and so, though celebrated as a secular global event, is measured from the birth of Jesus and is implicitly a Christian measurement of time which reinforces a largely Western hegemony that can be perceived as antagonistic towards other faiths (for example, the Islamic calendar, used in most Muslim countries, is measured from over 620 years later, marking Mohammed's flight from Mecca to Medina). Dates according to the Gregorian calendar are designated AD (*anno domini*, 'in the year of our Lord'),[3] but to oppose this cultural bias, in professional and academic circles, the designation CE is often used instead of AD, to refer not to the Christian Era but to a secular Common Era. A 'World Calendar' was considered but not accepted by the United Nations in 1954, yet this was primarily to make up for the defects of the Gregorian calendar.

Another aspect to the millennium that can be emphasised is its relation to multiple views of the socio-cultural measurement of time.[4] Appealing to different traditions, it is both an extremely prominent turning point on the calendar and a momentous date in the march of progress. However, it has an additional significance because of the apocalyptic anxieties that precede it, as witnessed, to take one example, in political commentator Peter Jay and economist Michael Stewart's 1987 'novel' *Apocalypse 2000: Economic Breakdown and the Suicide of Democracy 1989–2000*.[5] This kind of 'devastating vision of social collapse', to quote the book cover, is not unusual for a fin de siècle, the end of centuries having previously been gloomily associated with assertions of momentous endpoints within civilisation, but for a theorist such as Jean Baudrillard it is a habit that needs to be broken: '[W]e have to get used to the idea that *there is no end any longer, there will no longer be any end*, that history itself has become interminable.'[6] Baudrillard claims that 'history', the 'political', 'ideology', and so on, are not coming to an end but are continuing after their death as they are recycled and repositioned by postmodernism – a process exacerbated by the impulses to review that characterise the end of decades, centuries and inevitably, millennia. These large ideas find their meaning in consumerism as the grand narrative of history is fulfilled by its marketability: 'We wondered what the point of this coming *fin de siècle* might be. Here we have it: the sale of the century. History is being sold off, as is the end of history.'[7] The *New York Times* reflected on the coming millennium by noting that there was money to made in journals, candles, date books, mugs, t-shirts and more, selling to the general consumer looking for something to buy (into), but especially to the likes of New Agers and apocalyptic visionaries: '[I]n 999 feelings of gloom ran rampant. What the doomsayers may have lacked was an instinct for mass marketing.'[8] Which is to observe that, at least from the skewed point of view of its endpoint, the second millennium might be distinguished by, if anything, the rise of capitalism to the global proportions considered in the last chapter.

So, history and history's endpoint(s) are commodified and marketed, but what is it that is being sold at the second 'millennium'? The term means 'a thousand years' but in Christian eschatology (the theological study of endtimes) it is explicitly associated with the 'thousand-year' reign of Christ as foretold in the Book of Revelation of the New Testament, and so is less a chronological thousand years than the span of time that Christ would rule following the apocalypse, and so is wrapped up in Utopian visions of a time of peace and joy. The millennium celebrated in 2000 was thus simultaneously Christian (about two millennia since Christ's birth) and non-Christian – it was not the end of the world, neither was it a date of religious significance for most people in the West. As Baudrillard notes, nothing was coming to an end except the idea of endpoints: no apocalyptic *force majeure*, no nuclear holocaust, no computer catastrophe. Yet, for a secular society, the cultural baggage of Hegelian philosophy and Christian millenarianism was famously and effectively played upon by Francis Fukuyama in his Nietzschean 1992 book *The End of History and the Last Man* which foresaw the triumph of Western liberal democracy (following, for example, the collapse of the Soviet Bloc) eventually leading to an age of equality and universal enfranchisement that would be characterised by the political correctness of mutual recognition and respect but also by a potentially disastrous flattening of human experience.[9] If Fukuyama was right, the millennium had happened around 1989 and the celebrations of 2000 would best be seen as the mediated recognition of the coming age of not Christ but global liberal democracy.

From a broad cultural point of view, the millennium chiefly provided a unique occasion for marking and marketing, for public and private ceremonies and consumer events. The millennial celebrations were a global event, starting with the dawn of 1 January 2000 on the Pacific island of Kiribati and making their way round the world with thousands of TV cameras following in relay. In Britain the symbol of the millennium was the dome erected in London at Greenwich, to which Iain Sinclair marched beside the Thames to record his view quoted at the head of this chapter. For governments, production companies, marketing departments, firework manufacturers and expectant partygoers, the millennium was above all an 'opportunity', one that would certainly never come again for them. For cultural commentators of all hues from stargazers to historians it offered a watershed for accounting and assessment, for prognosis and for speculation.

None of which masks the fact that time itself had undergone a metamorphosis in the years immediately before and throughout the twentieth century, and had ceased to be a monolithic entity. In 1884, the Prime Meridian Conference (PMC) established Greenwich as the point from which British time would be measured. Though much of the rest of the world was initially resistant, and time was not centred on Greenwich by EuroAmerica until the International Conference on Time in Paris in 1912, the PMC also divided the world into twenty-four zones separated by an hour's difference, and enshrined an exact moment at which the universal space-time day would begin.

The 1884 Conference provided the sense of a standard time that would, over a century later, lead to the erection of the Millennium Dome at Greenwich as a spatial marker of temporal control. Yet, at the same time as the PMC, long before modern communications technology and virtual reality, the belief in a universal, fixed, measured temporality was being undermined by a distinction between public time, that of the clock, and private time, that of the individual. In *Time and Free Will*, published in 1889 only a few years after the Prime Meridian Conference, Henri Bergson maintained that 'reality' was characterised by the difference between the complex and varied experience of temporality in an individual's mind and the linear, regular beats of clock-time measuring all experience by the same gradations. Bergson argued that psychological time was measured by what he called *duration*, defined as the varying speed at which the mind apprehends the length of experiences according to their different intensities, contents and meanings for each individual. Thus, when Bergson distinguished between chronological time and 'duration' he did so by arguing that chronology is the time of history (hours, minutes and seconds) while duration encompasses those times in a life which are significant for each different individual, to which the backdrop of clock-time is irrelevant. After the turn of the twentieth century, time was also about to be changed by the intervention of Einstein: whilst in Newtonian mechanics, time was always and everywhere the same, according to the theory of relativity it depended on the observer's frame of reference, such that time was inseparable from space and velocity. While Bergson had pointed out that time was subjective mentally for the individual, Einstein observed that it was always relative physically too.

In Ian McEwan's novel *The Child in Time*, which is set just before the millennium, he explores the variety of twentieth-century scientific possible explanations for the phenomenon of time through the character of Thelma, a theoretical physicist. Trying to shed some light on the central character Stephen's strange experience of a curve in time, she reveals that 'there's a whole supermarket of theories these days.'[10] For example, one possibility 'has the world dividing every infinitesimal fraction of a second into an infinite number of possible versions, constantly branching and proliferating, with consciousness neatly picking its way through to create the illusion of a stable reality'. Another theory states that 'time is variable. We know it from Einstein, who is still our bedrock here. In relativity theory, time is dependent on the speed of the observer.' Yet another theory suggests that time is a separate entity in and of itself: 'In the big-bang theory, time is thought to have been created at the same moment as matter, it's inseparable from it.' The only certainty about time, Thelma says, is its uncertainty: '[W]hatever time is, the common-sense, everyday version of it as linear, regular, absolute, marching from left to right, from the past through the present to the future, is either nonsense or a tiny fraction of the truth.' As a literary exploration of scientific, artistic and religious explanations of temporal experience, *The Child in Time* exemplifies how time cannot be treated as a simple reality in the world. Which is to say that by the end of the second millennium, the notion of a 'fixed' moment in time having anything other than a cultural significance was logically absurd.

Yet, that cultural significance remains a strong spiritual and political force in numerous traditions. Here, the millennium is not a moment on the clock and calendar, but a powerful concept of 'new times' as compelling as that other idea which has marked much of the last thousand years, that of the 'new world'. As Asa Briggs points out:

> Other religions besides Christianity had millennial strands in their history. It was part of the Jewish tradition, taken over by Christians, that the Messiah would reign, the Prince of Glory, the Prince of Peace, and Islam inherited the tradition also. Outside this context, anthropologists identified religious cults, particularly Melanesian cargo cults, which trusted in a good time coming ahead – no Doomsday there – at a time unknown. So also did the South American Tupí-Guaraní, who searched for a 'Land without Evil'. New movements and 'new-age' cults of the late 20th century, stimulated by the imminence of 2000, focused upon the coming millennium. The Rastafarians formed one such movement. Others, as concerned with space as with time, anticipated it in what both Christian and secular groups regard as strange, even evil ways. As it was, the beginning of the year 2000 brought no more surprises than the year 1000, although in all countries there were people who claimed that the third millennium should begin not in 2000 but in 2001.[11]

Because the idea of the millennium is associated with a new world order and a second coming, idealists and politicians have employed it as part of their Utopian vision of a new tomorrow. This vision is conceived in eschatological terms because it seems to envisage some future point at which the years of hardship, social struggle or warfare will tip over into a largely static world of peace, such that the new visions, new deals, new worlds, and 'New' political parties all implicitly buy into the logic of millennialism. Which is to say that, in cultural terms, the 'millennium' stands for an apocalyptic overthrow of the present state of things and a transition towards a better future. Except that most cultures see this future as logical and inevitable, as in some way either natural or supernatural.

For a Western world that has undergone the digital revolution of the microchip, the apocalyptic anxiety attaching to the millennium was associated not with religion but computing. Y2K, as it became known, was the secular embodiment of mystical fears that the year 2000 held some special threat, and that the metaphysical world, or here the virtual (technology has been viewed, for example by Heidegger, as a form of metaphysics), would impact cataclysmically on the material: planes might fall from the sky, hospital systems fail, whole cities plunge into darkness. Any microprocessed action reliant on the progress of time could fail or cease, and all because many computer programmers, the architects of the postmodern world, had allowed for only two digits in their date codes, so that when the year turned from '99' to '00', instead of progressing, the world would be digitally decreed to have regressed one hundred years, such that the future would be a historical return. This is in many ways a virtual literalisation of the argument of postmodernist theorists that contemporary culture is marked by the frenetic and eclectic recycling of the past. Indeed the 'Millennium' with a capital letter appeared as a heritage event before it even occurred: unusually, a historic date under constant discussion was in the future not the past and so could be packaged and repackaged many times before it happened, or, more precisely, 'passed'. That the quasi-eschatological catastrophe of Y2K, sounding like one of the names of God via *Star Wars*, did not also come to pass in fact seems inevitable according to the cultural logic of the millennium, given that the event it marked was itself a fiction – a numerical non-event that would nonetheless be a global spectacle.

But, the things discussed here – Diana trauma, apocalyptic doom-mongering, and Y2K anxieties – help to point to what is perhaps the ultimate significance of the millennium. For Paul Ricoeur in his extensive work *Time and Narrative*,[12] time needs to be understood in relation to the human desire for story, or more particularly for the ordering of events into narrative. Which is to say that the function of narrative in social and personal lives is to attest to the coherence of temporal experience. Thus, according to Ricoeur: '[T]ime becomes human to the extent that it is articulated through a narrative mode, and narrative attains its full meaning when it becomes a condition of temporal existence.'[13] In between cosmic time, the scale of the historical, and the duration of psychological personal time, the task of narrative is to forge a continuum amongst these three perceptions of time. Deriving from an understanding of what is important in quotidian life, in terms of action, reflection or symbolism, narrative maintains a continuity between human ideas of the absolute, the historic and the day-to-day, and it is through this process that our sense of time is created.

As a consequence of the different narratives told by the media, the Churches, and by science, there have emerged two views of the millennium, which can be summed up by two pop lyrics that heralded its arrival from early in each of the preceding decades.[14]

> Yeah, they say two thousand zero zero party over
> Oops out of time
> So tonight I'm gonna party like it's 1999. (Prince, '1999', 1982)

> End of a century
> Oh, it's nothing special. (Blur, 'End of a Century', 1994)

In Prince's song, 2000 is the ultimate year of celebration, judgement and possible destruction. In Blur's song, the lyric to which was inspired by Martin Amis's millennial novel *London Fields* (1989), it is a non-event. For Prince it is momentous, drawing its significance from religious prophecy and ritual. For Blur it is a moment of artificiality imbued with a spurious and superstitious significance – the postmodern sublime of the illogical spectacle of an end that's not the end, because, as Baudrillard argues, it's never the end.

REFERENCES AND BIBLIOGRAPHY

Baudrillard, Jean, *The Illusion of the End*, trans. Chris Turner, Cambridge: Polity, 1992.
Gould, Stephen Jay, *Questioning the Millennium: A Rationalist's Guide to a Precisely Arbitrary Countdown*, London: Vintage, 1998.
Horrocks, Christopher, *Baudrillard and the Millennium*, Cambridge: Icon, 1999.
Kermode, Frank, *The Sense of an Ending*, Oxford: Oxford University Press, 1979.
Kumar, Krishan, 'Apocalypse, Millennium and Utopia Today', in Malcolm Bull (ed.), *Apocalypse Theory and the Ends of the World*, Oxford: Blackwell, 1995, pp. 200–4.
Ricoeur, Paul, *Time and Narrative*, trans. Kathleen McLaughlin and David Pellauer, vol. 1, Chicago: Chicago University Press, 1994.

NOTES

1. Iain Sinclair, *Sorry Meniscus*, London: Profile, 1999, pp. 43–4. J. G. Ballard wrote the novel *Crash* (1973) about people who find sexual excitement in automobile accidents, which was subsequently filmed by David Cronenberg. Jackson Pollock, James Dean, Jayne Mansfield and Princess Grace all died in car crashes.
2. Kermode, p. 96.
3. The birth of Christ was originally given as 25 December 1 BC, but theologians now place it about four years earlier.
4. This is aside from the many problems attendant on the creation and revision of the modern calendar, the most well known of which being the matter of whether the new century starts in 2000 or in 2001 given that there was no year 0. These are explored in detail in the second section of Gould's *Questioning the Millennium*, pp. 99–128.
5. Peter Jay and Michael Stewart, *Apocalypse 2000: Economic Breakdown and the Suicide of Democracy 1989–2000*, London: Sphere, 1987. This is a strange example of historiographical metafiction in which a post-Reagan and post-Thatcher EuroAmerican future is imagined in conjectural detail by two unlikely

novelistic Cassandras, who even add an index to their genre-defying hybrid of report writing and Dystopian vision.

6. Baudrillard, p. 116.
7. Ibid., p. 118.
8. *New York Times*, 26 December 1993, quoted in Gould, pp. 104–5.
9. Francis Fukuyama, *The End of History and the Last Man*, London: Hamish Hamilton, 1992.
10. Ian McEwan, *The Child in Time*, London: Picador, 1988. This and later quotations come from pp. 117–18.
11. Asa Briggs, 'Millennium', *Microsoft Encarta Encyclopedia*, 2003.
12. French philosopher Paul Ricoeur, *Time and Narrative* (published in English 1984 to 1987).
13. Ricoeur, p. 52.
14. For a discussion, history and overview of different political, philosophical and cultural Utopian and Dystopian millennial theories see Kumar, who argues in conclusion that humanity always needs a vision, whether apocalyptic or millenarian.

INDEX

A Room of One's Own, 91
A Thousand Plateaus, 132
Albert, Prince, 56
Al-Fayed, Dodi, 50
Alien, 31–9
Althusser, Louis, 2, 18, 66, 68
Amazon.com, 156–62
Amélie, 51
Amis, Kingsley, 148, 150, 152
Amis, Martin, 146–53, 171
An American Werewolf in London, 41, 43
Anarchy, State and Utopia, 17
Anderson, Benedict, 157
Another Country, 101
Anscombe, Elizabeth, 126
Appadurai, Arjun, 157
Arthurs, Jane, 62
Augustine, 151
Austin, J. L., 65
Avgikos, Jan, 89

Baker, Nicholson, 67
Bakhtin, M. M., 21
Ballard, J. G., 164
Bardot, Brigitte, 88
Barthelme, Donald, 128–36
Barthes, Roland, 2, 3–4, 37, 147
Baudrillard, Jean, 12, 13–15, 17, 18, 74–82, 109, 113, 167, 171
Berger, John, 90
Bergson, Henri, 168
Berkeley, George, 12, 13
Bernstein, Leonard, 44
'Beyond the Pleasure Principle', 56
Bhabha, Homi, 44, 105

Bierce, Ambrose, 128
Big Brother, 60–70, 76
'Black or White', 40–1, 44
Black Skin, White Masks, 44
Blade Runner, 11
Blair, Tony, 50
Blake, Andrew, 122
Blaxploitation movies, 41
Bloom, Harold, 8
Blur, 171
Booth, Wayne, 120
Borges, Jorge Luis, 14
Bourdieu, Pierre, 11
Branagh, Kenneth, 101
Branson, Richard, 152
Brass Eye, 81
Bricmont, Jean, 113–15
Briggs, Asa, 169
Bronfen, Elizabeth, 141
Browne, Thomas, 1
Browning, Robert, 139
Bulger, Jamie, 119
Burgess, Guy, 101
Burgess, Michael, 50
Burrell, Paul, 50
Burton, David H., 100
Butler, Judith, 15–16, 17, 18, 64–7, 91

'Candle in the Wind', 49
Caruth, Cathy, 57
Chariots of Fire, 101
Charles, Prince, 51, 54
Chekhov, Anton, 128
Chinn, Sarah E., 66–7
Chomsky, Noam, 77

Citizen Kane, 76
Clark, Henry, 97
'Cleanin Out My Closet', 137–43
Clinton, Bill, 152
Cohan, Alvin, 53
Colebrook, Claire, 135
Collett, Peter, 60
Conrad, Joseph, 36
'Conversations with a Cupboard Man', 137
Coupe, Laurence, 36
Couser, G. Thomas, 146, 148, 149
Coward, Noel, 63
Coward, Ros, 86
Critchley, Simon, 54, 55
Cronenberg, David, 164
Culler, Jonathan, 4

'Daddy', 140–2
Davis, Therese, 54
Day Lewis, Daniel, 101
De Man, Paul, 146
Dean, James, 164
Deleuze, Gilles, 50, 113, 132–6
Derrida, Jacques, 5–6, 132
Descartes, René, 12, 13
Diana and Me, 51
Diana, Princess, 9, 45–57, 99, 102, 164–5
Discipline and Punish, 68
Disraeli, Benjamin, 101
DuBois, W. E. B., 44
Duncan, J., 26
Duncan, N., 26
Dyer, Richard, 44
Dylan, Bob, 139

Eagleton, Terry, 9
Eminem, 137–43
Endemol, 60–3
Erikson, Erik, 56
Everett, Rupert, 101
Experience, 148–53

Fanon, Frantz, 40, 44
Farrell, Kirby, 56
Fichtelberg, Joseph, 146, 149
Finney, Brian, 146, 147
Firth, Colin, 101
Fish, Stanley, 4–5, 7–8, 32
Fisher, Elizabeth, 35
Fiske, John, 31–2, 37, 118
Fleishman, Avrom, 146
Foden, Giles, 139
Forster, E. M., 156
Foucault, Michel, 2, 7, 8, 24, 45, 68–9, 107, 147
Frankfurt, Stephen, 36
Freadman, Richard, 6–7
Freud, Sigmund, 56, 92, 134, 150
'From Work to Text', 3
Frye, Northrop, 148
Fukuyama, Francis, 78, 167

Gender Trouble, 16, 64–5
Gibson, Andrew, 123–4
Gibson, William, 12
Giddens, Anthony, 156–7
Gilligan, Carol, 126
Gilroy, Paul, 45, 98
'Good-bye England's Rose', 49
Gorbachev, Mikhail, 98
Gould, Stephen Jay, 165–6
Greenberg, Richard, 36
Gross, Paul, 112
Guattari, Félix, 132–6
Guerrero, Ed, 41

Hall, Stuart, 98
Hardt, Michael, 159–61, 162
Harrison, Bernard, 5–6
Harry Potter and the Philosopher's Stone, 118–26
Harry, Prince, 51
Harvey, David, 27, 91
Head, Dominic, 129
Heath, Edward, 101
Hockey, Jenny, 51

Hoggart, Richard, 2
Holmes, Su, 64
Holst, Gustav, 100
hooks, bell, 40, 45
Hopkins, Jeffrey, 25
Hurt, John, 35
Hussein, Saddam, 79, 80
Huxley, Aldous, 156

'I Vow To Thee My Country',
    99–102
I Walked with a Zombie, 43
Irigaray, Luce, 85
Is There A Text In This Class?,
    4
Isherwood, Christopher, 74
'It's Only Rock n Roll', 140

Jack, Ian, 49, 53
Jackson, Michael, 40–8, 143
Jagger, Mick, 140
Jameson, Fredric, 25–7
Jankovitch, Mark, 62
Jay, Peter, 166
Jenkins, David, 97
John, Elton, 49
Johnson, Richard, 57
Jones, Duane, 43
Joyce, James, 149

Kaplan, E. Ann, 45
Katz, Jeanne, 54
Keats, John, 139
Kellner, Douglas, 80, 81
Kellogg, Robert, 149
Kelly, Grace, 164
Kennedy, John F., 42, 50, 53
Kermode, Frank, 165
King, Martin Luther, 42
Klein, Melanie, 142
Kowinski, William, 21
Kristeva, Julia, 113
Krutnik, Frank, 91
Kubrick, Stanley, 11

Lacan, Jacques, 13, 62, 86, 92, 113,
    140
Landis, John, 41, 43, 44
Lawrence, D. H., 149
Lawson, Nigel, 96
Le Corbusier, 22
Le Guin, Ursula, 35–6
Leavis, F. R., 106
Lefebvre, Henri, 21, 27
Lejeune, Philippe, 150–1
Lem, Stanislaw, 33
Levinas, Emmanuel, 124–5
Levitt, Norman, 112
Libération, 75
Lingua Franca, 105
Lodge, David, 1, 2
London Fields, 171
Loren, Sophia, 88
Lowe, Stephen, 99, 102
Lucy, Niall, 133–4
Lumet, Sidney, 41
Lyotard, Jean-François, 109

Magnani, Anna, 88
Malebranche, Nicolas, 12
Mansfield, Jayne, 164
Mansfield, Katherine, 129
Marcus, Laura, 148–9
Marx, Karl, 34
Massumi, Brian, 132
Mathers-Briggs, Debbie, 138, 144n
Matrix, The, 11–20, 159
Maupassant, Guy de, 129
McEwan, Ian, 137, 168
McGrath, John, 66–7
Mejia, Cristina, 120
Mercer, Kobena, 41–3
Meredith, James, 42
Middlemarch, 126
Midgley, Mary, 126
Milgram, Stanley, 60
Miller, Arthur, 147
Miller, Seamus, 6–7
Monroe, Marilyn, 49

Moreau, Jeanne, 88
Morris, Meaghan, 22, 28
Multitude, 161
Mulvey, Laura, 87, 88, 89, 92
Myers, Tony, 68
Mythologies, 3

Negri, Antonio, 158–9, 161
Neill, Dennis, 55
Neuromancer, 12
New York Times, 167
Nice Work, 1
Nietzsche, Friedrich, 7, 109
Night of the Living Dead, 43
1984, 68, 74, 79, 156
Norris, Christopher, 75–6, 109
Nostromo, 36
Nozick, Robert, 17–18, 19
Nussbuam, Martha, 126

Olney, James, 146, 151
Orwell, George, 2, 13, 68, 74, 79, 156

Partington, Lucy, 148
Pascal, Roy, 153
Patton, Paul, 77
Paul, Henri, 50
Paxman, Jeremy, 51, 53
Persaud, Raj, 62
Plath, Sylvia, 141–2
Plato, 12, 13
Poe, Edgar Allan, 129
Poitier, Sidney, 41
Pollock, Jackson, 164
Price, Vincent, 40
Prince, 171
Pullen, Christopher, 66

Raban, Jonathan, 98–100
Raghuram, Parvati, 63
Reagan, Ronald, 98
Rees-Jones, Trevor, 50
Republic, The, 12
Richards, I. A., 109

Ricoeur, Paul, 125–6, 147, 170
Rivière, Joan, 67, 92
Roberts, Adam, 18
Robertson, Roland, 157
'Rock DJ', 140
Romero, George, 43
Rorty, Richard, 1, 6, 109, 123–4
Ross, Diana, 41
Rowling, J. K., 118–26
Rushdie, Salman, 119

Said, Edward, 1, 7–9, 45
Salih, Sara, 65
Scargill, W. P., 151
Scholes, Robert, 149
Schuler, Douglas, 159, 160
Schwarzkopf, Norman, 80
Scott, Ridley 11, 32–3
Seale, Delilah, 148
Sedgwick, Eve Kosofsky, 67, 70
Shapiro, Stephen, 147
Sherman, Cindy, 85–92
Shields, Rob, 23, 28
Shumaker, Wayne, 149
Signoret, Simone, 88
Simulations, 13–14
Sinclair, Iain, 49, 164
Sinfield, Alan, 67
Small, David, 51
Snow, C. P., 106
Social Text, 105, 106, 108
Soderbergh, Steven, 32
Soja, Edward, 27
Sokal, Alan, 105–15, 133
Spencer, Charles, 50–1
Spring Rice, Cecil, 100
Springer, Jerry, 140
Steedman, Carolyn, 152
Stevenson, Robert Louis, 129
Stewart, Michael, 166
Structuralist Poetics, 4

Tarkovsky, Andrei, 33
Taupin, Bernie, 49

Temperton, Rod, 41
Thatcher, Margaret, 95–102
'The Balloon', 128–36
The Bible, 96, 99, 119
The Child in Time, 168–9
The Day Today, 81
'The Death of the Author', 4, 147
The Golden Bowl, 126
The Planets, 100
The Prince and the Pauper, 44
The Production of Space, 21
The Satanic Verses, 119
The Sense of an Ending, 165
The Truman Show, 63
The Wiz, 41, 44
The Wizard of Oz, 41
The Young Ones, 62
This Life, 62
Thomas, Julia, 45
Thornton, Alinta, 156
'Thriller', 40–8
Time and Free Will, 168
Times Literary Supplement, 113
Tincknell, Estella, 63
Tolkein, J. R. R., 118
Trading Places, 44
Twain, Mark, 44
2001: A Space Odyssey, 11

Virilio, Paul, 81–2

Wachowski, Larry and Andy, 11, 12
Watkin, William, 49
Weaver, Sigourney, 32
Weir, Peter, 63
Welcome to the Desert of the Real, 19
Welles, Orson, 76
West Edmonton Mall, 23–6
West Side Story, 44
'What is an Author?', 147
White, Hayden, 151
William, Prince, 51
Williams, Raymond, 2
Williams, Robbie, 140
Williamson, Judith, 85, 89
Wilson A. N., 118
Winfrey, Oprah, 140
Woolf, Virginia, 2, 91, 129
Wordsworth, William, 135, 153
World Trade Center, 79

Yates, John, 97
Yeats, W. B., 1

Žižek, Slavoj, 19, 60, 68–70, 82

Journals *from* Edinburgh University Press

Translation and Literature

'has long been indispensable. It is a large intelligence flitting among the languages, to connect and to sustain. The issues are becoming archival; the substantial articles, notes, documents and reviews practise an up-to-the-minute criticism on texts ancient and modern.'
–Times Literary Supplement

Translation and Literature is an interdisciplinary scholarly journal focusing on English Literature in its foreign relations. Recent articles and notes include: Surrey and Marot, Livy and Jacobean drama, Virgil in *Paradise Lost*, Pope's Horace, Fielding on translation, Browning's *Agamemnon*, and Brecht in English. It embraces responses to all other literatures in the work of English writers, including reception of classical texts; historical and contemporary translation of works in modern languages; history and theory of literary translation, adaptation, and imitation.

Paragraph
A Journal of Modern Critical Theory

Publishes essays and review articles which explore critical theory in general and its application to literature, other arts and society. Regular themed issues highlight important issues and key figures in modern critical theory including Irigaray, Genet, Jacques Rancière, and The Idea of the Literary.

Themed Issues 2006

Paragraph 29.1
Theory and the Early Modern
Edited by Michael Moriarty and John O'Brien

Deleuze and Science
Edited by John Marks
Paragraph 29.2

Romanticism

A much-needed forum for the flourishing diversity of Romantic studies today. *Romanticism* publishes critical, historical, textual and bibliographic essays of the highest scholarly standard. And from 2006, each volume comprises three issues per year.

Comparative Critical Studies

(Formerly *Comparative Criticism* and *New Comparison*)
Published for the British Comparative Literature Association

Comparative Critical Studies seeks to advance methodological (self)reflection on the nature of comparative literature as a discipline. Contributions provide innovative perspectives on the theory and practice of the study of comparative literature in all its aspects, including:
- Theory and history of comparative literary studies
- Comparative studies of conventions, genres, themes and periods
- Reception studies
- Comparative gender studies
- Transmediality
- Diasporas and the migration of culture from a literary perspective
- The theory and practice of literary translation and cultural transfer.

Comparative Critical Studies will also regularly include sections with book reviews, the winners of the Dryden Translation Prize, the plenary lectures of the triennial BCLA conferences, and selected papers from other BCLA conferences and workshops.

Journal of Victorian Culture

An international forum for discussion of all aspects of Victorian culture, presented in a range of formats including articles, perspectives, roundtables and substantial reviews. Topics covered include architecture, social and economic history, history of science and technology, literature, music, theatre and the visual arts.

- Browse Contents Lists
- Subscribe Online
- Request A Sample Copy
  at **www.eup.ed.ac.uk**